| DATE DUE | | | |
|---|---|---|---|
| | | | |
| | | | |
| | | | |
| | | | |
| | | | |
| | | | |
| | | | |
| | | | |
| | | | |
| | | | |
| | | | |
| | | | |
| | | | |

# JOHN GALSWORTHY
## A Reassessment

# JOHN GALSWORTHY
# A Reassessment

Alec Fréchet
*Professor of English Literature*
*Université du Maine, Le Mans*

Translated from the French
by Denis Mahaffey

BARNES & NOBLE BOOKS
TOTOWA, NEW JERSEY

First published as
*John Galsworthy: L'homme, le romancier, le critique social*
by Librairie Klincksieck, Paris, 1979

First published in the USA 1982 by
BARNES & NOBLE BOOKS
81, Adams Drive, Totowa,
New Jersey, 07512

ISBN 0−389−20277−0

*Printed in Hong Kong*

**Library of Congress Cataloging in Publication Data**

Fréchet, Alec.
  John Galsworthy.

  Bibliography: p.
  1. Galsworthy, John, 1867−1933.  2. Novelists,
English − 20th century − Biography.  I. Title.
PR6013.A5Z56613  1982      823′.912      81−22900
ISBN 0−389−20277−0                          AACR2

# Contents

# Foreword

Professor Alec Fréchet's reassessment comes at an appropriate time, when John Galsworthy's reputation, after so many vicissitudes, seems at last to be permanently established. This has happened because of something that could never have been thought possible at the time when he was writing: television. Significantly enough, not the cinema (the film recounting Barry Lyndon's adventures did little to enhance Thackeray's reputation among the general public, just as *Tom Jones* had done little for Fielding's), but a serialised version which, week after week, repeated over several years, showed characters on the television screen that became like members of the family circle. If Soames has today taken on his full dimension in so many countries, including France, it is certainly through the agency of the BBC, which has made him as familiar to us as any Balzac hero.

Yet the popularity of *The Forsyte Saga* might not have been so widespread if the work itself had not crystallised a moment in the development of ideas. Galsworthy went through a long purgatory before people realised that, far from being a conservative bent on portraying an upper middle-class family reclining on its privileges, he had perceived the premonitory tremors of all that was to emerge in the explosion and aftermath of the sustained shock of two wars, and that has now come to form the very fibre of our day-to-day problems, in the fields of women's liberation, the religious crisis, the hypocrisies of the established order, or the demands of the exploited. Finally, with amazement, we discover that Galsworthy the gentleman, somehow rather too stoical, rather too stiff, in short rather too distinguished not to seem hidebound, old-fashioned, was, as it were, the litmus paper that was to reveal the great contemporary conflicts of society.

Such a realisation involved close study not only of his novels, but also of the stories, essays, plays and poems: an exhaustive undertaking which, combined with an investigation of the man's personality, and an assessment of the guiding principles that underlay his social criticisms, form a panorama of the Galsworthian contribution to literature.

Might I add that, for me, Professor Fréchet's work is eminently representative of what may be called the school of French Anglicists. This book, a revised version of what was originally a doctoral thesis, received with the highest honours at the University of La Sorbonne Nouvelle, necessarily reflects the requirements, so cherished in our academic tradition, of rigorous exposition, balanced proportions and priority given to ensuring clarity. So readers will not be surprised to detect a strongly architectural construction, and a constant discipline of elucidation. But there is something else. Echoing Alec Fréchet's own sensitivity, this study goes profoundly into its subject, with intuitiveness, warmth and the heart-felt fraternal force of the intellect.

RAYMOND LAS VERGNAS
*former Dean of the Faculty of Arts*
*La Sorbonne*

# Preface

I was thirteen when my father first sent me to England. He wanted me to acquire a good English accent. He chose a place in Norfolk where nobody for miles around spoke French. My host was a clergyman who had studied at Cambridge. He and his family gave me such a welcome that I have ever since loved and admired England.

Admiration is one of the keys to understanding. I respect and admire Galsworthy, and this has helped me throughout the many years of research that had to be devoted to a close examination of his works. A long time ago, Louis Cazamian, the greatest French scholar of his generation in English literature and civilisation, told me: 'Galsworthy has been unfairly treated, but one day his reputation will rise again.' He was right, and the English public has proved that he was right. In these hard and difficult times, Britain cannot afford to neglect any part of her heritage. Galsworthy's novels belong to that heritage. This is why I hope that this English translation of my work may satisfy the curiosity of English-speaking readers of Galsworthy, as well as those who have watched *The Forsyte Saga* on television with such interest.

I should like to pay tribute to the memory of several of the people who helped me gather my information, and provided me with invaluable personal reminiscences, and who have since died. Among members of the Galsworthy family, these included Frank Galsworthy (the novelist's cousin), Mrs Olive Galsworthy (Edwin Henry's widow), and above all Rudolf Sauter. Among Galsworthy's friends, they included H. V. Marrot (his official biographer), R. H. Mottram, former Mayor of Norwich, himself a writer and author of *For Some We Loved*, and Professor Gilbert Murray.

I owe so much to Rudolf Sauter. In conversations at his home, and in written answers to my questions, he extended my knowledge of his uncle considerably. More than this, his very sensitivity and tact helped me to understand Galsworthy better. I shall always remember his unfailing friendliness.

Frank Swinnerton, Richard Church and Angus Wilson gave me the benefit of their experience of English literary life.

I received wholehearted assistance in my research from several members of the British Council in Paris, London and Vienna.

Mr K. W. Humphreys, Librarian of Birmingham University, and Mr W. Evans, in charge of the Rare Books Department, made it possible for me to examine the Galsworthy Collection donated by Rudolf Sauter in 1962.

Lastly, I wish to express my deep gratitude to Professor R. Las Vergnas, former Dean of the Faculty of Arts at the Sorbonne, and President of La Sorbonne Nouvelle. Without his support and advice my work could never have been completed.

A. F.

# Acknowledgements

Mr Charles Pick, the Managing Director of William Heinemann Ltd, London, Mr R. Davies, the Sales Manager of Penguin Books Ltd, and Herr W. Polak, the Managing Director of Paul Zsolnay Verlag, publishers in Vienna and Hamburg, kindly supplied valuable figures concerning sales of Galsworthy's novels.

I wish to thank William Heinemann Ltd and the Society of Authors as the Literary representative of the Estate of John Galsworthy for allowing me to quote from Galsworthy's works.

# Introduction: the Literary Fortunes of John Galsworthy

Galsworthy was twenty-eight when he began to write, and thirty when his first book appeared in print. Success was slow in coming: the first two volumes had to be published at his own expense.

'In 1902,' he wrote, 'after seven years and four books I was still some seventy-five pounds out of pocket, to say nothing of incidental expenses, and had made no name.'[1]

His first financial success came with the publication of *The Man of Property* in 1906. Only small numbers of copies of his previous books had been printed, and they had never been reprinted, whereas *The Man of Property* was reissued four times between 1906 and 1911, and a cheap 'Sixpenny Edition' was available from 1907. After *The Man of Property*, subsequent novels were better received.[2]

This encouraging trend came to an end with the outbreak of the First World War. There was no fervent patriotism in Galsworthy's novels. Though set in the recent past or in contemporary times, they bore no relation to current events. And although they did not express any pacifist views, they were out of tune with the times simply because of the author's detachment from prevailing passions.

With *Saint's Progress*, the steady progress was resumed. Although the plot did not entirely cater to current tastes, the heroine's adventures, showing how the moral climate was deteriorating and conventional ties were slackening, were bound to interest many readers. *In Chancery* achieved no great commercial success, and it was not until *To Let* was published in 1921 that ten thousand copies were printed for a first edition.

On 2 May 1922, when both these novels, preceded by *The Man of Property*, came out in a single volume under the title *The Forsyte Saga*, Galsworthy's fame was finally established. He was fifty-five. From that year until his death in 1933, his popularity continued to grow, in spite of the weaknesses that flawed his later work. *The White Monkey* had a first edition of 15,000, *Caravan* 20,000, and

1

*The Silver Spoon* 40,000. And the last trilogy, *End of the Chapter*,
enjoyed the same success.

What is the explanation for this sudden popularity, and its
steady increase, in the last decade of a career that had begun
not only late, but also so slowly and laboriously? Likely reasons
are varied and complex. Initially, the uncompromising, harsh,
gloomy aspects of the early stories put readers off. But after the
First World War, circumstances turned in their favour. Following
publication of Lytton Strachey's biographies, *Eminent Victorians*
in 1918 and *Queen Victoria* in 1921, *The Forsyte Saga* provided
the most comprehensive, powerful and monumental expression of
the anti-Victorian climate of the immediate post-war period. So
many traditions and institutions had been swept away, and a storm
of fury and disrespect was shaking the foundations of those that
had survived. *To Let* showed 'those Victorian ashes scattered'.[3]

Another reason for *The Forsyte Saga* finding favour in 1922 was
the way it jumped from 1901 to 1920, passing over the sombre war
years in silence. People were only too pleased to forget them; like
the author himself, they took a hidden delight, in fact, in renewing
links with the past. The Victorian age was, of course, an object of
mockery; but it was also regarded with curiosity and a peculiar
pride. It was so reassuring to linger over the sense of confidence,
strength and tranquillity that had arisen from a supremacy which
had now vanished. Satire and nostalgia were, or appeared to be,
blended in just the right proportions to nurture self-esteem and
sensitivity. A people whose placid ways had been disrupted by war
longed, despite momentary querulousness, to regain its self-
confidence, reassert its identity, understand itself better. *To Let*
managed to combine contact with the present and continuity with
the past.

So it is easy to understand how attitudes crystallised in the minds
of many English people in the twenties. They recognised the
society Galsworthy was writing about, and identified it with the
society they came from. War years tend to seem longer than they
really are, and Victorian England was already remote in 1922. But
the most characteristic features of the Victorian age were still
present in people's memories. The remembered words of a grandfather, or an old aunt's ways, were enough. They stood surely for
the accuracy of the novelist's portraiture, like the nail on which a
painting is hung.

Individuals who were in their youth in 1922 spoke to me of the

Forsyte novels in such terms: 'That is why this great work had such a grip on us. It was through Galsworthy that we knew about Victorian England.' Some went further: 'We are indebted to him, not only for a picture of a past age. He gave us a feeling of what England itself was like then.'

Without intending to produce an historical work, he had tried to hold a mirror up to his country. And devoted public acclaim was indeed more than merited by the serious, conscientious and humble way he went about this task. The Forsyte Chronicles owed some of their influence, even authority, to their vast proportions. Neither before nor after their success did any of the eleven novels not belonging to the trilogies enjoy any comparable reputation. Despite their intrinsic merits, some of them have never been properly appreciated by the public.

While Galsworthy was first laboriously, then, during the last ten years of his life, effortlessly, achieving fame and fortune, his reputation in intellectual and literary circles was moving in the opposite direction. The moment when there was a change of heart towards him, when he ceased to be regarded as an avant-garde writer (or at least, considering how difficult it would be to define 'avant-garde' at that time, the moment when certain writers and critics stopped being interested in him), can be determined fairly precisely: around 1912. As he wrote in a letter to his friend and former adviser, Edward Garnett, in August 1913: 'I saw Conrad three weeks ago; we agreed that it was natural you should take no real interest in our productions because of our beastly success.'[4] It had been several years since Garnett had stopped reviewing Galsworthy's books in literary periodicals.

All this was fairly close to December 1910, defined by Virginia Woolf as the precise moment when a change occurred in human nature, sounding the knell of the three 'Edwardians', Wells, Bennett and Galsworthy, and inaugurating the 'Georgian' age. The date she chose is certainly historically significant, though as a demarcation line in the literary career of Galsworthy it is only partly valid. In some ways, his later works were still stoutly opposed to generally held opinions. It was in 1919, in the article entitled 'Modern Fiction' in *The Common Reader*, and in a lecture she gave in Cambridge in 1924, 'Mr Bennett and Mrs Brown', that Virginia Woolf made known her opinion of Galsworthy. She saw the change that occurred in December 1910 as a new interest by authors in the individual. The 'Edwardians' were not interested in their characters, but in external factors such as environment, social conventions, prospects or utopia.[5] Her husband, Leonard Woolf, had joined the Fabian Society in 1916, and taken part in Labour Party activities, and his opinion must have carried considerable weight with Virginia.

In 1927, D. H. Lawrence, undaunted by his lack of knowledge of the subject,[6] wrote an article on 'John Galsworthy', which was published the following year.[7] He also perceived a change within the general historical situation, though his dates differed from Virginia Woolf. He saw the present as a period of 'collapse', with the individual imprisoned within the psychology of his social being, and losing his freedom: 'The story is feeble, the characters have no blood and bones, the emotions are faked, faked, faked. It is one great fake.'[8]

This attack was far more damaging to Galsworthy's reputation than Virginia Woolf's rather hasty judgements.[9] It was more detailed, and far more penetrating. It contained more truth, as well as exaggeration. What made the onslaught so effective was that it was no isolated manifestation of hostility. F. R. Leavis, founder and editor of the magazine *Scrutiny* (1932–53) did not, as far as is known, intervene directly; convinced as he was that Lawrence was 'the best literary critic of our age',[10] he probably felt it unnecessary to add anything. The attitude of the 'Leavisites' has weighed heavily on Galsworthy's reputation.[11]

He was already being treated with scorn in his own lifetime. How many sheeplike critics simply followed the ideas of Virginia Woolf and Lawrence, repeating and embroidering on them year after year? As Angus Wilson pointed out to me, no major English critic has devoted any serious study to the author of *The Forsyte Saga*.

Unfortunately, he also laid himself open to political attack. His last six novels, forming the second and third trilogies, *A Modern Comedy* and *End of the Chapter*, contained real or apparent signs that he was turning to the conservative attitudes he had so savagely attacked earlier in his career. I hope my analysis will show that in fact he remained as sensitive as ever to the fate of society's victims. His other forms of writing also confirm that he remained true to his convictions and philosophy, which were, in some respects, radical to the end. Nevertheless, politics demands choices, which was exactly what he would or could not bring himself to make. When he showed some indulgence in describing London drawing-room society, or grieved over the lot of the rural gentry, he was unaware of the risks he was taking. In some cases it is not inaccurate to talk of betrayal.

The *Saturday Review*, which had been founded by liberals, was constantly hostile to him. The much more moderate antagonism of The *New Statesman and Nation*, the magazine of the Labour Party intellectuals, in which Leonard Woolf wrote, was more serious and regrettable. The leading liberal daily, the *Manchester Guardian*, had reservations, despite Galsworthy's connections with it. D. H. Lawrence added some political arms to the weaponry. His 1928 article criticised Galsworthy for being class-conscious, and he talked of prostitution to property.[12]

All this was unfair for a man whose generosity, including generosity of spirit, was seldom equalled. But it was perhaps an inevitable fate for the author of the Forsyte Chronicles. Can any writer devote himself, in his greatest work, to the meticulous, scrupulous and even nostalgic depiction of the past, without in the end becoming identified with it? So for the English, Galsworthy represents the past, because they are so conscious of all that is anachronistic in the world he describes, and of how fast it is all changing.

It is different for foreigners. They are quite aware that the Forsytes are old-fashioned, because the middle classes in most countries have moved along parallel lines. But they are much better at perceiving what remains true in Galsworthy's depiction of England, because they realise how slowly it has changed. Where else in Europe is it still almost impossible to go to the theatre on a Sunday?

The thirties and forties were years of purgatory and oblivion for Galsworthy. The fifties saw growing signs of his rehabilitation. A handsome illustrated edition of *The Forsyte Saga* was published in 1950, and its success was no fluke of literary fortune. It confirmed increasing public curiosity about Victorian literature and history. At the same time, several critics made so bold as to write articles favourable to Galsworthy.[13] Critical studies, variable in quality, appeared from 1956, showing that public indifference had ended. The first two studies of any real scholarly value, Asher Boldon Wilson's *John Galsworthy's Letters to Leon Lion*, and William Bellamy's *The Novels of Wells, Bennett and Galsworthy: 1890–1910*, were published in 1968 and 1971.

The year 1967 was the centenary of Galsworthy's birth. It was celebrated with resounding and quite unexpected success by the BBC, which produced a 26-hour long serialisation of the Forsyte Chronicles, at that time the most costly television production ever made. Soames and the other Forsytes first appeared on television screens on 7 January 1967, and continued to do so every Saturday evening until 1 July. Public reaction was so overwhelming that, by general demand, the serial was repeated from 8 September 1968 to 2 March 1969. Simultaneously, sales of Galsworthy's novels in Britain rose to levels never reached during his lifetime. And with more than forty countries (including the Soviet Union) buying the BBC film, new translations or large new editions brought him a vast new public. The scale of the success showed how wrong were those who had proclaimed him dead and buried.

Some critics have refused to back down. Since they cannot deny Galsworthy's fresh popularity, they claim that it is ill-founded, and maintain their own indifference. However, Galsworthy's literary fame seems to be assured of a long future.

# Part I
# Galsworthy the Man

# 1 Galsworthy and his Family Background

'I am, of course, a very dumb person, and liable to give people who meet me . . . a peculiarly dry and sketchy impression. Besides, to be quite honest, I greatly dislike being interviewed, and it rouses my perversity.'[1]

This was how Galsworthy warned a correspondent not to take seriously what claimed to be a portrait of him. Little is known of his life, and the man himself remained almost a stranger, except to a very small number of people: his wife Ada, his sisters Lilian Sauter and Mabel Reynolds, and his nephew and adopted son, Rudolf Sauter. In 1929, the German critic Leon Schalit wrote: 'He had been described to me as an inaccessible "iceberg", as a man of reserve carried to extremes.'[2] The mystery was to last even beyond his death in 1933, since the official biography by H. V. Marrot, *The Life and Letters of John Galsworthy*, did not appear until two years later. This bulky volume remains the basic source. It was commissioned by the family, and written in collaboration with Ada Galsworthy, using the novelist's papers. Marrot was not a professional writer, much less a critic. However, he was a fervent admirer of Galsworthy's works, and was familiar with them. The same was true of Ada, who had acted as her husband's secretary and typed out his manuscripts. But her involvement raises the delicate problem of deciding how objective the work may be. It is hardly necessary to say that it contains neither a comprehensive biography nor the complete correspondence.

So it was only in 1935 that the public learned that Ada Pearson Cooper had been married before, in April 1891, to Galsworthy's cousin, Arthur John Galsworthy. The marriage had not been happy, and Ada had found sympathy among her in-laws, particularly Galsworthy's sisters. The liaison with Galsworthy began in September 1895. Ada left her husband in 1902, and apparently he

9

sued for divorce before the end of 1904. On 10 January 1905, Galsworthy and Ada left England. They returned to London the following September, and were married on 23 September, the day the decree absolute was granted.

His novels, and what is known of Galsworthy's life, suggest that these were events of vital importance. His success in concealing them from the public in his lifetime is evidence of his determination and the effectiveness of his efforts. He had always been firm on this matter. He did not believe that simply by purchasing one of his books a reader gained any right to know about his private life. On 13 August 1912, he wrote to the young poet Ralph Mottram — towards whom he was always most friendly and generous — that it would be out of the question to supply biographical details; he felt that biographies during the life of those concerned were 'odious'.

So, all that can be done is to note the lack of information about Galsworthy's life. Too many of his relatives and friends have now died, and too many of his papers were destroyed by himself or his wife, to allow any accurate reconstruction of the real facts. Will it ever be possible to write any sort of comprehensive life of Galsworthy?

It is difficult, then, though not impossible, to apprehend Galsworthy. His natural reserve ruled out any sensational revelations, and his pride as a writer had the same effect. He wanted his background to have no bearing on any literary success. But this extreme reserve, which he could never entirely escape from, forced him to find other paths by which to express his innermost feelings. His writings have much to reveal about his life, if they are explored and interpreted with proper allowance for artistic transposition. And the different registers he employed make them all the more eloquent. Galsworthy was not only a novelist, he was also a dramatist, story-teller, short-story writer, essayist, publicist, letter-writer and even poet.

An unpublished letter from Galsworthy to his cousin, Edwin Henry Galsworthy, contains the results of his investigations into the origins of his father's family. The efforts made by Soames and other Forsytes to identify their own ancestors suggest that he must have been extremely persevering in his research. He gave up only when he had gone right back to 1598, and had met with insurmountable obstacles to further progress. The family tree that Galsworthy enclosed with his letter, and on which Marrot based his genealogical chart, bears the title 'Pedigree of Galsworthys from Wembury and Plymstock, South Devon'. He did not try to embroider on the facts, or give any grounds for snobbery. He made no mystery of the fact that his forebears were of humble though honest origin ('wholesome' was his word for it). This also applies to the Forsytes, whose ancestors are described as 'small beer'.

Why did Galsworthy carry out these investigations? He appears to have taken an early interest in animal pedigrees, as a keen huntsman and betting man. And this may have led him, quite naturally, to extend his curiosity to human lineages. The idea of racial purity, nowadays so misplaced, was deeply rooted in him. He was delighted to have succeeded in establishing that he was of purely English stock.

His paternal grandfather, John Galsworthy, the second to bear the name (Galsworthy himself was the fourth), was born on 7 January 1782 at Plymstock. For six generations his family had been small farmers. He became a successful merchant and shipper, and left Devon for London in 1833. He entered the booming property market in London, where judicious speculations turned his Devonshire savings into a fortune.

The little that is known of him may be supplemented by a few details supplied in 'Superior Dosset', the first of the stories in *On Forsyte 'Change* (1930). Superior Dosset was Young Jolyon's grandfather, and he had begun as a mason, a trade that was of use to him later. On his death, he left thirty thousand pounds to be divided among his children. Most of the facts and dates suggest that Galsworthy's grandfather was the model for Superior Dosset. The only other reminiscences of the period prior to the departure for London are to be found in the second story in *On Forsyte 'Change*, 'Sands of Time 1821−63'.

Galsworthy's mingled affection and admiration for his father is expressed in a subdued, even constrained way, in his novels. But all the texts relating to him are most impressive. John Galsworthy senior was the model for Old Jolyon, like him the eldest member of the family, and by far the most estimable of all the Forsytes. Old Jolyon's old age and the close of his life are beautifully described in *The Man of Property* and *Indian Summer of a Forsyte*. He was a proud man, with a strong personality, held in some awe by all around him, but also loved, particularly by children. Without possessing the critical turn of mind that his son displayed in a more progressive and sceptical age, he had enough intelligence and taste to succeed in life.

Galsworthy's father was a solicitor and company director in London, who suffered some misgivings about the huge fortune he had acquired in the exercise of his profession. Few clues are given to this dissatisfaction. The short story in *On Forsyte 'Change* entitled 'A Sad Affair' tells how Old Jolyon pays a debt incurred with a moneylender by his son when a student. The story reflects the difference between two generations, almost two social classes, for Old Jolyon had not been to university. But the most striking feature is the efforts of both father and son to come close to each other, and maintain their mutual affection and understanding. Galsworthy was no Samuel Butler: he was never moved to hatred of his father, even by the desire to go against his wishes. There was indeed some disagreement as to the choice of a career. But when his parents realised that they could not turn him into a lawyer, they hid their disappointment, and did not try to impose their authority, or make him suffer in any way.

The text 'A Portrait' in *A Motley*,[3] reprinted in *Caravan*, is completely stripped of any novelistic or imaginary elements, and yet is as inspired an account of his father as the finest pages of *Indian Summer of a Forsyte*. It was written in 1908, only four years after his father's death, and is extremely precise. It places special emphasis – perhaps even with an overtone of envy – on the excellent balance between the man of action and the man of reflection, on his art of living life to the full, but with moderation.

Far less is known about Galsworthy's mother, born Blanche Bailey Bartleet in 1837. She was twenty years younger than her husband, whom she married when she was twenty-five. She died in 1915, eleven years after him. She was of loftier lineage than the Galsworthys: the Bartleets belonged to the rural gentry of Worcestershire.

Documents available about her are very limited. There is a short chapter in Marrot's biography, entitled 'Interlude: Mother', consisting mainly of an unpublished text in Galsworthy's hand, 'Note on my Mother'. In his fiction, she appears in the guise of the Freelands' mother in his novel *The Freelands*. She is also 'The Grey Angel', title of a short story in *Caravan*.

Galsworthy's near silence on the subject of his mother is eloquent. His feelings towards her were mixed. Even in his childhood, there had been no great intimacy between them. Yet in the three texts in which he spoke of her, *The Freelands*, 'The Grey Angel' and 'Note on my Mother', he tried to be fair. He admitted his mother's charm, elegance, taste, distinction, goodness: in short her nobility of character. He believed that he owed her his respect for form, his own sense of dignity. But he could not stand her lack of critical spirit, her dreadful conventionalism in every way, her maternalism. Indirectly, she exerted a major influence, arousing a reaction against the type of family life she had imposed on him.

But things must not be over-dramatised. There is no evidence of any real conflict between mother and son. On the contrary, after her initial disappointment, she took a lively interest in her son's literary ambitions, and subscribed to a cuttings agency which sent her press reviews of his work. And he showed suitable concern when his mother became ill in her old age. He admired her calm and stoical courage.

She had never concealed her strength of character, but never used it in a tyrannical way. This is why, in the two texts in which he uses her as a model, he judges her with some mischievousness, but never unkindly. The Grey Angel and Frances Freeland are both charming and quite inoffensive old ladies. They have to be accepted as they are, and this was clearly Galsworthy's attitude to his mother. He wrote: 'My father really predominated in me from the start, and ruled my life. I was so truly and deeply fond of him that I seemed not to have a fair share of love left to give my mother.'[4]

On the whole, then, he had good parents, and was fortunate in his relations with them.

# 2 Galsworthy's Legal Training and Background in Literature

Galsworthy's solicitor father decided that his son should be a lawyer. Galsworthy read law at Oxford, somewhat lackadaisically, from 1886 to 1889. He continued his studies in London, at Lincoln's Inn, from 1890 to 1894, and was called to the bar on 29 April 1890. He had already been introduced to legal practice, for his father entrusted him with several cases in which his clients were interested. Among other things, he had to draw up his own family tree, in order to sort out a particularly thorny inheritance dispute.

It was probably in 1892 that his father encouraged him to turn to maritime law. His 1892–3 voyage to the South Seas was also intended to familiarise him with certain aspects of maritime affairs. His father obviously had ambitions for him, hoping that he would specialise and become an authority on maritime law. These hopes were to be disappointed. From the meagre information available about Galsworthy the man of law, Marrot concludes that he practised very little. Some time in 1894 he abandoned his profession.

His novels and plays give considerable space to lawyers, judges, surveyors, solicitors, notaries and clerks, as well as to accounts of prisons, prison staff and conditions. What he was mainly interested in was legal practice, and jurisprudence, and for this purpose he used his knowledge of the procedures and arguments that lawyers are prone to engage in. It was a vast field, on which he could exercise his sense of humour, and often his satirical gift.

He made discreet though effective efforts to bring about changes in legislation in several areas. He was particularly concerned with divorce law, and with regulations on solitary confinement. On both these points he argued passionately for liberalisation of the law. And the reactions aroused by his play *Justice* did, indeed, lead to changes in rules governing solitary confinement.

So he looked hard at the system of justice, in many cases found it extremely unjust, and denounced it or helped to reform it. In this humane attitude he was well ahead of his time.

He was, himself, greatly influenced by his legal training. The accuracy, meticulousness and consummate skill with which he relates so many trials and legal procedures of all kinds, pleas, cross-examinations, inquiries, verdicts, identification of victims or guilty parties, hearings of witnesses, jury deliberations, show that, in spite of appearances, he had not been an entirely idle student of law. When his sister Lilian reproached him for giving away family secrets in *The Man of Property*, he replied that, for him, it was not a matter of being for or against any particular character: 'I feel more like a sort of chemist, more cold, more dissective.'[1]

The reference to practical anatomy, in which the medical student trains himself to achieve the greatest possible insensitivity, is significant. Looking for clues, analysing circumstances, understanding motives, immediate or remote causes, may have been a purely intellectual game for him at first. Later, when he felt involved, certain habits of rigour and fairness were already ingrained, and they conferred greater subtlety and depth on his work.

His descriptions of legal proceedings show how skilfully he could put himself in the place of the judge, or of either counsel. Both barrister and judge are seeking the truth. But the barrister is interested in only the part of it that is favourable to his client. It may well have been this obligation to be one-sided that made the legal profession so distasteful to Galsworthy. He would rather have seen himself as the judge, and would have made a good one.[2]

Galsworthy's philosophical and paraphilosophical reading will be discussed later. At present, I want to deal with his introduction to literature, describe the actual circumstances in which it took place, and assess his background in literature and its extent.

At Harrow, as he says, he was given no taste for literature or history. At the age of twenty-two, he wrote in an album belonging to a female cousin that his favourite authors were Thackeray, Dickens (he was particularly fond of *The Pickwick Papers*), and Whyte-Melville. His fondness for Dumas's *Three Musketeers* and *Count of Monte Cristo*, Robert Louis Stevenson's novels (*Catriona* and *The Master of Ballantrae*), and one of Mark Twain's greatest stories, *Huckleberry Finn*, no doubt dates from his youth. He believed that Hardy's novels could not be compared with those of Stevenson, which he found far livelier. He also said that he loved Conrad's 'greatest works'.[3]

His 1892–3 voyage did much to awaken his literary vocation. One of its purposes was to meet R. L. Stevenson. Part of the voyage was on board the *Torrens*, where the first mate was Joseph Conrad. This began a friendship that lasted thirty-two years, until Conrad's death. Galsworthy was immediately attracted by the personality of Conrad, eleven years his senior. Conrad already had twenty years of roving to relate, and Galsworthy was a spellbound listener. Conrad had the as yet uncompleted manuscript of his first novel, *Almayer's Folly*, in his cabin, but this was not discussed. Three years after being on the *Torrens*, Galsworthy published his own first work, a collection of short stories entitled *From the Four Winds*. The figure of Conrad is illustrated in one of the stories, 'The Doldrums'. Galsworthy no doubt read Conrad's novels eagerly as they came out in the closing years of the century.

Of another story in the same collection, he wrote: 'From the title of that story, "Dick Denver's Idea", you can tell how much of it can be traced to the inspiration of Bret Harte and how much to the influence of Rudyard Kipling.'[4]

No firm conclusions can be drawn from these rather eclectic, youthful tastes. However, at this stage it may be useful to recall his fondness for two novelists who were very popular in their time, and are far less well known today: the Scotsman George John Whyte-Melville and the American Francis Bret Harte.

In a reference to Whyte-Melville, Galsworthy tells that, by dint of reading novels about imperturbably stoic, even though debt-ridden, young dandies, he had come to believe that wearing side-whiskers, being impeccably dressed, and remaining unaffected by the whims of Fortune, were the golden rules of life.[5]

Bret Harte, founder of the 'school of local colour', presented strongly contrasted characters, adventurous rogues, gamblers, consumed with a lust to win, but in whom a predilection for good-ness and devotion lay dormant. And precisely, 'Dick Denver's Idea' offers a very simple and clear moral: woman is sacred. This con-ception of the weaker sex is to be found in the story 'A Knight' and, indeed, throughout Galsworthy's writings. His heroes are always chivalrous towards women.

During his 1893 voyage, Galsworthy also read and reread a little book of quite a different kind, *The Story of an African Farm*, by Olive Schreiner. It is the first sign of his search for a more sober, sparer style, and also of his interest in agnosticism.

The next phase of his introduction to literature began in 1898. In his attempts to learn the craft of writing, he studied Maupassant and Turgenev intensively in French. These two 'masters' were, he said, 'the first writers who gave me, at once, real aesthetic excitement, and an insight into proportion of theme and economy of words'.[6]

These are the only two authors to whom Galsworthy recognised any great debt. In general he denied having undergone literary influences, although such denials cannot be fully accepted. In particular, he never admitted his debt to Conrad, whose name should surely be added to those of Maupassant and Turgenev. According to Marrot, 'The bookish discussions at Elstree under the presidency of Conrad had brought him among the ranks of those to whom technique mattered.'[7]

This seems only fair to Conrad the stylist. But the role of literary mentor was played by Edward Garnett, with whom Galsworthy began a regular correspondence from 1900. Garnett did not simply criticise the manuscripts his new friend sent him. He was extremely knowledgeable about contemporary literature, and guided Galsworthy's reading. In a letter of June 1903, for example, he advised him to read *Hampshire Days* by W. H. Hudson, and told him, without delay, of the publication of a 'remarkable book', *The Way of All Flesh* by Samuel Butler.[8] Both these writers were, in different ways, to excite Galsworthy, to such an extent that he heaped over-lavish praise on all their writings. In addition to Hudson's best work, *Green Mansions*, he read *El Ombù*, *The Land's End*, *Idle Days in Patagonia*, *Afoot in England*, *Adventures Among Birds*, *A Shepherd's Life*, and others, in fact probably all his works. He also read the 'nature authors' whose names are often associated with Hudson's: Richard Jefferies, Henry Woodd Nevinson, whose *A Modern Slavery* impressed him 'enormously', and Henry Williamson, whose *The Old Stag* and *Tarka the Otter* he praised.

Garnett's wife Constance published translations of the Russian classics, which Galsworthy admired tremendously. Meanwhile, Garnett himself was publishing articles on Russian literature, and a book on Turgenev. On 14 June 1901, he advised Galsworthy to read the French translation of Gorki's *The Vagabonds*. On 24 April 1910, Galsworthy told him that he had read Maurice Baring's *Landmarks in Russian Literature*, and of his intention to improve his knowledge of Dostoyevsky by reading *The Idiot*, *The Brothers Karamazov* and *The Possessed*. Among Tolstoy's works he had read at least *War and Peace* and *Anna Karenina*.[9] Another friend, the classical scholar Gilbert Murray, introduced him to ancient Greece, and to Greek drama in particular.

Bret Harte is not the only American author mentioned by Galsworthy. There are also Henry James, Emerson, Longfellow, Hawthorne, Whittier, Thoreau, Motley, Holmes, Lowell, Sinclair Lewis and Mark Twain, already mentioned.[10]

In a letter in 1914, in which he recognised the merits of Lawrence's *Sons and Lovers*, while criticising its indecency, there is a longer list of 'masters' than before. The list shows fuller knowledge of Russian and French literature: it includes Tolstoy, Turgenev, Chekhov, Maupassant, Flaubert, Anatole France.[11] As time passed, the range of authors became even wider, and more English authors are mentioned. In 1920 he advised a young writer to read W. H. Hudson, the Bible, Walter Pater (while putting him on his guard against Pater's preciosity), Samuel Butler, Masefield and Siegfried Sassoon.[12] A list of major literary and dramatic characters, probably dating from 1923,[13] throws further light on his interests: Don Quixote, Sancho Panza, Hamlet, Lear, Falstaff, Tom Jones, Faust, d'Artagnan, Sam Weller, Betsy Trotwood, Mr Micawber, Becky Sharp, Major Pendennis, Bel Ami, Irina, Bazarov, Anna Karenina. There is a further list of short stories which Galsworthy considered masterpieces, and whose authors, according to him, had been less successful as novelists.[14] The context shows that he was far from regarding the short story as a minor *genre*.

The conclusion to be drawn is that Galsworthy's knowledge of literature was both extensive and restricted. He was familiar with only a short period of French literature. He appears to have known nothing of German, Italian and Spanish literature (except for *Don Quixote*). On the other hand, he was far more at home in English literature than his own statements might lead one to expect. He loved the Greek and great 19th century Russian classics. Details of all his reading would cover many pages, and provide a most impressive catalogue of literary works.

# 3 Aspects of Galsworthy's Life

## THE SPORTSMAN

The most appropriate starting point might have been a discussion of Galsworthy's health and constitution, but very little direct information is available. When one enjoys good health, as he did, there is nothing to say; and, anyway, in the circles in which he moved, it was not 'done'. At most, people might mention taking the waters at some fashionable spa.

The best approach to the subject is to consider his sporting activities — an acceptable, even a recommended subject of conversation in such circles.

His healthy appearance is confirmed by Rudolf Sauter: 'My uncle was never one to make much of such ailments as he had, and on the whole they were remarkably few.'[1]

Mabel, speaking of her brother's childhood, though admitting that her memories were vague, wrote:

> The general impression is that of a normal, not at all unusual kind of boy. I know that he was healthy and active, good at games and school sports — as a number of cups and other trophies can testify; captain (in due course) of 'footer' and 'gym' at Harrow; a bad cricketer, but good tennis-player, horseman and shot.[2]

He was to bring his athletic career to a triumphant conclusion in 1886, beating the Harrow record for the mile, in 4 minutes 43 seconds. He relates how he let his two rivals lead the field, overtaking them in the last 200-yard sprint. He also claimed that he owed his victory to an excellent meal of which he had partaken the previous evening, accompanied by champagne and port.[3] He had only one more term to spend at Harrow School, and pointed out that he never ran again.

19

His biographer, though a firm admirer, admits wryly — and
other evidence abounds to the same effect — that Galsworthy
never showed much interest in studying at university. He was far
more interested in other aspects of undergraduate life. The £300
yearly allowance from his father, although a handsome sum for
the time, was not always enough to cover his expenses.[4] If he incurred too many gambling debts, he could always, like his friends,
pawn his watch. . . .

Oxford, as characteristic an institution of the governing class in
Victorian England as Harrow, adopted a completely different
approach in order to form an élite. The university left its students
considerable freedom to spend their time at agreeable pastimes,
while qualifying for the jobs and responsibilities that awaited
them. There was no better way of convincing the sons of the upper
classes of their superiority, and of the legitimacy of the privileges
they enjoyed.

Not surprisingly, Galsworthy's first reaction to the enjoyment of
these extraordinary rights was to adopt current conventions, and
embark on his brief period as a dandy.

During the summer vacation of 1887, he went walking and
climbing with a friend in Cumberland. Fortunately, Ada was to
show the same enthusiasm for walking. From what they said, they
seem to have continued this activity until very late in life.
Although it may lack physical thrills, rambling requires good
muscles and plenty of free time. In the timetable for an average
day which he once wrote down, 'two hours at least' are reserved for
walking and riding when in the country, and 'one hour at most' for
walking when in London.[5]

So there is no reason to doubt the general truth of the travel
stories told by Ada Galsworthy in *Over the Hills and Far Away*, in
1937. It is a charming book to read, and even her slight exaggerations are instructive. Both of them, she said, preferred the
countryside, and they much preferred mountains to the seaside,
which failed signally to attract either of them. They loved hilly
country, both for its beauty and for the exercise it offered.[6]
Neither was a real mountaineer, however. Their love of the Tyrol
will be mentioned later, since it was so deeply motivated, making it
of considerable interest to the student of Galsworthy. The medium
altitudes that they liked were healthy, and the tranquillising
effects were sought and appreciated by both of them, being
endowed with more physical strength than nervous resistance.

Galsworthy also enjoyed riding, though Ada was a less frequent companion. Rudolf Sauter describes the morning ride he and his uncle used to take before breakfast, when they were at Manaton; the afternoon was kept for walking. Galsworthy was very fond of strenuous and even, occasionally, dangerous gallops.[7] In London, apparently, he never appeared on the highly fashionable Rotten Row, in Hyde Park. As long as he actually lived in the inner city, until 1918, he did not do any riding there.

Given his athletic tastes, it is not surprising that Galsworthy was also fond of shooting. This began when he was sixteen or seventeen. There were plenty of opportunities, for in the social class to which he belonged — the upper middle class but also, on his mother's side, the landed gentry — there were many house parties and long weekends. Shooting parties moved on from one country house to the next. And in about 1883 his father began to rent land during the grouse-shooting season, in Devon and later in Scotland.[8]

While his other sporting enthusiasms were never to fade, his passion for shooting — such a favourite sport in England that many refer to it simply as 'sport' — came to a sudden end, usurped for ever by a horror of bloodshed and all violence. In one of his most delightful and most autobiographical short stories, *Memories* there is a humorous account of the way he changed after 1895, and how it affected the life of his favourite dog, the spaniel Chris:

> It was strictly in accordance with the perversity of things, and something in the nature of a calamity that he had not been ours one year, when there came over me a dreadful but overmastering aversion from killing those birds and creatures of which he was so fond as soon as they were dead. . . . But as *he* grew every year more devoted to dead grouse and birds and rabbits, *I* liked them more and more alive.[9]

On the whole, then, Galsworthy enjoyed excellent reserves of health and strength, which he preserved and maintained through his enjoyment of life, lived with discrimination and moderation, thanks partly to the various forms of skill he practised, but mainly because of his consistency and conscientiousness. By nature he was privileged, and he never misused this privilege.

## HEALTH

Information referring explicitly to Galsworthy's health is very sparse, as has been said. When none at all exists, the logical conclusion should be drawn from such absence.

Chronologically, the first complaint to be mentioned is shortsightedness. Mabel attributed it to his voracious childhood reading of history and adventure stories. He read lying on the floor, his eyes down.

The second ailment to be reported is just as commonplace, and it is not clear how serious it was. Galsworthy suffered from rheumatism fairly early in life, in his twenties. He treated it with a portable shower of his own invention, which caused sweating.[10] His rheumatism did have one result, which will be mentioned later.

In 1908, just after alighting from the train at Charing Cross, he and Ada were in a cab that was overturned by a pair of runaway horses. Ada opened the door and leapt out, but Galsworthy was buried under the luggage. A moment later, however, with Olympian calm, he surfaced, emerging unharmed through the window. He seems to have enjoyed the protection of Providence in such cases, for, as a small child, his pony had run away with him, and he had escaped death by a miracle.[11] It continued to smile on him to such effect that it was not until he was in Arizona that he was stung by a scorpion. He was unwell for six or seven days, wrote Ada in a letter on 22 March 1926. A blow on the chest from a cricket ball was a little more serious, and he was incapacitated for two or three weeks.

But these are all minor disabilities. An occasional cold, a headache, the little irritations that are noticed only in the absence of greater misfortunes. He knew how fortunate he was: he wrote to André Chevrillon, about an attack of paratyphoid that he and his nephew's wife Viola both contracted on holiday in Morocco, 'We pay, as usual, for luxuries.'[12] But for this letter, the event would not even have been heard of. As far as is known, it was the only price he had to pay in the course of innumerable travels to every corner of the globe.

Galsworthy can almost be seen as one of those rare and blessed beings whose life is like a quiet sea on which they sail.

## CONFINEMENT IN LONDON

In an attempt to understand what may be called Galsworthy's 'change of heart', the circumstances in which it occurred must be reviewed. If a title were to be given to these circumstances, it would probably be 'Confinement in London 1890—1905'.

Why 'confinement'? To explain it, some reference must be made to Galsworthy's way of life, described in another chapter. He was no town-dweller: his deepest instincts led him to flee the city where his grandfather had come to make his fortune, and retrace his steps back into the country. He dreamt constantly of retiring from business life, and succeeded, after showing as much obstinacy as his grandfather had in entering the world he wanted to leave.

His father, well aware of the financial benefits of the legal profession, set him to study law as soon as he went up to Oxford. From 1890 on, this meant living in London, having a room in the Inns of Court — or being sent off to Russia or America whenever his watchful father's eye saw the advantage of so doing, to put an end to an undesirable attachment. The young Galsworthy had no objection to travelling. Between 1891 and 1894 he went on three such trips. But he always ended up coming back, to practise a profession which he regarded only as a way of making money.

In 1904, an event of considerable importance occurred. During a long solitary ramble through his beloved Devon, he discovered Manaton, a village right on the edges of the wild stretches of Dartmoor, within sight of the coast, and a few leagues from 'Great Galsworthy', the field where his forebears had grazed their livestock. The great thirty-volume edition of his works took its name from the village of Manaton. In the hamlet he found Wingstone Farm, part of which he rented as a country home. For fifteen years, from 1908 to 1923, he was to spend his happiest days there.

In very simplified form, this was half of Galsworthy's life. Thirty-three of his sixty-six years lay between 1890 and 1923. It was the central period of his life, comprising his 'change of heart', and the First World War. Before examining these two events, the significance of his 'confinement' in London from 1890 to 1905 needs to be explained. And this can be done only by answering the precise question: was Galsworthy a town-dweller or a countryman? It is impossible to understand what a constraint living in London was for him without realising that, previously, he had been neither forced nor used to urban living. Information on this involves the first twenty-three years of his life, from 1867 to 1890.

## TOWN-DWELLER OR COUNTRYMAN?

Galsworthy was born at Kingston Hill in Surrey, now part of the outer London suburbs, but a century ago in the heart of the country. Marrot suggests that his father moved to Surrey, from his London house in Portland Place, in 1864, three years before John was born, because he wanted his young family to enjoy a natural, healthy environment. He himself was passionately fond of the country. This is confirmed by his daughter Mabel and grandson Rudolf, who writes: 'From my grandfather . . . they inherited . . . a love of beauty and nature.'[13] He had chosen the site of his house for the lovely view over the Surrey Downs. He turned the place into a rural paradise, neat and cared-for, in the landscaped style dear to English landowners, with grounds, kitchen garden and domestic animals to amuse the children, and provide fresh produce for the whole family.

Galsworthy lived there till he was nine, beginning his education with a series of governesses, in the usual upper middle-class way. At the age of ten or eleven, he went to a small boarding school at Saugeen, near Bournemouth, also well away from factory chimneys and the overcrowding of large towns. The children continued to enjoy the delights of nature — nature kept on a tight rein by gardeners, healthy and placid. Harrow, attended by the children of the aristocratic and wealthy, was also in rural surroundings.

Mabel confirms the story told by Galsworthy in *Awakening*, the second interlude in *The Forsyte Saga*. In these pages, with their admirably poetic and imaginative style, Jon, she points out, is quite clearly John: 'It is easy to form an idea of his childhood, for although some details are distinctly different, the picture he has drawn in the sketch called *Awakening* of the little boy Jon's early life is practically a description of his own.'[14]

His period in Oxford was too brief and superficial to be called town-dwelling. Anyway, very little of his time was spent in the library, at lectures or in the High. The rest of the time he was out in the country. This is confirmed by *The Island Pharisees*, where undergraduate memories are used, if not recounted. Most of the action takes place in the country.

If there was any period of his life when Galsworthy lived mostly — though never uninterruptedly — in town, it was during the four years after he came down from Oxford. From 1890 to 1894 he read for the bar. He showed a distinct lack of enthusiasm, but appears to have suffered little distress from having to comply with his father's wishes, and with the obligation to reside in chambers. By predilection he was rather like a lawyer without a brief, and in 1894, during his fourth year of study, he gave it all up.

It is hardly an accident that his biographer should know so little about the next period of his life. The frequent changes of address become significant, and everything becomes clear, when it is realised that his liaison with his cousin's wife began in 1895. What better place to conceal it all than in a city like London, with its many opportunities for anonymity? Once Ada had taken advantage of her husband's departure for the Boer War to quit the conjugal home, each of them had a small flat in London. Not surprisingly, London represented for Galsworthy the city above all cities. If one has to stay in town, why not seek there the adventures that one has not been able to go after in Australia?

It was all the easier to resign himself because he and Ada proved uncommonly good at snatching trips to the country, and even farther afield, to other countries, during the first nine years they were together, until the death of Galsworthy's father in December 1904 enabled them at last to appear together in public. They at once offered Ada's deserted spouse an opportunity of divorcing her. Once wed, they set up home in a small house in Addison Road in the West End.

There is no need to study Galsworthy's changes of residence in any further detail. Far from weakening in subsequent years, the same tendencies grew stronger. He kept a house in London but, apart from long visits to Manaton during the summer, he fell into the habit of going to Littlehampton to work, when there was not enough time for the long journey down to Devon. The name of this small seaside resort begins to appear in Marrot's biography in 1907, and it is mentioned frequently in Galsworthy's diaries. It must have been a very small place at the time, with few people around when they went there, in the off season. The series of long trips abroad began in 1911. Every year until his death, and from 1924 on in the company of their nephew Rudolf and his wife Viola, the Galsworthys spent the whole winter outside Britain, visiting Europe, America and Africa.

On 27 September 1918, Galsworthy finally left inner London, and settled in Grove House in Hampstead. This was at the time a haven of fresh air and greenery, with everything he needed for riding at his doorstep. This was even more important during the last three years of his residence in Hampstead, after the lease on Wingstone Farm ran out in 1923. He felt this as a dreadful blow. For sixteen years this corner of his beloved Devon had provided him with an ideal retreat. 'Alas for us! — or for me, rather, because I think Ada is almost glad to be quit of Devonshire damp — Wingstone will be reft from us next month. . . . To me it's a blow, *I don't say so however.*'[15] This was in a letter to his friend H. Granville Barker. Leaving Manaton meant giving up the peaceful solitude that so suited him, though it may have weighed on Ada (like the lack of amenities, to which he was quite indifferent). Far more cruelly, it meant losing the contact with nature, animals, the farm where, during the war and at harvest time, he had always so enjoyed lending a hand; never in any other place had he felt such profound emotions, such close, personal contact with nature.

So, in a kind of gloomy revenge, in the autumn of 1926, he decided, for the last of many times in his life, to move house. He left Grove Lodge for the country, where his last home was Bury House, on the Sussex Downs. Rudolf Sauter tells how his uncle chose this large house, without even entering it, simply from seeing the wonderful view from the terraces. 'This is the place,' he said at once.[16] He was soon to be striding over his own lands. Seven years and a few months later, he died.

What conclusions can be drawn from this account of Galsworthy's homes? He spent most of his life in the country, and if he did so, it was from choice. Does this mean he was hardly ever in town, and disliked it when he was? Not at all. This is why allowance has to be made for subjectivity in Rudolf Sauter's comment on Galsworthy's love of nature. Speaking of Wingstone, he wrote: 'Here, the rain and the sun and the scent of the land became . . . a part of my uncle's own nature. . . . Without these, he seemed to be deprived of some integral current of life, some sustaining force, little understandable in our present, largely urban existence.'[17]

The implication of the foreign nature of urban surroundings for Galsworthy, and his inadaptability to city life, is clearly inaccurate. Admittedly, Galsworthy himself constantly expressed such views. The inexorable urbanisation of England repelled him: not that he had a phobia of towns, any fear of life there, simply that they filled him with distaste, and, above all, distrust. Does that prove that Rudolf Sauter was right in what he said?

In fact, Galsworthy was constantly in contact with towns, through his very frequent short visits, and in his correspondence and thoughts, even when he was physically absent. He even loved the town for itself, though he continued to fear its effects on his fellow-men. None could deny the eminently sociable character of his writings, particularly his plays, evidence of his own sociability and even urbanity. All that he disliked was the ugly outside face of a city, and the overcrowding. His imaginative gifts were stimulated and enriched by his great sensitivity. So he experienced the existence of towns of his day, with their slums, smoke, blackness and dirt, without living among them.

There could be nothing more untrue than the idea of Galsworthy the misanthrope, withdrawing to a solitary life in the country, hating towns, firmly intending to forget them and never go back. He did have great delight in contact with the countryside, but was capable of discovering equally intense pleasure in London, Manchester, Birmingham, Liverpool, Nottingham, Cologne and New York, where he attended performances of his plays, after taking a very active part in production work at every stage. It was on a theatre stage that he met the young choreographer Margaret Morris, and their relationship took place entirely in London.

His many other charitable, intellectual, international and journalistic activities in cities, his lecturing, his work as founder of the PEN Club, all go to show his intense participation in urban life. He knew where power lay, even if his own tastes took him elsewhere to live. So the answer to the question of whether he was a town-dweller or a countryman is a complex and illuminating one. But the approach that is opened up by studying the question stops before reaching its goal. The events that marked the year 1895 must now be examined.


## GALSWORTHY'S CHANGE OF HEART

In his chapter entitled '1895: Crisis', Marrot writes:

> Although at first there was much unhappiness mixed with the rapture that it brought, its effects were in every way beneficial. Moreover, it exacted of him an emotional and imaginative toll which endowed him with pity and comprehension; and it

yielded him as perfect a mate as ever man had. Again, both the
man and the writer are the better understood through the story
of his love; for without Ada Galsworthy he might never have
become a writer.[18]

In the short chapter that follows, Marrot provides very little
evidence of substance about the 1895 'crisis'. There seems to have
been some over-dramatisation, for which Ada was probably partly
responsible. She and Marrot worked together, and she cannot
have been averse to appearing as her husband's muse and inspiration. What does remain clear is that Galsworthy went through
a troubled period, and underwent wide-ranging changes in his
life.

The two main sources of information are the unpublished
diaries, and his novel *The Island Pharisees*. Neither should his first
novel, *Jocelyn*, be ignored. It is valuable for two reasons, both of
which concern its date of writing, 1898. At that time, the
memories of 1895 were far fresher in his mind than when *The
Island Pharisees* was published six years later, in 1904. In
addition, his lack of literary experience made the autobiographical aspect of *Jocelyn* much more revealing.

It is all mysterious, even obscure. It is hard to distinguish
sentiment from passion, and emotion, though emotion seems to
predominate in the character who may be taken to represent Galsworthy in the triangular plot. The tormented situation arouses in
him not a moral conscience, but at least awareness of his partners'
sufferings. And as the path embarked on in *Jocelyn* widens, so in
*The Island Pharisees* there is, if not a social conscience, then at
least a realisation of his fellow men's sufferings.

Given what is known of him, it is certain that Galsworthy must
have spared no effort to conceal and destroy every clue to his
personal relationship with Ada. Nothing precise is revealed in
*Jocelyn* or *The Island Pharisees*. His correspondence contains no
trace of a single letter exchanged by the lovers, and even the unpublished diaries and note-books give very little information.

Galsworthy's change of heart was caused by the feelings aroused
in him by Ada, probably from 1893, when the first recorded
private meeting between them took place.[19] These feelings were a
mixture of compassion, respect, gallantry, anger and desire, no
doubt. The fact that Ada was married turned her lover into something of a rebel against the established order. And Ada's fateful

words, 'Why don't you write? You're just the person', were pronounced at the Gare du Nord in Paris, in 1895, only a few months before their wedding.[20] The advice was soon carried into effect, and John, Ada and Literature were to form a blissful *ménage à trois*.

There were two outward signs of the gradual transformation that was invading Galsworthy's mind and feelings. Some time earlier, he had formed the habit of walking at night in the poor districts of London, seeking contact, which was easy to find, with human wrecks, victims of the industrial revolution and drink. This fascination with the unfortunate had begun when his father had sent him to collect rent in the working-class houses for which he was agent. Long afterwards, Galsworthy still went roaming those neighbourhoods, which so fired his senses and imagination.

The other outward sign was his sudden horror for shooting, as profound as his former youthful zest for a pastime that was a privilege of the class he came from. Reference has already been made to the story telling of his change of attitude. His enthusiasm seems to have been at its height between 1884 and 1892, after which other ardours took him away from his gun, in the English woods and Scottish moors. It was not until the early years of the new century, some time between 1899 and 1911, that his lack of enthusiasm became an actual antipathy.

Although his compassion for animals and their sufferings may have been slow in developing, it later knew no bounds. The texts grouped together under the title 'On the Treatment of Animals', in the collection *A Sheaf*, published in 1916, reflect his ideas. There could be no more striking example of repentance, persistent remorse or at least regret, than the nightmarish 'Reverie of a Sportsman', in which a huntsman is suddenly assailed by the vengeful ghosts of all the animals he has slain. Galsworthy's horror of violence and suffering, inflicted in any way on any living creature, human or animal, gave rise to feelings that became all-embracing. Not content with giving up shooting, he took pity on all animals, domestic and wild. He overcame his deep repugnance, and visited slaughterhouses, so that he could advance serious and well-documented arguments in favour of reform. The list of good causes which he supported[21] includes twelve different campaigns for animals, among them one in favour of mining ponies, another against the use of osprey feathers by dressmakers, and another against experiments on live dogs.

## NEW TENSIONS: THE FIRST WORLD WAR

Between the first crisis, around 1895, and the second period of tension, from 1914 to 1918, is there any period recalling the first or presaging the second? Any answer to this question means discussing Galsworthy's romance with Margaret Morris.[22] It took place only seven years after his marriage to Ada (though admittedly seventeen years after the start of their liaison). To think that their union was described as perfect, and that he was said to have been completely devoted to her! It is true that the affair had not exactly been voiced abroad, and Marrot may very well have known nothing of it. But I was told the same thing, far later.[23]

The facts must be regarded more realistically. What a reader of Galsworthy might take as rather vaguely erotic, slightly tasteless descriptions of female beauty, reflected something far more precise. Galsworthy was very interested in sex, very sensual, indulgent, particularly where young women were concerned. He did not always have his feet on the ground. Otherwise, how could he ever, as he did for a short time, have envisaged a *ménage à trois* with Ada and Margaret, before breaking off the relationship?[24] Ultimately, his lack of duplicity, and his candour (he talked far too much about each woman to the other) are reassuring. His fundamental honesty and kindness emerged intact (though not enhanced) from the affair. Once he had realised how much Ada was suffering, he ended it, gently but firmly, without any resentment.

Time was passing, and Galsworthy was approaching fifty. The First World War broke out in 1914, as unexpectedly for Galsworthy as for most of his fellow countrymen. Even before hostilities began, he was seized with profound uneasiness, even anxiety: his imagination moved fast and far enough for him to be able to picture the slaughter, the destruction of the world as he had known it. For two more years, until conscription was introduced in 1916, the nation as a whole still believed that it could remain on the sidelines of the battle, and merely bring in its all-powerful fleet, small professional army, its industry and money, backed up by the whole Empire. But Galsworthy, with his lucidity, could not indulge for a moment in such illusory hopes.

As his diary shows, he was immediately so upset that his inspiration, one of his greatest vital forces, was imperilled: 'August 6 . . . Find it impossible to settle to anything.'[25]

A little over three months later, on 15 November, he wrote:

The heart searchings of the War are terrible; the illumination of oneself rather horrible. I think and think what is my duty, and all the time know that if I arrived at certain conclusions I shouldn't do that duty. This is what comes of giving yourself to a woman body and soul. A. paralyses me and has always paralysed me. I have never been able to face the idea of being cut off from her. . . . Luckily for my conscience I really believe my game shoulder would not stand a week's training without getting my arm into a sling. Moreover I suppose there is no one yet training as short-sighted as I am. Still I worry − worry − all the time − bald and grey and forty-seven and worrying. Funny![26]

Remembering what was said about Galsworthy's robust health, one is surprised to read this extract from his diary. Why is he suddenly complaining of being old, unfit, grey, stricken with worry, afflicted with a pain in his shoulder that makes him nearly an invalid? With so much evidence to show that, on the contrary, he was a vigorous practitioner of several sports, and lived a healthy, reasonable life, how is this declaration of disability to be explained? Ultimately, he answers his own question in far too circumstantial a way to be quite convincing. Yet there is a revealing photograph,[27] taken at Martouret in 1916. The strange ageing, already mentioned earlier, is quite evident on his face. There is a sharp contrast between his drawn, mask-like features, and Ada's radiant complexion, beside him in the group.

It was the exceptional circumstances, by temporarily upsetting his normal balance, that laid bare his most profound and permanent nature, so difficult to perceive on ordinary occasions. During such a disturbed period, certain painful, exaggerated emotional states burst into the open and dominated everything. Time took on the most extreme importance, for two reasons, one subjective, one historical. Galsworthy's uneasy nature meant that, from the first day of the war, his imagination made him see the future as catastrophic. He also had to cope with that secret weapon of anxiety, time passing, prolonging the ordeal of millions of fighting men for four years, and of many non-combatants, soldiers' mothers and wives and relatives. As fate would have it, no close relation of Galsworthy's was in danger. But imagined sufferings can be just as terrible as actual ones, if they disorganise the victim's life, if he can no longer operate effectively. Galsworthy was a man who did not need to live in a town in order to suffer from claustrophobia, nor to be physically wounded in order to suffer cruelly.

His state is illustrated by a well-documented episode during the war, which can be referred to as the Martouret affair. It reflects his sometimes pitiable efforts to carry his ideals of disinterestedness, courage and fraternity into effect.

On 8 September 1916, he met an old acquaintance, Dorothy Allhusen, at a Red Cross meeting in London. She suggested that he should go to France and work in her rehabilitation centre for wounded or sick soldiers. It was a kind of small private hospital, run by convalescents on family lines, with the help of a few British volunteers. It was near the South of France, at Die, near Valence. There were to be no more than thirty-five patients, all cases of neurasthenia, shell-shock and rheumatism.

The decision was taken three days later. He would bath and massage the patients, and Ada would look after the linen. He at once enrolled for Swedish massage classes, while pursuing his literary activities. They left England on 13 November. Galsworthy records that on arriving at Le Havre at midnight he felt great joy and emotion at the idea of leaving Britain. They took up their functions at Martouret on 20 November. His timetable, in his own hand, has survived. It shows that he spent four hours a day (five, he told his sister) giving three massage sessions. There was half an hour's gymnastics with the patients. He also helped serve meals. Six days after his arrival, he said that he was happy with the men and everybody. He was interested and gratified to find that his massage actually helped them.

They worked for three and a half months, with only Sundays off, and left on 3 March 1917. No explanation can be found for their departure. On the day they left, Ada wrote a laconic note to her sister-in-law: 'We are feeling a little tired and there are many letters to write.'[28]

From Die they went to visit Arles, Marseilles and Cassis. Ada was lame as the result of a fall in Marseilles, and Galsworthy was suffering from sciatica. They stayed in Cassis for eleven days, in 'a nice clean little hotel',[29] and once they had recovered sufficiently they went on walking expeditions. Even in Marseilles, 'walk' appears in the timetable. They were back in England by 27 March 1917, after a profitable stop in Paris, where Galsworthy met his French publisher, Calmann. But for the first two weeks after their return they were 'both seedy'.[30] This was their only trip outside Britain during the war.

Moral reasons no doubt lay behind the whole event. Galsworthy was anxious to contribute personally. Looking after the sick and wounded corresponded to his preoccupations and natural bent. So why did he not persevere? Leaving aside Ada, the most prosaic reason may be the right one: at his age (he was in his fiftieth year), and with his lack of training, he may have found the massage sessions more exhausting than he had expected.

But the real question perhaps lies elsewhere. Is it not superficial to judge any man without taking account of his real occupation and vocation in life? Is it cynical to claim that Galsworthy was best doing his duty by sitting down and writing? There was nothing heroic about his action, but on the whole it was reasonable, serious and useful. The war situation, as has been said, had had a deleterious effect on his inspiration. And one cannot but be struck by the range of subjects covered in his writings directly inspired by the French experience, not to mention the indirect influences aroused by the trip. They include 'France, an Impression 1916–1917', 'Poirot and Bidan', 'Flotsam and Jetsam' and 'Cafard'. In these last three sketches, he deals with the drama of wounded men who have become mentally handicapped. Every word shows how predisposed, ready and sensitive he was. He had no difficulty in finding familiar ground in all the impressions he had gathered, and particularly in finding himself.

None of this should suggest that Galsworthy was a pacifist. He suffered on behalf of all men, and was by conviction and reason as internationalist in outlook, at a time when this called for far-sightedness and intellectual courage. So he was among those for whom the dragging-out of hostilities became a betrayal of the noble intentions that had accompanied the declaration of war. Heart-sick at the useless killing, he was in favour, probably from 1916, of negotiations to end the war.

In other words, he was far from being in full agreement with official policy. But he was fortunate enough to live in a country where, even in war time, political thought remained free and censorship fairly liberal.[31] There was one topic on which he was never short of ideas, and about which he never tired of speaking out: the myriad grave problems that would follow the end of the war. To many people such considerations are highly subversive.

There are innumerable short texts from his pen, particularly those typically British 'appeals' to the generosity and kindness of his fellow countrymen. These appeared in daily papers or periodicals, and they reflect the active part that Galsworthy wished to play in national life and, particularly during the war, his desire to intervene and bend events in what he considered the right direction. His favourite role, in fact the only one he would accept, was that of a freelance.

Another example, quite different from the Martouret episode, but recalling it in several ways, was the 'Reveille' affair, another war-time undertaking that similarly reflected Galsworthy's convictions, wishes and deepest preoccupations, and his need for generous action.

In 1918, in agreement with the authorities, he decided to launch a periodical, to be called 'Reveille', where the problems of treatment of war victims could be discussed. He was to be the editor, and he persuaded a number of his fellow journalists and writers to collaborate. Its pages contained both literary contributions and technical articles. Unfortunately, he and the Ministry of Pensions did not see eye to eye. At the end of six months, publication stopped, after three issues. Again, there was this difficulty in fitting in with an organisation, a system.

All this activity, only some significant aspects of which have been mentioned, saved his balance. If he had been reduced to silence, or had lost his inspiration and enthusiasm, he might have broken down. What is true of his whole literary career applies even more to the war years. Pursuit of his literary goals was beneficial to him. His novel *The Burning Spear*, which is little known and well-nigh unreadable, is revealing. It reflects his inner turmoil. It seems likely that this chaotic work had a therapeutic effect, freeing him, and releasing him from even stormier currents of consciousness. In the end, Galsworthy's heart and mind survived. And this might not have happened had he abandoned his pen, taken a gun and gone off to the front, as he reproached himself for being unable to do. His nerves could never have stood it, and he might have been driven to open, tragic revolt, or been completely crushed. Violence was already unbearable to him in peace time. What would have happened at the battlefront?

## SUCCESS, AND THE END

The man may now be seen more clearly behind the myths. Some of his own myths collapse: the assertion of perfect happiness with Ada, or happiness in the country, especially at Manaton. Not that they were imaginary, but they were not all-consuming or adequate passions. The propensity to worry, the anxiety that nagged so persistently at him, hindered the scale, intensity and duration of any passion in Galsworthy. In normal times he lived with his uneasiness; to some extent he was accustomed to it. But in times of strife or acute distress, it overwhelmed his consciousness, leaving him anguished, reducing him to the condition of many of the male characters in his novels, particularly in *Fraternity*. Like the Russians (whose temperament in some ways he shared), he was haunted by the spectre of powerlessness, impotence. The difference between him and his characters was that he actually experienced this frustrated and unhappy mood.

Fortunately, it was only a temporary neurosis, even if prolonged and painful. As soon as the Armistice was close, in September 1918, five or six weeks before the actual cessation of hostilities, Galsworthy proved that his health had not been organically affected, even that he still had reserves of strength. He threw off his anguish without waiting for his hopes to be confirmed in military and political terms. He gave up his flat in town, and moved to the edge of Hampstead Heath. He opened the door of the prison he had built round himself, and went out to regain what he had loved in earlier times.

About two and a half months before the departure for Hampstead, an event had already occurred that did much to relieve his mind: 'Examined for the Army at the age of 50 years and 343 days. Was totally rejected on score of sight.'[32] He knew that in any case he could not be enrolled in a fighting unit. The preoccupation from which he was released by the decision was a purely moral one. He had not been able to settle the internal debate that had gone on since the start of the war, unable to see where his duty lay. His uncertainty on this point was the intellectual aspect of the state of anxiety in which he had been plunged. The recruiting board, in settling the problem in this way, ended his doubts and consequently his anxiety.

From a literary standpoint, his recovery was equally rapid. It provides striking confirmation of the importance of what has been discussed above. Galsworthy was reborn. Not content with 'recovering his speech', he was to surpass his former achievements. In a flash, he was to conceive and begin work on what was to be his *magnum opus*, *The Forsyte Saga*. Quite incredibly, this happened in July 1918, only a few days after his final rejection for military service. The diary even makes it possible to define the exact interval between the two events: six days!

> We stayed on at Wingstone till the end of August, during which I began the Second Part of *The Forsyte Saga*, to be called *The Second Flowering*. The idea of making *The Man of Property* the First volume of a trilogy cemented by *Indian Summer of a Forsyte* and another short episode came to me on Sunday July 28th and I started the same day. This idea, if I can ever bring it to fruition, will make *The Forsyte Saga* a volume of half a million words nearly; and the most sustained and considerable piece of fiction of our generation at least.[33]

He could hardly have found a more meaningful title than *The Second Flowering* (though it was in fact later replaced by *In Chancery*). The relationship between life and works is confirmed with exceptional force. *The Man of Property* arose from the first crisis in his life. The second novel in the *Saga*, another masterpiece, was conceived as the second crisis ended. The relationship is again very close, though quite different. The word 'recovery' is appropriate: a spontaneous, joyous return to his original wellsprings, after a long break, providing undeniable evidence of deliberate, conscious, inner reconciliation, a regained sense of continuity.

The huge success of *The Forsyte Saga* was partly a tribute to the author's character. The British public nearly always gives recognition to a long work. Galsworthy in turn was greatly affected by the way his best writings at last succeeded. The trilogy was completed with the ending of *To Let* on 28 September 1921. Sales really began to expand with the appearance of the *Saga* in a single volume, on 25 May 1922.[34] Galsworthy was in his fifty-fifth year. Was that too old to become self-infatuated? Although he was never guilty of overweening pride, he was not proof against natural vanity. From then on he seems to have become over-sure of himself. He was no longer prepared to examine the advice of critics on its merits. The second and third trilogies were written by a man who could make no mistakes. It is a pity to see his personal charm a little tarnished so late in life by this failing, or weakness.

It is well known that old age protects nobody against neurosis, particularly depression. On the contrary, many people end up enmeshed in the toils of neurotic anxiety. On the other hand, substantial and well-earned gratifications, even if they come late, can strengthen and improve the balance of a personality, and release it from nervous stress.

This was what happened to Galsworthy. It even gave him greater strength for the final, cruel struggle, against the disease that was to prove fatal. He had achieved an enviable poise.

More is known about his death than about his life.[35] His courage, lucidity and perseverance, which enabled him when already seriously ill to pursue an active life, and complete an estimable novel, *Over the River*, prove his mental toughness, which was greater at the end of his life than it had ever been. Considering his passionate love of life, and his disbelief in any afterlife, his end was worthy of a Stoic.

He died of a brain tumour on 31 January 1933, in his sixty-sixth year. His physical sufferings were fairly short, but the mental ordeal was severe and prolonged: the first symptoms had appeared in 1930 and had worsened the following year.

In the face of illness and death, he remained true to his habits of thought, particularly his conscientiousness, and to his own ways of behaviour. He refused to be taken in by any idle distractions from reality, or any miracle cures promised by quacks – among whom he firmly included *all* doctors. His family had to deploy great patience and all kinds of ruses in order to have him examined. He hid his illness like a dog hiding its bone, to keep it for itself. Already naturally taciturn, he withdrew increasingly into himself. He made no complaints, but neither did he put up any falsely cheerful front, and those close to him could not expect any euphemistic talk. He gave free rein to his whims and eccentricities, and required them to be complied with. Just as he had moved his armchair onto the lawn at Wingstone, to enjoy the last rays of sunshine before going to bed, so he had his bed moved for the same purpose. He had been moved back from Bury House to Grove Lodge, where he even thought of buying the house opposite and having it demolished, to let more sunlight into his room.

In other words, he showed the obstinacy of those who know what they want. In the final ordeal, he showed no signs of the inner confusion and mental turmoil of earlier periods of crisis. The most eloquent of his last wishes was revealed by a poem, left prominently placed among his papers. It was called 'Scatter My Ashes'. It was a clear instruction to have his remains cremated and the ashes strewn on the Heath.

# 4 Galsworthy's Emotional Nature and Artistic Tastes

The available information has shown Galsworthy's tendency to worry, which, in critical circumstances, made him a prey to anxiety. But although this uneasiness affected certain aspects of his emotional life, it by no means dominated.

There are a thousand forms of worry and uneasiness, and some people move constantly from one to another. This was not the case with Galsworthy. There are many kinds of anxiety that he was never subject to. The excellent portrait of James in *The Forsyte Saga* shows that Galsworthy was detached enough to be able to point out how ridiculous James was with his permanent state of generalised anxiety. His heroes never let themselves be intimidated. There is every reason to think that Galsworthy was not personally of a nervous disposition. In fact, he rather tended to overawe those he was in contact with. He had no fear on his own account, but for others, or for his own conscience, which amounts to the same thing. This was what made him sometimes taciturn and often pensive, even almost melancholy.

Both a broader and more accurate definition of his emotional temperament needs to be established. Rudolf Sauter writes: 'It was only most reluctantly that he could bring himself to look upon disfigurement or deformity. To one of his imagination, this was not physical repulsion alone; it was something at a much deeper level, which hurt him so profoundly that he shrank from the experience.'[1]

Even more significant, because it was purely emotional, without any physical repugnance involved, was Galsworthy's reaction, as reported by both Ada and Marrot, to the showing of his plays on the stage. As the *dénouement* approached, again and again he fled the theatre. But he could also draw great vigour from his emotions, and express himself with total self-assurance. His outbursts of bad temper were rare but fearful to behold. Mottram and

Sauter told me that they were triggered by the sight of cruelty to a human being or an animal. It is this kind of rage that governs the narrator of the story 'The Black Godmother'.

Galsworthy's temperament was not sentimental, as has been claimed, but emotional. There is a vast difference between the sentimental and the emotional. Not that there was nothing sentimental about Galsworthy, but it was far outweighed by his emotional side. The emotions are by nature in a constant state of ebb and flow; whereas sentimentality involves a psychological fixation that mummifies the emotions. If Galsworthy had been more sentimental, his uneasiness would soon have subsided, and the crises would have been impossible. It would also have made him more faithful.[2]

He retained great freshness of emotion, and his affection for Ada did not diminish as the years passed. The interlude with Margaret Morris is easy to understand in a man of his temperament. It was a serious emotional urge. But the attraction of something new and the temptation to grasp it were soon cancelled out, and more than counterbalanced, by a conflicting emotion. The sight of the neglected Ada's suffering deprived the escapade of its charm.

Galsworthy's feelings towards his parents have already been discussed sufficiently. Of his two sisters, he preferred the elder, Blanche Lilian. She was literate and extremely sensitive, and her intelligence had contributed to his intellectual growth. He was greatly affected by her death under painful circumstances. It was the First World War that caused a family break-up and forged very close links between Galsworthy and Lilian's son Rudolf. Lilian's husband was of German origin. Despite his marriage to an Englishwoman, and his long residence in England, he was interned as an enemy alien in 1916. Rudolf was interned in 1918. This struck a fatal blow at the marriage. Lilian died brokenhearted in 1924.

The two novels that date from this period, *The Burning Spear* and *Saint's Progress*, but particularly the short stories 'The Dog It Was that Died' and 'The Bright Side', originally published in the collection *Tatterdemalion* in 1920, and reprinted in *Caravan*, express his feelings of pity for the victims, and the anger aroused in him by the cruelty that some of his contemporaries revealed in the atmosphere of the war.

He and Ada were childless, and his affections were transferred to his nephew, whom he later adopted. He had lavished his affection on Rudolf, whom he called 'Rudey' or 'Rudo', from infancy.[3] Galsworthy suggested that Rudolf and his wife Viola should come and live under the same roof, and he bought Bury House for the four of them. Rudolf, who was a painter like his father, and an occasional poet, long thought that he did not have it in him to write a book about his uncle. But in disgust at the unscrupulousness of a critic to whom he had entrusted some documents, he finally set to work. His book, *John Galsworthy the Man: an Intimate Portrait*, published in 1967, adds to the very valuable information with which he supplied me in conversation. What is known about Rudolf himself and what he tells of his uncle make a major contribution to understanding Galsworthy. Important points of similarity can be discerned between the two men. His friendliness and sensitivity make the figure of Galsworthy more human. The publication of his correspondence with Margaret Morris had the same effect. These practical, familiar details, and obvious signs of spontaneous affection, are what the author's memory most needs. They endow his image with a sense of vividness and truthfulness that had been somewhat lacking, largely because of his own secretiveness.

There remain Galsworthy's friendships. Any exhaustive examination of this subject is impossible in the absence of the collected correspondence. As it is, the names of his principal correspondents already constitute a long list of friends, for a man who has sometimes been said to have been incapable of friendship.

A completely false idea of his social situation would be given if only writer friends were mentioned. Edward Garnett tells that, during the discussions between them about *The Patrician*, Galsworthy reduced him to silence by sending a list of a hundred and thirty people in high society who were known to him. Later on there was an exchange of letters with Winston Churchill, when Home Secretary, concerning penal reform. Social small talk increasingly gave way to more serious purposes in his correspondence.

This explains why the bulk of the letters are to literary friends. These included, to begin with, Joseph Conrad, then, through him, Edward Garnett from 1900, E. V. Lucas from 1901, and W. H. Hudson from 1904. Galsworthy and R. H. Mottram also became acquainted in 1904. Gilbert Murray and John Masefield appeared slightly later, followed by Thomas Hardy and Max Beerbohm.

Still later came Hugh Walpole. Richard Church told me that he had received help and advice from Galsworthy in his youth — like many other writers, he said. Of all these people, his closest friends appear to have been Conrad, Murray, Mottram and Masefield. He knew George Bernard Shaw, H. G. Wells and Arnold Bennett, but varied in his appreciation of them, and was never intimate with them. His only French friend was André Chevrillon, whom he knew from before the war.

Originally, his letters were utilitarian, referring to literary or social problems. But as time passed signs of friendship and mutual trust could appear. As people knew him better they tended to like him more, and he showed himself a true friend, affectionate and generous, once the ice was broken.


The large number of artists among the characters in Galsworthy's novels, and frequent allusions to the arts in his stories, require some consideration of the contribution of the aesthetic sense in his make-up. The matter of literary creation will be left aside here.

On 9 December 1971, Rudolf Sauter, in response to a question from me, provided some useful details:

> J. G.'s interest in painting was not as great as in music. But then he had a goodish voice and sang a little in his early days. Then there was Ada's connection with music and her very fine playing, which kept that side alive all the time. They went to concerts together, of course, and *Carmen* was his favourite opera . . . he (with Ada's help) made a new English text from the original French. This was performed several times, though not often. He specially liked Ada's playing of Chopin, and Brahms, Schubert and Schumann. The Brahms *Songs* and the *Songs of the Hebrides* were often on the piano of an evening. He did not like Wagner; but Ada would play Debussy and Ravel, and often some Spanish music, mostly with rhythm and tune. From all of which you will infer that his taste was limited but genuine . . . the following come to mind as pictures which he particularly liked: Goya's *La Vendimia*, Titian's *Death of Procris*; Botticelli's *Primavera* and *Venus Rising from the Sea*; *The Mona Lisa*, Piera della Francesca's portraits; in fact Renaissance pictures generally, and in addition de Hoogh and Vermeer. Of course he came up against more modern painting

in his relationship with my father, and I think that any appreciation he had of 'modern' work came through him. They did not
always agree, by any means, and I think my father thought his
views on painting rather immature. . . . No, he did not collect
paintings as such. But he purchased or acquired contemporary
paintings from time to time. . . . Their rooms were always
beautiful, pictures and curtains so arranged as to fit in and
harmonize, for both had taste.

He also sent me some unpublished extracts from his diaries for
1925.

15th December 1925 (Chandler, Arizona). J. G. is always
oppressed by things majestic and towering (and A. G. too). To
him beauty is only in grace and charm . . . in birds and flowers,
in blue skies and sunlight, in quiet night. The wild sea, the
stormy sky, the sheer fastnesses of Nature have no attraction,
but are rather repulsive to him.

26th December (Riding with J. G. partly on the desert in a
beautiful light). J. G. remarked suddenly: Lovely the desert is
where it borders on this — 'this' at which he was pointing being
where fields edged the desert. It is a half-tamed Nature he likes.
He would give a touch of cultivation, a bit of human handiwork,
the squirming figure of a loafing dog (man's friend) for all the
wild fastnesses I love.

Rudolf's opinion of their good taste in interior decoration is confirmed by Margaret Morris. She provides a description of their
house, which differed substantially from the standard Victorian
décor: '14 Addison Road had all-white walls and white paint (this
was quite an innovation in those days); the furniture was good
dark "period" stuff but there was not too much, and I think one or
two pictures.'[4]

So Galsworthy enjoyed music and painting, although he does
not seem to have played an instrument or wielded pencil or brush.
He was very interested in Rudolf's paintings and those of other
contemporary artists, despite rather limited and conservative
tastes. In fact, modern painting seems to have had little attraction
for him, and he was extremely aggressive about living painters in
*The Man of Property*. So if he took an interest in new forms of
graphic art, it was through a personal interest in the painter.

But Rudolf Sauter would seem to be over-restrictive when he mentions the Renaissance painters as Galsworthy's favourites. Admittedly, Botticelli is more frequently alluded to in his works than any other painter, but he was also devoted to the great 17th century Spanish masters, so remote from the Italian Renaissance. Furthermore, the number of 19th-century English and French paintings in Soames' collection suggests the interest Galsworthy took in the painters and schools of that period.

Rudolf felt that his uncle was more interested in music than in painting, but this may simply mean that music played a greater role in his everyday life. Ada was an excellent pianist, and he liked to listen to her playing every day, while he was working, or as recreation. But he had no great theoretical knowledge. Ould reveals two errors in his references to musical works.[5] His comments are always brief and usually rather vague. Only two musicians play any important role in his novels: Fiorsen in *Beyond* and Pierson in *Saint's Progress*. Pierson's musical taste is one of the forms his sentimentality and escapism take. Fiorsen is a hard worker, but a man of no virtue, dignity or heart. In neither of them does the analysis of the musician's inner experience in playing reach the profundity of Thomas Mann's depiction of Hanno Buddenbrook.

Galsworthy seems to have had little interest in the other arts, particularly architecture.

# 5  Galsworthy's Way of Life

It is much easier to describe Galsworthy's daily way of life than to study his character. All the necessary documents are available, without much need to interpret them. It is Galsworthy himself who provides the details, set out perfectly clearly, showing his daily timetables and methodical lists. It is almost as if he wanted, in this way, to make up for the silence about his private life. Or perhaps this serious, systematic attitude towards drawing up accounts and summaries reassured him that he was carrying his convictions into practical effect.

Here is the 'Analysis of Average Day' in the life of Galsworthy:[1]

| | |
|---|---|
| Sleeping in bed | 7 hours |
| Thinking in bed | 1 hour |
| Trying not to fall asleep in chairs | $\frac{1}{2}$ hour |
| Eating, and listening to others talking | 2 hours |
| Playing with dogs | $\frac{1}{4}$ hour |
| Playing without dogs (on the telephone) | $\frac{1}{4}$ hour |
| Dressing, undressing, bathing, and Muller exercising | $1\frac{1}{4}$ hours |
| Exercise in country (riding or walking) | 2 hours at least |
| Exercise in London (walking) | 1 hour at most |
| Imagining vain things, and writing them down on paper: | |
|     In the country | 4 hours |
|     In London | 3 hours |
| Correspondence, and collecting scattered thoughts: | |
|     In the country | 2 hours |
|     In London | 4 hours |
| Skipping newspapers | $\frac{1}{4}$ hour |
| Reading what I don't want to, or otherwise attending to business | 1 hour |
| Reading what I do want to | $\frac{1}{2}$ hour |

| Revision of vain things; and of proofs say | 1 hour |
| Education by life | the rest |
| Call it an eight to nine hour day. | J. G. |

There is no possibility of error: it is copied out in Ada's hand-writing, and initialled 'J. G.'. This timetable was obviously com-piled in a humorous mood, designed to conceal modesty, when intimate details are being given, but which may also allow one or two small inaccuracies to be slipped in, among plausible and very useful figures. Is it possible that his considerable literary output (not all of which is included in the thirty-volume Manaton Edition) was written in only four or five hours a day? Has this not something to do with an author's vanity? Rudolf Sauter says that the morning was reserved for actual creative work. Revision and letter-writing were done between tea-time and dinner.

He describes Galsworthy at work, out of doors whenever pos-sible, a writing pad on his knees, a quill in his hand (he detested fountain pens), and nothing else but blank paper nearby. Indoor photographs never show him sitting at a desk, but always in a leather armchair, using the same pad. In Bury House there was a room called the library. But Rudolf Sauter never remembers seeing any large reference books there, and does not believe Gals-worthy consulted encyclopaedias. His diaries provide details of his wide reading, but he never mentions visiting a library to do research on a specific subject. Anyway, he was often travelling. Winter was always spent abroad, and he said that he was perfectly happy to go off with nothing more than his paper and pen. Several of his favourite places abroad were particularly congenial for working.

Two facts should be underlined: Galsworthy was born at a time when people belonging to his class in society knew how to live. His father travelled from his country villa by train every morning, appearing at his London office by 11 a.m. He would be back home or in the grounds by 4 p.m. No doubt he had had to work harder to amass his fortune in the first place, but his son would hardly see that as a necessity any more. Galsworthy had too much common sense (and affection for his father) to refuse what he was given. He even knew how to take advantage of the situation. In the England of that age, all was designed to cater to the pleasure and content-ment of the upper classes.

Galsworthy started off in life with a fortune, at the peak of

Victorian prosperity. He asked no questions. Why should the son of an upper middle-class family ask any, when British power and influence were all-pervasive? He began to write for the reasons related earlier. He did not write to make money. That must never be forgotten. Galsworthy was never forced to write out of material need. But his uneasy temperament forced on him a moral obligation to write, as pressing a motive as poverty, the driving force behind so many men of letters.

Authorship gradually transformed his way of life. From the wealthy, leisured young man of 1895, he turned into a hard worker. This change has completely escaped the notice of some critics, who claim that he subsided back into his former conventionalism and conservatism once success was assured. Rather than basing an opinion on the amounts of money he made, it would be better to examine what use he put it to.

There were two main stages in the transformation of his way of life. The first dates from around to 1906 to 1912, when he became a playwright. He laboured more over his novels than over his plays, but, once written, the plays had more effect on his daily life. He attended rehearsals, thought of everything, dealt with everything. This activity began with his first plays, *The Silver Box*, produced in 1906, *Strife* in 1909 and *Justice* in 1910.

But this was only a beginning. The second stage began around 1920–2. With the huge success of *The Forsyte Saga*, he became as over-worked as any debt-ridden Balzac. His very wealth, combined with his well-known kindheartedness and generosity, helped to make his life harassed and vexatious, far more like an American businessman's life than he cared for, and the contrary of what he liked by nature. But although hostile critics lightheartedly ignore the fact, the day-to-day motivation was not to earn money. He was trying to help others, not himself. The cash transactions noted in his diary were outgoings, not income. The lists are not lists of clients, but of charities to which he contributed.[2] Even before the war, he rarely spent more than half his income on himself.

So it was without any external constraint, but through a sense of duty, because he believed in what he was writing, that Galsworthy completed the change of heart begun twenty-five years earlier, during his first 'crisis'. He was pleased to find himself sensible and balanced enough not to let his head be turned by success, as has happened to so many. He retained some of the wholesome habits acquired from his social background: the practice of sports,

regular interruption of work for rest, relaxation, solitude and
reflection (this was the function that Manaton and Littlehampton
performed), and a categorical refusal to yield, beyond certain
limits that he had set himself. He had become involved in the great
causes of his age, out of a sense of duty, and it made his life one of
toil and struggle. But amid the fracas he kept to his own deeply
rooted ways.

# Conclusion to Part I

A kind of initial contradiction in Galsworthy's temperament has to be noted. This anxious, emotional man both loved and feared emotion. An indissoluble blend of happiness and unhappiness, pleasure and pain, both disheartening and invigorating, was to be found in Galsworthy, especially at the sight of the beauty he was forever in search of. This strange commotion can be sensed in every action or literary production of any scale or duration. In conditions of stress, he could become a prey to acute anxiety, the permanent, extreme form of the dull uneasiness he was subject to by nature.

Even mildly neurotic individuals like Galsworthy can endure considerable distress; but certain stabilising factors, forms of behaviour inherited from his family — neither of his parents ever showed any lack of balance — and habits acquired during youth and adolescence made these nervous tribulations bearable. He kept them quiet, and this was possible in that they never seriously affected his capacity to operate normally.

Galsworthy found salvation in action. His great good fortune was to find the type of action that best suited him, literary creation. His seriousness and conscientiousness turned this into an obligation to write. This intellectual labour immediately conferred all the benefits of work on him, particularly the greater poise it brought. No one among the millions that knew him as a best-selling author, a leading national figure for at least ten years, suspected the secret drama that gnawed at him. After his death, they learnt of his liaison with his cousin's wife, and their subsequent marriage. Yet even this knowledge of the intimate facts still did not betray his secret, for they were only its outward manifestations. Even those closest to him, who held him in the greatest affection, did not really understand what lay inside him. Perhaps with the lapse of time, it is possible to see him more clearly today.

His temperament made it impossible for him to withdraw into

the ivory tower that his financial resources could have made available. Once or twice, whenever circumstances demanded, he pointed out, perfectly coolly and frankly, that his income did not depend on his literary work. Few writers can say as much; and it is a good thing for literature that some should enjoy the independence of mind such means procure. There is no way of denying that Galsworthy wrote from a sense of vocation, which was completely disinterested. It does much to enhance his dignity.

Character is destiny, he often said. As an extrovert, he could not avoid plunging into discoveries which, because of his emotional temperament, were bound to affect him deeply. His shyness could not keep him at a distance for long: it was soon replaced by pity, scruples or remorse. He was to be found in places where he might well have been the last person to venture, which caused him unspeakable repugnance, and which most people keep well away from, unless they are forced to go there: hospitals, internment camps, gaols (where he investigated the terrible effects of solitary confinement in private discussions with the inmates), East End slums and slaughterhouses, revolting and sickening establishments at that time. His highly developed sense of smell, for example, was constantly outraged in such places. Yet he never uttered a word of complaint about these experiences. They were part of his secret.

The main motive behind such activities was his compassion, which, as the word indicates, brings observer and victim close together. It is sometimes mistaken for sentimentality — 'a mere parrot cry', Galsworthy said of such an accusation, usually quite unjust.[1] The sentimentalist stands on the sidelines of the game of feelings. Galsworthy was completely committed to what he was doing.

His compassion sometimes knew no bounds, and he realised himself that it occasionally turned him into a sort of latter-day Don Quixote. Both the name and the idea are to be found in *The Burning Spear*. Obviously, however, he was unable to put names to the windmills he was tilting at so wildly.

His unbounded pity for animals should be remembered. (He once spent a night on a couch in his drawing-room to stop a stray dog feeling lonely.)

Then there was his extreme solicitude towards women. He always took their side in divorce cases. Quiller-Couch reminded him harshly that some women take unfair advantage of men. But for Galsworthy, cruelty was a monopoly of the male sex. He could not conceive of it in a woman; though, like every Englishman, he recognised his right to exaggerate his case.

These are small frailties, compared with the way his original sense of compassion contributed to the realisation of his personality. How did the process of self-fulfilment begin? The first victim to be rescued was his future wife, Ada. She never forfeited the pre-eminent position this entitled her to, and the privileges that accompanied it. Apart from the other bonds between them, why did Galsworthy feel this debt of gratitude? By arousing his compassion and putting him in the role of saviour, she revealed to him his real and hitherto unsuspected nature. Moments like that are never to be forgotten, and they mould a whole existence. Another even more extraordinary revelation came when Ada encouraged him to write. After releasing his energy potential, she guided it towards the right outlet. These were two victories she had every reason to be proud of.

Galsworthy's temperament, character and personality have been widely discussed here, while the same aspects of Ada have been left out. Sadly, all that can be said is that nothing is known of her. Many of those that knew her say that Ada was lovely. She was also an excellent pianist. Galsworthy is unlikely to have been insensitive to such charms. In his book *The Man of Principle: a View of John Galsworthy*, published in 1963, Dudley Barker uses a number of known facts to attack Ada. He argues that she was selfish, capricious, vain and haughty, at times bad-tempered. Then in 1976, the novelist and playwright Catherine Dupré published *John Galsworthy: a Biography*. It does not provide any new information. The author claims that near the end of his life Rudolf Sauter supplied her with verbal information, which differs in some ways from what he had told me a few years earlier. She quotes no sources for Chapter 7: 'Ada'. According to this chapter, Ada was an illegitimate child, whose father was unknown, and for this reason her childhood was very unhappy. This is supposed to have affected her whole married life. The hypothesis turns suddenly into a thesis, thereby reinforcing the image of Ada already advanced by Barker.

Catherine Dupré even claims that if Galsworthy had been released from her malevolent influence when he met Margaret Morris in 1910, his career would not have ended on 'a failure', and that his work would have been infinitely richer. These are rash claims, and in any case would require very serious study of the novels, which this book fails to do.

There are other points to be put in Ada's defence. She was a great help to her husband in his work, reading and commenting on all his manuscripts, then typing them out — no small task, some idea of which may be given by the thirty thick volumes of the Manaton Edition, and the huge correspondence, not all of which has yet been traced. This role made Ada an early exponent of a job that women are traditionally good at, and is certainly incompatible with laziness, inconsistency or selfishness. It is also a humble job. Galsworthy does report in his diary that he sometimes had to look after her when she had colds, or 'flu, or bronchitis. These are minor indispositions, but if they are chronic they can be an ordeal for sufferers, and they require care and attention.

The case of Galsworthy shows how an uneasy, emotional person can engage enthusiastically in action, if he is an extrovert. It was Galsworthy's nature to fling himself into action, whenever he shared the suffering of those he wanted to help. Given the countless sufferings of humanity, his task was bound to be endless. The intensity of his sympathy and his complete sincerity made him a practical man. After succeeding in having legislation on solitary confinement amended, he returned from his interview with the Home Secretary, Herbert Gladstone, and began adding up and multiplying, to work out the total number of hours of solitary confinement that would disappear as a result of the successful campaign. In other words, his passion never turned to hatred. He could get angry, furious, with those responsible, but he had no time to hate them. In someone so extrovert, hatred was unlikely anyway. Consideration of his philosophy[2] will complete the view of the spiritual life of this serious and dignified man.

# Part II
# Galsworthy the Novelist

# Introduction

Galsworthy's career does not include any period when one particular literary *genre* predominated, even temporarily. He began by writing short stories about 1896. Without awaiting their publication, he started work on his first novel, *Jocelyn*. The second novel, written in 1899–1900, was published in October 1900. September 1901 saw the publication of a first version of *A Man of Devon*, a second collection of short stories (one of which bore the title 'The Salvation of Swithin Forsyte'). During this same year, 1901, he was working on a play, *The Civilised*, which remained uncompleted and unpublished.

So Galsworthy was already thinking of the theatre, even before he had achieved anything decisive in the field of the novel.

But the plot of *The Civilised* is over-burdened with material. At least two novels, *The Island Pharisees* and *The Man of Property*, a play, *The Fugitive*, and a short story, 'The Stoic', were needed to exploit the potential themes of this first play. Galsworthy realised that it was all too complicated for the stage, and he turned to the novel as a way of presenting the Forsytes. For four or five years, apparently, from the end of 1901 to the end of 1905, he devoted himself entirely to writing his first two major novels, *The Island Pharisees* and *The Man of Property*. At the beginning of 1906, before *The Man of Property* was published, he wrote his first complete play, *The Silver Box*. This play was written and produced eight years after the publication of his first novel, *Jocelyn*, in 1898. This lapse of time is important, establishing the primacy of the novel over drama in Galsworthy's works.

But examination of the twenty-eight years of his full-time writing career (1904 to 1932) shows few years in which a novel was not completed or a play produced. Both events often occurred in a single year. The average interval between the publication of one novel and the next was one to two years. Collections of short stories were also published at fairly regular intervals throughout his career. And the dates of his three collections of poems, 1913, 1926 and 1934, show that this was also quite a regular activity. In other words, Galsworthy spread his literary output fairly evenly over all the forms he practised, moving from one to another apparently at will, and without any preconceived plan.

# 6 Galsworthy's Career as a Novelist

The preface written by Galsworthy in about 1924 for the Manaton Edition of *Villa Rubein* contains these words:

> Looking back on the long-stretched-out body of one's work, it is interesting to mark the endless duel fought within a man between the emotional and critical sides of his nature, first one, then the other, getting the upper hand, and too seldom fusing till the result has the mellowness of full achievement. . . . My early work was certainly more emotional than critical. But from 1901 came nine years when the critical was, in the main, holding sway. From 1910 to 1918 the emotional again struggled for the upper hand; and from that time on there seems to have been something of a 'dead heat'.[1]

The facts are too complex and the variety of his output too great during the years from 1910 to 1918 to allow this period to be defined simply as 'emotional'. Anyway, because of the date, the suggested classification is incomplete. Finally, Galsworthy's use of words leaves some ambiguity. However, the table of his literary career, as Galsworthy drew it up, can be useful, provided some amendments and additions are introduced. The term 'critical' will be retained. It is clear enough in its context, since the word 'satirical' is also used. The word 'emotional' will be replaced by 'lyrical' − and the particular features of Galsworthy's lyricism will be considered later. Table 6.1 incorporates Galsworthy's own interpretation of his career, especially as far as the first part is concerned. By 1924 he had a clear enough perspective on those early years, and they also covered a period when the ideas that motivated him were fairly straightforward. It would be much less defensible to apply simple, abstract criteria to the second half of his career. Accordingly, the table uses purely factual criteria to

TABLE 6.1    *Galsworthy's career as a novelist*

|                                   |           |          |          | *Dates of Publication* |
| --------------------------------- | --------- | -------- | -------- | --------------------------------- |
| The early writings                | 1896–1900 | 5 years  | 2 novels | (1)  *Jocelyn* (1898)             |
|                                   |           |          |          | (2)  *Villa Rubein* (1900)        |
| The 'critical' novels             | 1901–9    | 9 years  | 4 novels | (3)  *The Island Pharisees* (1904) |
|                                   |           |          |          | (4)  *The Man of Property* (1906) |
|                                   |           |          |          | (5)  *The Country House* (1907)   |
|                                   |           |          |          | (6)  *Fraternity* (1909)          |
| The lyrical and war-time novels   | 1910–19   | 10 years | 6 novels | (7)  *The Patrician* (1911)       |
|                                   |           |          |          | (8)  *The Dark Flower* (1913)     |
|                                   |           |          |          | (9)  *The Freelands* (1915)       |
|                                   |           |          |          | (10) *Beyond* (1917)              |
|                                   |           |          |          | (11) *The Burning Spear* (1919)   |
|                                   |           |          |          | (12) *Saint's Progress* (1919)    |
| *The Forsyte Chronicles*          | 1920–28   | 10 years | 5 novels | (13) *In Chancery* (1920)         |
|                                   |           |          |          | (14) *To Let* (1921)              |
|                                   |           |          |          | (15) *The White Monkey* (1924)    |
|                                   |           |          |          | (16) *The Silver Spoon* (1926)    |
|                                   |           |          |          | (17) *Swan Song* (1928)           |
| The end – the third trilogy       | 1929–32   | 4 years  | 3 novels | (18) *Maid in Waiting* (1931)     |
|                                   |           |          |          | (19) *Flowering Wilderness* (1932) |
|                                   |           |          |          | (20) *Over the River* (completed in 1932) |

The first trilogy, *The Forsyte Saga*, consists of nos 4, 13 and 14.
The second trilogy, *A Modern Comedy*, consists of nos 15–17.
The third trilogy, *End of the Chapter*, consists of nos 18–20.
*The Forsyte Chronicles* comprise the first two trilogies.

distinguish later phases: completion of *The Forsyte Chronicles*, and writing of the last trilogy, *End of the Chapter*. In any case, no dogmatic division of the thirty-four years of Galsworthy's writing career into five periods is intended. The only purpose is to illustrate the unity and diversity of his literary output.

## THE EARLY WRITINGS (1896–1900)

This is a short period, when Galsworthy considered that he had not yet really mastered his art. But it would be misleading to limit it to the dates of publication of his first two novels. An earlier collection of short stories, *From the Four Winds*, had already been published in 1897. And above all it must be remembered that Galsworthy began writing very slowly and laboriously. It is not certain exactly when he started. Either 1895 or 1896 seems most likely. Ada Galsworthy hesitated between them. In the table of contents of

*Forsytes, Pendyces and Others*, she put the date 1895–1896 after
the title of the short story 'The Doldrums', from *From the Four
Winds*. This is repeated on page 206, though in her introduction
she puts 1896. The year 1896 will be adopted here as the hypo-
thetical date for the start of this phase of Galsworthy's career.

Is it consistent, in other words is there an actual close relationship, between the two novels it comprises, *Jocelyn* and *Villa
Rubein*? In fact, any such relationship is limited. To begin with,
neither novel is particularly original. Strangely enough, the first
novel seems to be more personal than the second. But this may be a
false impression, arising from the fact that the model Galsworthy
used as inspiration for *Jocelyn* is unknown, whereas Turgenev's
influence on *Villa Rubein* is well documented. But there is another
significant difference between the two stories. There is almost no
family or social background to *Jocelyn*. The hero and heroine are
soon the only characters involved. *Villa Rubein*, although still
mainly lyrical, comprises a simple, but within its limitations
effective, collective setting. However, comparison of the first and
third phases of Galsworthy's career reveals a real continuity. There
is a direct line from *Jocelyn*, and to some extent *Villa Rubein*, to
*The Dark Flower* and *Beyond*.

## *Jocelyn* (1898)

Giles Legard, a well-to-do 35-year-old Englishman of private
means, lives abroad with his wife Irma, who is dying of consump-
tion. Giles falls in love with an English girl called Jocelyn, and she
becomes his mistress. Irma's death, under suspicious circumstances, separates them. Ten months later, Jocelyn is finding life
very tedious in London. Giles comes to her and begs her to marry
him. She says she is unworthy, but admits that she is in love with
him, and offers herself to him. It is his turn to refuse, and he leaves
for Singapore. Jocelyn overcomes her doubts and catches up with
her lover at Ismailia.

Galsworthy's first novel was published in 1898 under the
pseudonym of John Sinjohn. It was not well reviewed, and Galsworthy soon accepted the critical verdict. He tried to eradicate
even the memory of it. It was never reprinted in his lifetime, and
there cannot have been more than a few hundred copies in existence by the time it was reissued in 1976.

And yet it was worth bringing back to public attention. Why

was Galsworthy so determined to wipe out all trace of his first novel? His reasons were less aesthetic than personal. When he had become famous, and more adept at using his own memories while disguising their origins, he may have turned against his first hero. Giles is a self-portrait. But there were to be many others in later novels. Jocelyn remains mysterious, difficult to understand. The plot has only remote similarities with the events leading up to Galsworthy's marriage to Ada, and is quite inventive.[2] Irma's timely death removes the eventuality of divorce. So it must have been Giles' often violent and direct expression of his feelings that later displeased Galsworthy, and seemed to him incompatible with his ideas of 'good form'.

But the book is full of interest for Galsworthy admirers. With no transition from his first published work, a collection of exotic, colourful stories entitled *From the Four Winds*, it shows Galsworthy capable of writing a purely psychological novel. *Jocelyn* is a love story, with little action in the plot and only two characters. Irma's death might have been a dramatic event, but it is underplayed. The situation is simpler than in real life. The few secondary characters are soon packed out of the way. There are no family complications. The basis of the plot is almost purely subjective. The situation is also easier than in real life: abroad, with money, anything is possible. Galsworthy unconsciously turned *Jocelyn* into wish fulfilment, with freedom achieved happily and quickly.

But there is more to the novel than might be suggested by this simplified account of autobiographical facts and the changes made to them. Little information is available on the novel. Galsworthy had known Conrad since 1893, and had been introduced to Russian literature by him. Turgenev's influence is apparent in the next two novels Galsworthy wrote, and may also have affected *Jocelyn*, though I cannot detect it. Unlike *From the Four Winds*, Jocelyn appears to owe little to Kipling or Bret Harte, except in its idealised view of women. On the whole the story is told effectively, capturing the reader's attention by its subtlety, and holding it by its intensity. Ignorance of how the story will end gives added interest. At times the setting is described realistically, at others with a certain exotic charm. At that time the town where most of the action takes place, Menton, was a kind of English colony.

But this is not the essential interest of the story. The apparently insignificant detail often turns out later to provide a clue to the advancement of the inner drama, governed by a discreet but meticulous chronology, with a sense of brooding fatality. The effect of the mystery can be understood by noting how the chapters are divided up, and how two different actions sometimes happen simultaneously. For example, Chapter 21 takes place in Jocelyn's place in London, and Chapter 22 on the same day in Spain, where Giles is staying.

The sense of fatality arises from the psychology of the characters. The book describes how two people who cannot love each other freely are initiated into suffering. The obstacles to their love may be insubstantial, but it is clear that the spiritual experience being described is exactly the situation resulting from a lengthy, painful separation. This situation further accentuates the divergence of temperament that arises from the difference in sex. The heroine is so unpredictable, incomprehensible, uncertain, that the result is sometimes highly improbable — a romantic concept of woman that is to be found in all Galsworthy's heroines.

The whole novel is filled with tension. This contributes to obscurity, since overblown language is always confusing. Over-excitement and obscurity are two aspects of the same defect, simply because all certainty departs from an over-excited mind. 'His brain was in an exhausted state of nervous excitement,'[3] says the author of his hero, no doubt describing his own experience. Yet despite its flaws *Jocelyn* is more pleasant to read than certain later works, because of its candour, impetuousness and youthfulness. The subject is simpler than in the other novels, but the novelist's skill can already be detected.

## *Villa Rubein* (1900)

A young Austrian painter, Harz, falls in love with Nicholas Treffry's niece Christian, who lives with him and some relatives under the same roof, in the Villa Rubein in Bolzano. Harz tells her of his life as a poor student. He had belonged to an anarchist group. The family is split. Christian's stepfather denounces him to the police, but Nicholas Treffry takes him to the Italian frontier. Harz and Christian are united at the end of the novel.

Galsworthy used the same pseudonym as for *Jocelyn* when the second novel was published in 1900. It was revised twice, and appeared in its final form in 1909, under his own name. Edward Garnett, in his preface to *Letters from John Galsworthy*, writes that when they met Galsworthy was writing *Villa Rubein* in the

style of Turgenev. Without in any way doubting Garnett's knowledge of Turgenev, it must be said that his opinion of Galsworthy's
novel is an over-generalisation, to be explained partly by the fact
that he had no hand in its composition. Galsworthy probably
borrowed from the Russian novel *On the Eve* for Harz's tale. But
he also recognised the influence of Maupassant.[4]

He also borrowed extensively from family sources. According to
Marrot, 'the hero and heroine were largely drawn from his
brother-in-law and sister, Georg and Lilian Sauter'.[5] It remains
short of the truth, as far as Georg is concerned anyway. The predominant factor in the novel is that Harz is, like Georg, a painter,
and similarly in revolt against academic art.

Georg Sauter was a man of strong personality, and he had made
a powerful impression on the whole family when he married into
it, as I learnt from Rudolf's personal reminiscences of his father.
Galsworthy was particularly intrigued by this first person from
another world that he was able to observe.

Harz is the first of a long series of artists of various kinds to be
found in Galsworthy's novels. All of them are more or less outsiders, dogmatic individuals on the fringes of society. These
aspects of Harz's character overburden the story. They are more
important than the love story. His stiffness, resulting from his
origin, detracts seriously from the book's credibility and interest.
The plot is slight, and its ending slides towards sentimentality. The
anguish of Christian, torn between love and loyalty to her uncle, is
unconvincing. There is none of the conflict or suspense of later
Galsworthy novels. *Villa Rubein* is his slightest novel.

There is a sort of regression, compared with *Jocelyn*. It is not just
a love story. It contains careful portraits of several members of a
family, revealing their characters in the new situations in which
they are placed by the two protagonists, a rich vein that Galsworthy
was to mine fully. Nicholas Treffry is actually a former partner of
Old Jolyon. A year later, there was a Forsyte as the main character
of a short story,[6] prior to their all coming together in a novel.

*Villa Rubein* reveals Galsworthy's already extensive resources
and several of his major themes: a family, still small, the opposition between artist and society, between young and old, between
love and death. But these conflicts are often merely subjects of discussion. The novelist's real skill appears in the description of the
natural setting, and the creation of atmosphere, with rapid, frag-
mentary strokes, mingling feeling and perception.

## THE 'CRITICAL' NOVELS (1901–9)

The first of these novels, *The Island Pharisees*, was only published in 1904 although it had been begun in August 1901. Galsworthy is therefore entitled to mention the latter date in his preface to vol. IV of the Manaton Edition. This novel, by its virulence, breaks with the past, taking Galsworthy into his violent period.

A letter he wrote to Garnett in 1905 contains the first outline of what amounts to a working plan. He was in the throes of preparation for *The Man of Property*, his fourth novel, but was looking forward rather than back. The idea at the back of his mind, then and already while writing *The Island Pharisees*, was nothing less than 'the feeling of the utter disharmony of the Christian religion with the English character'.[7] He tells Garnett:

> I've got it in my mind now to carry on this idea for at least two more volumes. Just as the theme of the first book is the sense of property, the themes of the next (or rather the national traits dealt with) are (1) the reforming spirit, (2) the fighting spirit . . . the theme of the third book would be the spirit of advertisement, self-glorification, and impossibility of seeing ourselves in the wrong, and it would deal with the Boer War. . . . Six years elapse between each book, and I carry Young Jolyon through all three as commentator.[8]

He was then planning to give *The Man of Property* a subtitle such as *National Ethics I*, or *Christian Ethics I*, or *Tales of a Christian People I*, to announce a series on this central theme. Unfortunately, his letters give no clue as to why he dropped this plan in 1907, when he turned to other characters, in *The Country House*, where religion is secondary and the Boer War completely absent.

However, this new novel does partly contain what Galsworthy had envisaged for the third volume. It is even possible to regard the next novel, *Fraternity*, as illustrating 'the reforming spirit'. The original plan was changed rather than abandoned. Admittedly, Young Jolyon had to wait another fourteen years before reappearing in *In Chancery*. But the important thing was that Galsworthy was already thinking of a series, although he was less interested in linking it by using the same character or characters than in choosing a central theme, and illustrating several aspects in turn. This second phase of Galsworthy's career contains several of his most characteristic stories. Whatever one thinks of their qualities, the 'critical' novels are at the heart of his work as a novelist.

This group of 'social' novels overlaps into the third phase, with *The Patrician* (1911) and *The Freelands* (1915). This means that the series based on the 1905 plan does not tally with the 1924 classification. In 1910, when he completed *The Patrician*, he wrote to Garnett that this novel completed the series of critical novels begun with *The Island Pharisees*. In fact this was not even accurate: he was to publish two more that were to some extent critical novels, *The Freelands* in 1915 and *Saint's Progress* in 1919.

## *The Island Pharisees* (1904)

This novel tells how Dick Shelton, son of wealthy parents, breaks off his engagement to Antonia Dennant. The first part is entitled 'The Town', namely London, where Shelton lives, and the second part 'The Country', meaning the Dennant manor-house near Oxford. The hero meets a kind of Flemish tramp named Ferrand, whose influence deeply disturbs him. His convictions and prejudices are gradually undermined by Ferrand's subtle but pitiless criticism of his social privileges. He finds his own way of life in London, and the attitudes of mind that prevail in the Dennant household, unbearable. He is convinced that Antonia does not love him. She writes to tell him that she will keep her word. Seeing her ready to sacrifice herself to preserve the proprieties, he breaks off their engagement.

Extensive borrowing from Turgenev's *Rudin* (1856) can be detected. Galsworthy had read the book, and regarded one of the characters, Natasha, as among the finest creations in fiction. *Rudin* is the story of a broken engagement. The plot is slight. Much of its substance is provided by the speeches of the hero, who represents 'superfluous men'. But the two authors have rather different attitudes to their heroes. Shelton's taciturnity contrasts with the eloquence of Rudin, who is not treated sympathetically by Turgenev. Shelton's giving-up of Antonia could also come from another Turgenev novel, *Andrei Kosolov*, which is as personal and autobiographical as *The Island Pharisees*. There is also Turgenev's play *A Month in the Country*, where the hero similarly decides to leave after discovering his own agitation, and the uneasiness it is causing around him.

Galsworthy wrote of the novel, which he believed he had begun in 1901:

> The first draft of *The Island Pharisees* was buried in a drawer; when retrieved . . . it disclosed a picaresque string of anecdotes told by Ferrand in the first person. These two-thirds of a book were laid to rest by Edward Garnett's dictum that its author was not sufficiently within Ferrand's skin. . . . He started afresh in the skin of Shelton. Three times he wrote that novel.[9]

Galsworthy was right when he called this novel his 'tug of war'. It contains, in embryo, the four novels that followed it from 1906 to 1911. There is even a fifth, later novel, *The Freelands*, of 1915. It is not that plot and characters are similar, but their themes and theses are foreshadowed in *The Island Pharisees*.

And yet when he says that he started afresh in the skin of Shelton, Galsworthy did not realise that this was a vital factor in his art. This is where the artistic transformation occurred. The book is in fact an astonishing testimony to two, well-nigh simultaneous transformations: the achievement of moral and social awareness, and the discovery of the best form of expression. He was to keep to this indirect method from then on. Like *The Island Pharisees*, his later books are spiritual autobiographies. Obviously, it is regrettable that this development eliminated so much of the picaresque element. All that is left of Ferrand are a few remarks and letters.[10]

Despite and even because of this two-fold transformation, *The Island Pharisees* is not a good novel. It is full of obvious flaws. Galsworthy, so good at evoking love, deprived the book of this, in describing how the hero's love fades. And although he discovered his own way of writing, he was as yet unable to deploy all its effects. The descriptive poetry, charm and mystery already discernible in the first two novels are lacking.

There is no lack of characters but they fail to act. In chapter after chapter, the plot is little more than encounters that lead to discussions. Nothing could be more disastrous from an artistic viewpoint, and this it the most tedious of all Galsworthy's novels. Seen from the inside, however, it takes on a kind of lyrical unity, from its prevailing mood of anger and disgust. The satire is brought out, and from the pen of a member of the privileged classes it has the bite and effectiveness of a *roman à thèse*. For the first time Galsworthy published under his own name. In conservative circles the novel was regarded as scandalous, even treacherous. As was done for the portrait of Galsworthy, it can be taken as a reflection of his ideas, being the frankest of his novels. For once, with bitter disgust and sustained anger, he says a number of brutal things that were later to be put far more subtly.

The character of Shelton provides one of the most accurate self-portraits in the whole of Galsworthy's writings. There are two major differences: Shelton is not a writer; and, by a kind of imaginative sleight-of-hand, Galsworthy has turned his own romantic problem upside-down. Instead of achieving awareness through an attachment, Shelton frees himself by leaving his fiancée. But the passion, though leading in another direction, remains. And it is no accident that the matter of women's status is obsessively present throughout the novel. Its very awkwardness and incoherence show its authenticity: Galsworthy released his critical spirit only slowly, laboriously and empirically.

Shelton is a man of his age, reflecting a *fin-de-siècle* pessimism and discouragement. His conversational gifts are meagre, and his flight from Antonia inglorious, not to say shameful. He leaves the house unbeknown to all, without even leaving a letter like Ferrand. It foreshadows Hilary's departure at the end of *Fraternity*, and is less gloomy only because of the hero's age and a certain vitality in his anger. But his fate confirms the same moral. Shelton is put among the 'men of inaction', and it is even added that action makes him dangerous. The man who thinks destroys himself.

### The Man of Property (1906)

This novel tells of the conjugal misfortunes of a wealthy London notary, Soames Forsyte. The action takes place in London from June 1886 to December 1887. Soames' sensual passions are frustrated by his young wife's coldness. Her love is awakened when she meets Philip Bosinney, the architect commissioned by Soames to build him a luxury house at Robin Hill. Soames' efforts to assert his rights over his wife drive her into adultery. Bosinney is so disturbed at learning that Irene has been raped by her husband that he is knocked down and killed by a cab in the fog. Irene returns home like a bird to its cage.

In 1906, marriage, divorce and the rights of **marriage partners** were highly topical matters. Some people wished for greater justice and freedom, others were alarmed at the dangers new legislation and new ways could create for family traditions and the interests they involved.

When Marrot's biography of Galsworthy was published after his death, it became clear that the Forsytes represented his own family. The biography contains a family tree very similar to that of the Forsytes, though even more ramified, and going back far further. In particular, John Galsworthy (1782—1855) and Jolyon Forsyte (1770—1850) are almost contemporaries and their lives are very similar. Both had large families and moved to London at the same period, when urban expansion offered the best opportunities for making a fortune.

I shall try to put together the invaluable testimonies supplied by four members of the family whom I met, together with my own speculations. The novelist's mother and his forebears on that side do not appear in the Forsyte Chronicles. His father is faithfully reproduced in the character of Old Jolyon, while his father's brothers and sisters provided models for the Forsyte aunts and uncles. Except for Timothy, who is imaginary, the portraits of the uncles appear to be largely true to life. The aunts, however, are caricatured. The distinction between the obvious admiration for Old Jolyon and the satirical attitude to his brothers and sisters would appear to be justified partly by the facts. Swithin represents William, and James is Frederick. The aunts did not live with an uncle. Frank Galsworthy told me that Galsworthy's father was less concerned with money, and had a finer mind than his brothers. They were all gifted and successful, and had made a lot of money, mainly through financial speculation. Sir Edwin had become an important businessman, well-known in the City. On the whole, the characters are partly true to life, then, although their circumstances have been altered or entirely invented.

With the second generation of Forsytes, Galsworthy's creativeness held greater sway, even in the delineation of the characters. No one can say who Soames is, or Young Jolyon, or Bosinney. Each of them contains something of the author. Obviously, he speaks most clearly through Young Jolyon, who defines the typical Forsyte and the upper middle-class made up of Forsytes.[11] He also observes the other side of the coin. Emancipation of the young leads to degeneration of the species, from the end of the 19th century.

June is an exception to this general absence of models. She is probably based on Galsworthy's younger sister Mabel. Young Jolyon and Bosinney may owe something to Frank, who gave up being an architect to become a painter.

Together with Old Jolyon, Soames is the most capable and serious of the Forsytes. Either could have become a leading financier or politician. Citizens of Lübeck like Thomas Mann's Buddenbrooks, they would have been consuls or senators. Soames' vital mistake was to believe that he could own another human being, his wife, like some object. But the theoretical aspect of *The Man of Property* has often been exaggerated, as has its criticism of the idea of ownership, while too little attention has been paid to the fundamental truth embodied in Soames, made human through his sufferings, despite the blinkers he wears.

The abstract aspect of the book does exist, but it is limited: it is Old Jolyon who ironically bestows the name 'the man of property' on Soames. It imposes nothing; whereas the problem of women's rights is constantly raised and illustrated.

Galsworthy and Soames Forsyte have a complex relationship. There is the professional side. Galsworthy was a cultivated man, who had pursued the studies needed to become a lawyer. Soames is on a slightly lower, though more lucrative rung of the ladder. Galsworthy regards him, not with superiority, but with detachment. However, he would not, or could not, pursue satire and realism to any extreme. This would have meant describing the professional activities of Old Jolyon and his brothers, when they were still making their fortunes during the period of English industrialisation and uncontrolled urbanisation. This covered the beginning and middle of Victoria's reign, which lasted from 1837 to 1901. The novel starts in 1886, with the Forsyte brothers already in or on the point of retirement. Galsworthy probably found this more tactful.

The character of Irene is not actually a portrait of Ada. She is only one aspect of the model, chosen and sublimated to the point that it becomes a symbol. According to my informants, Fleur shows some of the features of Ada, while Jon was inspired by Rudolf. Another important literary influence is that of Thomas Hardy. The scene in Chapter 14 of Part II, where Irene takes refuge behind her locked door, must be inspired by the passage in *Jude the Obscure* (IV, 2, 3) in which Sue withdraws, far less brutally, through physically repugnance for Phillotson. Soames is an insensitive Phillotson.

The *Man of Property* is generally regarded as Galsworthy's best novel, and it is certainly the most widely read. The numerous satirical portraits it contains make it lively and amusing, while its tragic side comes from the growing anxiety that leads to the climax. But it cannot be considered in isolation. It is set off by what is best in the rest of *The Forsyte Chronicles*.

The plot is simple and almost flat, given that the only event that is dramatic in the accepted sense is Bosinney's death. But the story is complex, interrupted by flashbacks, and complicated by the number of characters. There are flaws, such as characters who have nothing to do with the plot, like Mrs Baynes or Mrs Macander, or others like Old Jolyon who are over-developed. The subplot centred on him takes up too much room. Interest is dispersed in Chapters 5 and 7 of Part I, and in Chapter 3 of Part II. Finally, the author shows a lack of taste in the fate meted out to June by Irene. But Bosinney is not a failure, as Galsworthy feared.

When Galsworthy extended the Forsyte family to take in half of England, he conferred an epic dimension on his novel. There is something Tolstoyan in the qualities and defects of *The Man of Property*. *Anna Karenina* may well have influenced the combination of a multitude of characters and vast horizons, but particularly the conception of the heroine's sufferings and passion.

## *The Country House* (1907)

George, the son of Squire Pendyce, lives the leisured life of a wealthy young man in London. Suddenly, his mistress's husband, Captain Bellew, sues for divorce. The Squire, horrified at the thought of his name, authority and the future of his family being endangered by the prospect of legal action and all its accompanying scandals, threatens to disinherit his son. Mrs Pendyce, worried about her son, leaves her husband and goes to London to find George. Mrs Bellew tells her that she has broken off her affair with George. She manages to persuade Bellew to drop his suit. All returns to normal in the Squire's house.

According to Marrot, *The Country House* was praised on all sides when it came out. Understandably, some of the most conservative critics were rather relieved to find this new book free of the satire and bitterness of *The Man of Property*. But their lucidity may be questioned. Admittedly, Marrot is right in saying that it is more pleasant to read, and that some of the characters are more

sympathetic. Most are rather unintellectual, and this helped Galsworthy keep discussions to a minimum. But it is so concise that it is
not easy to read. Galsworthy may even occasionally have gone too
far in his desire for sobriety. There is no clearer example of how
laconic he could be than the masterly three-page chapter entitled
'Mrs Bellew squares her accounts'.

The character of Helen Bellew is a resounding success, and
unique for a writer who tended to over-idealise women. He shows
consummate art in the way he makes her pronounce her own
opinion of the Squire and his class: 'You and your sort are only half
alive!'[12] H. G. Wells was quite mistaken in criticising Galsworthy
for his portraiture of George Pendyce. Admittedly he is partly
'wooden', but this does not prevent him from suffering, and therefore being alive. The Squire is splendidly obtuse, and his ally, the
Reverend Hussel Barter, is ferociously treated. The main driving
force, Mrs Pendyce, is Galsworthy's finest female character, like
Dinny in *End of the Chapter*, and, together with Soames, Fleur
and Miltoun, one of his greatest creations. He has told how he lost
control of Mrs Pendyce while writing the novel, and how she took
over as heroine. This in no way spoils it. Gregory Vigil is the only
failure.

This is the most perfectly constructed of all his novels. The
action is more substantial than usual. It starts far more briskly,
when George's situation is upset by Bellew's initiative. It provides a
dramatic turn of events, and there are few of these in the novels.
The other possible dramatic event, George's arrival at the house,
does not take place. His absence, just when the Squire has sum-
moned everyone, is the opposite of a *coup de théâtre*. But the
scene remains dramatic, recalling certain unspoken scenes in Galsworthy's plays, where the emotion is stepped up by the silence. It is
George's very absence that precipitates the crisis, creating tension
between father and son, then between husband and wife. The
tension and anxiety are increased by the ignorance of George's
address in London. It is the culminating point of the story, if the
word can be used to describe an inextricable tangle of emotions,
which paralyse opposing wills. By skilfully dividing the action
between the house in the country and London, Galsworthy points
up the rivalry between the static principles that the rural gentry is
trying to maintain, and the shifting attractions of the city. Everything in the book rounds out and concentrates the action. At the
end, silence regains possession of the country house. But its fate

is known: someone unworthy and incapable will succeed Squire Pendyce. The country house is lost.

This novel is one of the peaks of Galsworthy's career. Unlike Wells, Galsworthy knew and understood the world he was describing — as well as he knew that of the Forsytes. But having lived less in it, he had fewer connections, and it was this that enabled him to achieve a classical bareness, lightness and elegance not to be found elsewhere in his work.

## Fraternity (1909)

The action takes place in London. Two well-to-do brothers, Hilary and Stephen Dallison, are married to two sisters, Bianca and Cecilia. While one couple is happy and successful, the other is sterile, and mysteriously disunited. Hilary takes a young country girl, Ivy, under his protection. The 'little model' worms her way into his heart, by her acceptance of his advice and her dumb gratitude. Frightened, he tries to get rid of her. She fails to understand, and offers herself to him. He wavers, but is too fastidious. Finally, realising the failure of his marriage, he decides to leave England. Ivy asks him to take her with him, but he goes alone, giving her £150. The novel also tells of the misfortunes of Mrs Hughs, a poor seamstress who works for the Dallisons.

There is no definite proof of the influence of Turgenev's *On the Eve* (1859) on *Fraternity*, but the two plots are so alike that little doubt is possible.

'The title *Fraternity*,' wrote Galsworthy, 'was originally *Shadows*, for it was from watching those dogging counterparts of well-to-do lives that its author . . . conceived the scheme of this book.'[13] However, the novel starts in a drawing-room, and only seven of the forty-one chapters tell of the lives of the 'shadows', and Hilary's visits to them. Galsworthy was no more than complying with Garnett's advice during the writing of *The Island Pharisees*. He was right to do so, for the sections on the Hughses and their world leave much to be desired. Mrs Hughs is extremely weepy, and her misfortunes, which have no bearing on the plot, leave the reader cold.

So the main aspect of the novel is the personal relationship between the privileged and their shadows. The problem is confined to Hilary, the only person really concerned. How does Galsworthy handle him? Although the word is not uséd, he is a pure

intellectual – even if the authenticity of this may be doubted: the
only evidence that he is intelligent and full of ideas is that the
author says so. Might Galsworthy have presented a conventional
intellectual in the abstract? Might Hilary have been created as the
counterpart to Soames? Unfortunately, there is no precise record of
how the character was conceived. He is partly a self-portrait, to the
extent that Galsworthy took a trait of his own character, enlarged
and isolated it from the rest. But he did not realise the falsity of this
distorted projection. It is the trait already found in Shelton, 'the
man of inaction', generalised and taken to an extreme. Galsworthy
confuses something else. If Hilary is impulsive and erratic in his
behaviour, it is not because of his intelligence, but because of his
excessive delicacy and refinement, a defect that arises from the
temperament and senses, not the intellect.

The behaviour of this anti-hero can be judged from many view-
points, as was clearly seen by Conrad, whose splendidly sincere
and extraordinarily violent reaction, in a letter quoted by his
biographer Jean Aubry, was that of a moralist. But the character
may also be seen as the result of dreadful self-hatred in the author,
a frenetic confession, an indirect confession of the inadequacy of
his generosity, and this, indeed, would be my own opinion. It
makes *Fraternity* a premonitory forerunner of *The Burning Spear*.
Galsworthy was into his forties, and may have been a victim of
middle-aged restlessness, as was to be shown even more clearly in
'Autumn', the third episode of *The Dark Flower*. On the other
hand, Hilary's abstinence may be respected.

One thing is evident: in describing Hilary and Bianca, Galsworthy is giving an example of psychological impotence that has
nothing to do with his own case, and which he judges severely. He
condemns Hilary's 'hamletism', while finding it less objectionable
than Antonia Dennant's or Squire Pendyce's blindness.[14]

The weakness of the novel is the inevitable result of its psychological basis and the thesis it illustrates. Hilary and Bianca are
insipid – Bianca even more so than her husband – and their
actions are insignificant. Consequently, the story leaves a persistent taste of ashes in the mouth. It is less tedious than *The Island
Pharisees*, since some of the secondary characters are quite vivid,
but harder to read because it is gloomier. Galsworthy's pervasive
and boundless pessimism is less bearable than Hardy's, because the
blackness of the picture is not compensated for by his imaginative
vision.

The presentation of the concept of fraternity in the character of Sylvanus Stone, and in the extracts quoted from his great work, is not a great artistic success. But Galsworthy constantly adopted a comical style when he wanted to express his most dearly held convictions. An extremely interesting parallel has been drawn by Samuel Hynes between C. F. G. Mastermann's *The Condition of England* and *Fraternity*.[15] The contrast with E. M. Forster's novel *Howards End* is also instructive. All three books were published in 1909. E. M. Forster is far more inventive, imaginative and engaging than Galsworthy, but they share a large number of ideas.

The emptiness of Hilary's life holds no fascination. It would have been wrong to end his story with a suicide. *Fraternity* contains an acceptance of powerlessness, a lucid attitude to failure, that can touch contemporary readers. This may be why the book is more widely read than other Galsworthy novels that have greater charm.

## THE LYRICAL NOVELS AND WAR-TIME NOVELS (1910–19)

The beginning of this phase is not marked by any break comparable with that observed in 1901, but Galsworthy was still justified in choosing the date 1910. *The Patrician* which, looking back from 1924, he saw as lyrical rather than critical, was written during 1910, though published in 1911.

When he was writing his preface for the Manaton Edition of *The Patrician*, thirteen or fourteen years later, he considered that the change of direction had been too sudden and deliberate: 'Aesthetically speaking, I consider that a certain forcing of the "beauty" note . . . and a sort of "softness" in the love stories, detract from its merits.'[16]

There is further confirmation of the change mentioned by Galsworthy in three other very significant works that he wrote at this time in three other *genres*: *The Little Dream*, an 'allegory in six scenes', a collection of poems, *Moods, Songs and Doggerels*, which was to be published in March 1912, and a collection of sketches, stories and essays, *The Inn of Tranquillity*, in which he tries to express the serenity he feels.

Another sign of the reality of the change in Galsworthy's attitudes at this time is the prelude to the novel *The Dark Flower* in his

own life, his interest in the young dancer and choreographer
Margaret Morris. He wrote his first letter to her on 9 February
1911. So is this the right moment to ask: why, and why then? The
reason might be the drying-up of Galsworthy's satirical inspiration, or, more precisely, the exhaustion of the vein he had worked
up to then. This interpretation in no way means that he abandoned the convictions and ideals he had adopted. Nor does it imply
a final end of his satirical style. It takes account of circumstances
at the time, and of a change of register. As Galsworthy himself
does, it would be wise to admit that not all the causes and exact significance can necessarily be grasped.

In any case, two of the novels in the third phase are entirely representative: *The Dark Flower* (1913) and *Beyond* (1917). they can
even be said to mark the summit of Galsworthy's rather personal
form of romanticism. To some extent, both novels are escapist.
But, as will be shown, even in romantic stories his critical mind is
not entirely absent. It still operates perhaps unconsciously.

Publication between these two works of another, rather different
novel, *The Freelands*, in 1915, is understandable when one knows
of the unsettled conditions of writing and the unfortunate fate of
this novel, finished out of a sense of duty during the war. It is worth
pointing out the organic link between *The Freelands* and novels in
the previous phase. However, this unexpected extension is by no
means to be welcomed: it is the most mediocre of his novels. But a
sixth title to be classified with the 'critical' novels, and completed
reluctantly, provides final proof that Galsworthy really conceived
nothing outside the two categories of works and two forms of inspiration defined by him. In fact, *The Freelands* occupies the same
position in the complete works as *The Patrician*. It is a (late)
transitional work between the 'critical' and 'lyrical' novels. The part
concerned with return to the land (and satirising the local Squire) is
limited, despite Galsworthy's passionate interest in the problem.

An author of such sincerity and integrity as Galsworthy was
bound to be affected by the war in his writings. But critics failed to
perceive the gravity of its effects on his very life and health, which
made it even harder for them to appreciate the extent of its
influence on his work. Marrot does not provide much help concerning the effect of the war on Galsworthy's career. Understandably (given his knowledge), he saw no more than a slight drop in
quality resulting from general current difficulties: 'Little wonder if
the books of this period fell below his normal level.'[17]

Talk of any momentary drop in Galsworthy's vitality is both exaggerated and inadequate. It is inadequate because it reduces what was in reality a profound spiritual upheaval to a passing event. And it is exaggerated, because the actual quantity of work produced during the war years showed no slackening: on the contrary, more than four novels in four years. And it is also exaggerated to suggest any falling-off in quality. This is at least arguable for the novels. Admittedly, they are unequal, but the same may be said of every phase in his career. *The Freelands* is weak, *The Burning Spear* is less a work of art than a kind of satirical autobiography. But *The Dark Flower* is an interesting and engaging attempt. Above all, *Beyond* is a notable success, as work of art and as character study, with the heroine, Gyp. Not even Marrot has been fair to this novel. I place it very high among the novels. It is as original as *The Dark Flower*, but better.

One thing is clear. If *Beyond* has been so neglected by most critics, not to say ignored like *Jocelyn* and *The Burning Spear*, it is precisely because it is different from what may be called the 'typical' Galsworthian novel, *The Man of Property*. More than one critic has passed judgement on the whole of Galsworthy, on the sole strength of reading *The Man of Property*. If other works have been read, they are those that follow the first Forsyte novel, or at least those that resemble it. Since the lyrical novels raise other problems, it was often considered more expedient not to mention them. Garnett had stopped giving his opinion by the time they were written. Bellamy in 1971 also leaves out this part of Galsworthy's works, in his book *The Novels of Wells, Bennett and Galsworthy, 1890–1910*.

Admittedly, Galsworthy did not bring these books together in a single series, as he had intended to do for his 'critical' novels. Neither letters nor diary draw any comparisons similar to those between *The Island Pharisees* and all succeeding novels up to *The Patrician*. In the preface to the Manaton Edition of *The Dark Flower*, however, he groups together the heroines of three of the novels of this period, and pronounces the same verdict on them. Replying to attacks against him when *The Dark Flower* was published, he writes: 'Women of the type of Olive and Nell in the *Dark Flower*, Gyp in *Beyond*, and Noel in *Saint's Progress* are rather rare, especially in these days — one can hear the "Thank God" of ten thousand readers — but they exist.'[18]

In this way he recognises a common inspiration for the three novels. If he had not decided to keep silent about his first two novels, he would probably have mentioned the heroines of *Villa Rubein* and particularly *Jocelyn*.

*The Burning Spear* and *Saint's Progress* remain to be situated in the works of this phase. They were both published after the end of the war, *The Burning Spear* on 24 April 1919 and *Saint's Progress* on 16 November. So they may be regarded as contemporary.

With these stories, the war enters Galsworthy's novels, though both late and in a limited way. Neither of them contains any account or description of actual war events. As always, they are concerned with heart searchings and the consequences of facts, not the original crude facts — which does not prevent the consequences and heart searchings from being grave and anguished.

War is either dramatically present in the works of this period, or totally absent. The contrast between *The Dark Flower*, *The Freelands* and *Beyond* on the one hand, and the other two novels on the other, has not been pointed up. And yet it is easy to explain. The war obsessed Galsworthy, and either invaded the whole book, or was excluded from it. There was no middle way.

On the contrary, *The Burning Spear* in particular, but also *Saint's Progress*, show a kind of concentration and exaggeration that recall the most passionate and violent works of youth, *Jocelyn* and *The Island Pharisees*, at least in certain psychological aspects. *The Burning Spear* may be completely unclassifiable, but it can still be seen as a perfectly logical and coherent culmination of trends already apparent in the 'social' novels. It should, no doubt, be regarded as the ultimate manifestation of that critical spirit that had inspired Galsworthy in the series of five novels beginning with *The Island Pharisees*, and in a sixth, *The Freelands*.

Is *The Burning Spear* not the final stage in satire, in other words self-criticism and self-satire? Just as Shelton takes leave of the 'Pharisees', John Lavender wishes to take leave of England at war, but above all of himself, for his existence is a challenge to his beliefs and standards. In wanting to end it, he is consistent.

*The Burning Spear*, then, is related to the other novels only through the personal aspect of the problem it raises. *Saint's Progress*, on the other hand, with its story of Nollie's passion, the development of the feelings of the man who ultimately weds her, and Leila's misfortunes, contains much of what Galsworthy called the emotional side of his nature, even though the basic theme remains a determined and sustained attack on the Church of

England and Christianity. Galsworthy's verdict on his 'saint' is satirical and severe, without being sour. Through him he is criticising an institution and habits of thought that are centuries old.

The two separate critical themes of *The Burning Spear* and *Saint's Progress* are accompanied by another, less important, but common to both novels. Galsworthy once again exercises his critical gifts on the new human, social and even political problems arising from the war. Once again, he does not share the majority view. He speaks out against the hatred that was being unleashed, and the injustices of the present, and expresses his anxiety at the dangers of the coming peace. So the 'emotional' phase from 1910 to 1918 ends with a renewal of the critical spirit. Galsworthy is guilty of an error in failing to mention this in the 1924 text quoted at the beginning of this chapter.

## *The Patrician* (1911)

Miltoun, eldest son of Lord Valleys of the Caradoc family, is destined for an outstanding career as a statesman. His future is compromised by his love for Audrey Noel, who is separated from her husband. He gives her up, but falls ill. She looks after him and saves him. They became lovers. Miltoun abandons his career. Fearing that this may in the end cost her his love, Audrey leaves England.

This novel is an illustration of the principle of hereditary authority in a family of the nobility. The Caradocs are politicians. But their political action is not shown; in fact, even their political ideas lead to only two developments, one of which is of some importance, in Chapter 22 of Part II. The whole of the rest of the book is concerned with the human problems that Patricians are faced with through submission to their own dogmas.

Miltoun is of particular interest, because, of all Galsworthian heroes, he is the most different from the author himself. He is a tortured being, where Galsworthy was merely anxious. He believes in God. He is dogmatic and headstrong. Did Galsworthy have a real-life model? Did George Meredith inspire this passionate creature? One cannot tell. The most likely influence was Carlyle.[19] There was little affinity between the two writers, and any influence must have been ill-defined. But it did colour and perhaps enrich Galsworthy's imagination.

There is also something exaggerated about Audrey that distinguishes her from his other heroines. Her passive attitude to love and to her relationships with the other characters, her devotedness and her self-denial, appear unbelievable. The dates of Galsworthy's correspondence suggest that in Audrey he drew for his contemporaries a portrait of the anti-suffragette.[20] She shows great nobility and, although a commoner, she gives a lesson in nobility to the nobility.

The novel is helped by half the action being located in Galsworthy's ancestral countryside. Without even using the name Dartmoor, he provides a very powerful and emotional description of the wild charm and primitive beauty of that landscape that moved him so deeply. The setting was perfect for the dark and tragic plot of *The Patrician*, the novel that most recalls the stories of Hardy. The profound influence of Gilbert Murray's recent translations of the Greek drama is also to be seen in the feeling of implacable fate. With an even greater sense of restraint than usual, Galsworthy sought and obtained tragic effects, with little action, and with no physical violence, death or injury.

The argument is stated perfectly clearly in the text. However, the criticism of the aristocracy is far less biting than that of the country gentry in *The Country House*. This is a sign of the change in Galsworthy's mood and manner already mentioned. His criticism in fact is not wholesale. Changes affecting the nobility are illustrated through the trio of Lady Casterley, Miltoun's grandmother, a living and still formidable vestige of the 'die-hards'; at the other extreme, the irreligious and rebellious young Barbara, Miltoun's sister; and between them Lord Valleys, the aristocrat with nothing of the domestic tyrant. He has effected the change proposed to his class by Edward VII, adapting to modern ways, science and trade. Galsworthy's picture is historically valid, all the more so because so few of his contemporary writers had the same opportunity of mixing with the aristocracy.

The double plot of *The Patrician* is not completely successful. There are some disadvantages in the parallel and simultaneous love affairs of Miltoun and Barbara: the second is not very interesting. Courtier is a failure, as Galsworthy admitted. But he comes over better than Gregory Vigil in *The Country House*, or Hilary in *Fraternity*. In spite of these reservations, and the author's own later ones, I must confess my own particular liking for this novel, with its severe but pathetic beauty, and the tragic poetry that fills it. Dialogue is good, but there is little of it, and the book could be compared to a long recitative. In one sense it is a dream, in which

Galsworthy imagines a perfectly noble being, overcoming love as he himself had never been able to do, and committing himself entirely to duty. Its very anachronism adds to its charm. Among the novels, I would put it not far below *The Country House*.

## *The Dark Flower* (1913)

This novel contains three episodes: 'Spring', 'Summer' and 'Autumn'. It describes the romantic attachments of Mark Lennan, aged nineteen, then twenty-six, finally forty-six. The women in his life are, first, Anna Stormer, the wife of his professor, supplanted by Sylvia, who becomes his wife; then Olive Cramier, his great love, who has a short and tragic history — she drowns the day before she is to elope with Mark; and finally Nell Dromore, who is only seventeen.

In 1905, eight years before *The Dark Flower* was published, Arnold Bennett had produced *Sacred and Profane Love*, which recounts three crucial times in the life of his heroine, Carlotta Peel. Galsworthy had probably not read the book but must have known of its existence. He may have borrowed the construction and even the theme from Bennett, though he handled it in quite a different spirit and far more successfully, because more sincerely.

According to Marrot, the book met with a general outcry on publication. This is not surprising, given its real or apparent amoralism, which was so shocking. Although Galsworthy considered that he had abandoned satire for poetry, his plot once again flouted conventions. Mark, like all his heroes, is a man of his own class. It was unforgivable for such a man, with every appearance of respectability, to prove completely indifferent to it. The author had used an Austrian woman to denounce 'English Grundys'. He had made Cramier such an unattractive husband that even Soames seemed preferable. Worse still, he had written: 'In love, there are no little bits — no standing still.'[21]

The distinguished and discriminating poet and critic Arthur Quiller-Couch wrote, in the *Daily Mail*, that Galsworthy was seeking refuge in free love, and lamented the fact that he had written a book about a marriage where there were no children.

As might be expected, there is nothing to shock the reader of today in *The Dark Flower*, and it can now be studied more objectively. The author's response to Quiller-Couch[22] is quite justified: Anna in 'Spring' and Mark in 'Autumn' each offer an example of self-sacrifice motivated by respect for others. The ageing Mark conquers his desires in order to spare his wife. Galsworthy's most deeply held belief is that love and hypocrisy are not compatible.

The hero's character is not explored in any depth. He provides the only link between the episodes, and since they share neither unity of place nor unity of time, it would not be a novel at all, but three separate stories, were it not for sustained unity of action and tone, as great as possible, given the theme.

The essential theme is not marriage, though the author's customary considerations on the subject are to be found. Even less does it depict a conventional lover, a Don Juan, or a particularly sensual man. Mark is distinguished by his outstanding sensitivity, and the extreme delicacy of the feelings he shows. In this, like other Galsworthy heroes, he illustrates a feature of his author's character. The subject is handled without any over-fastidiousness, but with considerable discretion and unfailing good taste. Some of his other novels are less reticent: the air of eroticism that clings to Irene, Helen Bellew, Barbara and others can become tedious and irritating. *The Dark Flower* is free of this.

The plot is admirably straightforward. Galsworthy does not follow those who try to describe passion through the innumerable adventures into which it leads their heroes. There is a touch of the exotic in *The Dark Flower*, with its evocation of Hyères and the Tyrol. But the most attractive and delightful qualities are its poetic style and shades of feeling. The most beautiful scenes take place in the English countryside, among the trees in the wild grounds around the old manor, in 'Spring', and on the river, in 'Summer'.

The recent publication by Margaret Morris of the seventy letters that Galsworthy wrote to her from 1911 to 1913, under the title *My Galsworthy Story*, throws new light on 'Autumn', but not on the other two episodes. However, the whole book was written while their relationship was in progress. As Margaret Morris says, she was not in the same position as Nell. And yet, she says, every scene was illustrated in her mind by a matching scene that actually occurred. Mark's behaviour and thought processes correspond to those found in, or which can be deduced from, the letters. Margaret Morris' personality and initiatives seem to have been very similar to those attributed to Nell.

'Autumn' is not the only autobiographical part of *The Dark*

*Flower*. 'Summer' quite obviously relates Galsworthy's meeting with Ada, and the beginning of their love. But there is far more artistic recasting of the event, making it almost completely fictional. Finally, even the first episode may have a slight auto-biographical basis.[23] *The Dark Flower* is perhaps a poem rather than a novel, though it is very engaging as a novel. All three episodes have their charm. The finest is 'Summer', not because of its central position, but by virtue of its special tragic and poetic qualities.

## The Freelands (1915)

Tryst, a morose and boorish widower, who suffers from epilepsy, and who lives in a Worcestershire village, is threatened with eviction by the lady of the manor, on moral grounds. The farm-workers go on strike, and there is some violence, burning of hay-stacks, scuffles with the police. Tryst is arrested, tried, and sentenced to prison. He dies, and there is doubt as to whether it was an accident or suicide. The main part of the story concerns the repercussions of the event on the four Freeland brothers, who belong to the upper middle classes.

Fewer copies of this novel were sold than of any other. For one thing, the agrarian question did not cater to public tastes in 1915. But the indifference persisted, and in the end it was a fair verdict. Galsworthy was no more familiar with the rural poor than with the urban proletariat. He confused and distorted the situation by making Tryst an epileptic, and made matters worse by making him suffer from claustrophobia. Only in stirring monologues, where the tranquil beauty of the English countryside is contrasted with the sufferings he sees hidden there, did he really deal with the injustice of working-class conditions in the country.

Kirsteen Freeland and her children Sheila and Derek go farther than any other Galsworthy character in their sympathy for the oppressed and along the path of revolutionary action. The words 'revolutionary' and 'rising' are used several times. It is exaggerated, but not entirely misplaced. This is unusual enough to require some explanation. It is to be found in Turgenev's novel *Virgin Soul* (1876). Galsworthy never mentions this influence, but his close paraphrase of the Russian title in his own title, and similarities between the two novels, support my belief that he borrowed extensively from it. He simplified Turgenev's plot, greatly reducing its tragic character. However, Sheila and Derek do not spare themselves. There is also a model in the Turgenev novel for Felix Freeland, the novelist. He becomes more important than Paklin, for Galsworthy always enjoys scourging himself.

Galsworthy approves neither of Felix, whom he dismisses as a 'hamletist', nor of Kirsteen and her children, whom he does not forgive for inciting the labourers to violence. They are condemned through the mouth of the good-natured giant Tod Freeland, an interesting and well-delineated character who very probably owes something to another Turgenev hero, Fedor Lavretzky, protagonist of *A Household of Gentlefolk* (1859). Here Turgenev's influence is in harmony with the natural predispositions of his English disciple, who took such delight in farm work when he was at Manaton. Tod is neither a tenant farmer nor a gentleman farmer, but a nature lover. He and Kirsteen form one of those slightly eccentric well-to-do couples that are to be found in the heart of the country.

Turgenev's overwhelming superiority as a writer shines out in his wonderful depiction of humble country people. Only in the love story of Derek and Nedda, and in the very beautiful, poetic description of the countryside, does Galsworthy rise near the level of his master. The character of Frances Freeland, mother of the Freeland brothers, should also be mentioned.[24] But basically the book never amounts to more than a well-intentioned effort.

## Beyond (1917)

Gyp, illegitimate daughter of an officer, Winton, marries a great Swedish violinist, Fiorsen, with whom she is unhappy. She bears with his vanity for two years, then leaves with her baby daughter. The following spring she falls in love with Bryan Summerhay and lives with him as his wife. But she is temperamental and demanding, and becomes suspicious. Their life together becomes fraught. Bryan dies accidentally and Gyp contemplates suicide. But her strength of character enables her to regain her health, and maybe even her zest for life.

There are two versions of *Beyond*. In the first version it was his longest novel. Galsworthy abridged it by a quarter. The final version, without containing any important changes in the story, is better. The plot differs from the usual ones found in Galsworthy's writings: the action is longer, and more spread out in space than is customary.

Galsworthy is less than frank in the preface he wrote for the Manaton Edition. It praises the three masters to whom he says he owed most: Turgenev, Tolstoy and Maupassant. He alludes twice to Maupassant's novel *A Woman's Life*, but there is no information about his other borrowings in *Beyond*. To complicate matters further, nine years earlier, in 1908, Arnold Bennett had published *The Old Wives' Tale*, which was also inspired by the Maupassant novel – an influence that Bennett admitted. However, there are only superficial resemblances between *Beyond* and Bennett's masterpiece.

The basic idea they borrowed from Maupassant was of a sensitive romantic woman. This was perfectly in accord with Galsworthy's fundamental romanticism, while at the same time it took him out of a certain rut, for he had never chosen a female character as the protagonist of a novel (and except for *Maid in Waiting* he never did it again). In doing so, and in making Fiorsen a Maupassant-like Bohemian bereft of any social awareness, he was completely overturning the normal situation in his novels. The standard Galsworthy protagonist was a man, tormented by his scruples. The change was all the more beneficial in that Galsworthy otherwise retained his full independence. The spirit of the book, its psychology and philosophy, are far from Maupassant's style. Galsworthy rejected the French writer's pessimism, and regarded realism only as a means to an end. He handled the character of Gyp in his own way, opening himself to influences other than Maupassant.

Gyp is a typical Galsworthy heroine, except that certain traits of character are taken to an extreme, while other unaccustomed ones are included. She is quite lacking in any reasonableness or common sense to counterbalance her emotional excesses. The secrets of her subconscious are revealed. It is not the physical side of marriage that she objects to: even when she realises that she does not love Fiorsen, she is still quite ready to yield to his sexual demands.

This is in complete opposition to Irene's, Audrey Noel's and Olive Cramier's refusal and revulsion. They are sexually unsatisfied or even traumatised by their husbands. Gyp's attitude is entirely post-Victorian and 'modern', heralding Fleur's acceptance of her husband in *A Modern Comedy*. But it is also Tolstoyan.

Next to *War and Peace*, *Anna Karenina* was Galsworthy's favourite Tolstoy novel, and is mentioned by him several times. Gyp strikingly resembles Anna, though they are also quite different in some ways. As Gyp points out, she never suffers from Anna's remorse. Neither is she a society woman. This explains the difference in the novel endings. Tolstoy's story is more romantic and tragic, infinitely vaster and more epic in its proportions than *Beyond*.

Apart from these signs of Tolstoy's influence, what information is available about the origins of this fascinating character? It is rather like the problem of sources for Miltoun. Do these unusual personalities owe something to Meredith? Or to Anatole France?[2]T Both hypotheses are valid, and compatible.

Like *The Dark Flower*, *Beyond* is more critical than Galsworthy realised. The social background is still his own. Gyp is on the fringes of society rather than an outsider. Fiorsen is ridiculed. There is a biting satire of the lower middle classes, in the person of Daphne Wing. There are excellent comic scenes.

*Beyond* is a most estimable novel in itself, and is ultimately quite distinct from all the works to which it owes something. It is one of the least gloomy of all Galsworthy's writings. It shows a human being so full of natural vigour that death becomes only a passing shadow.

## The Burning Spear (1919)

During the First World War, John Lavender, his head filled with the patriotic rallying cries he reads every day in five leading daily papers, yearns to ape journalists and official orators. He is recruited as a voluntary propagandist, and is regarded by everyone as a madman. His grandiloquent spoutings are ignored. The audience is usually imaginary: he addresses a scarecrow, or sees a crowd where there is only one person present. His misadventures convince him of his powerlessness to carry through his mission. In despair, he makes a huge pile of all his newspapers, sets fire to it and, perched on top, decides to commit himself to the flames. He falls, but his neighbour Isabelle, 'a tall young lady of fine build and joyous colouring'[26] catches him in her arms.

The novel was completed in 1918 and was published anonymously after the end of the war. It was a complete failure, and had no greater success when Galsworthy had it reissued in 1923 under his own name. And yet he included it in the principal editions of his works, and never thought of disowning it. It is undoubtedly the most peculiar and hermetic of all his writings. Hardly any critics ever mention it. The significance and interest of the book are in the light it casts on the depiction of Galsworthy the man, in Part I of this study. Looking back on it, Galsworthy called *The Burning Spear* 'a revenge of nerves', which it certainly is.[27] Every excess of the war-time hatred and chauvinism is railed against, particularly the exaggerations of which some newspapers were guilty.

But it is far more than a revenge. Like most of his novels, it is a self-portrait, as self-critical as any of them. John Lavender is John Galsworthy made clownish, ageing and wretched. Like him, he has private means that free him from his profession as a lawyer. Like him, he is made miserable by the war and his part in it. Galsworthy is so bitter that he ignores his own work as a writer, treating it as utterly idle rantings. He exacerbates the feeling of dissatisfaction by showing his hero incapable of committing suicide properly.

The novel is abortive, as its brevity shows. And yet Galsworthy made use of two great literary models: he tried to make his hero an amalgam of Don Quixote and Mr Pickwick, Don Pickwixote. Galsworthy was an admirer of Dickens. He used to read his books aloud in the evenings, emphasising their comic side. He borrowed several comic effects from *The Pickwick Papers*, as well as Dickens' sense of exaggeration. But the effect of his book is quite different. He also admired Cervantes, and always tended to compare Don Quixote with his own idealistic characters; he even saw himself in him, in a poem called 'Errantry' from *Moods, Songs and Doggerels*. He also alluded to him several times in *Castles in Spain*. He had probably read Turgenev's discussion of Hamlet and Don Quixote as human types. This would explain the attraction these two heroes exerted on his imagination. Cervantes' cruelty to Don Quixote and his conception of madness — as two aspects of the same thing — had a powerful effect on him. He also shared the cult of beauty. The very title of the book seems to be inspired directly by Cervantes rather than by echoes of Elizabethan literature.

In reply to a letter dated 18 May 1919, and quoted by Marrot, Gilbert Murray attributed the failure of *The Burning Spear* to the influence of *Don Quixote*. I feel that this burdensome influence is rather a sign of failure. The same could be said of Dickens.

Galsworthy's talent was too personal and delicate to be adapted to such powerful geniuses. The fact that he tried to do so suggests that he was unable to find his own way of expressing his mock-heroic intentions. *The Burning Spear* is the most authentic reflection of Galsworthy's state of mind during the war, his mental confusion, and the destructive effect on his inspiration.

Galsworthy called *The Burning Spear* a novel, and I have no hesitation in accepting the term. He cared little about defining it, however, and also described it as 'a comedic satire'.[28] It could also be termed a philosophical tale, or a mock-heroic tale. But 'novel' is probably the best definition, even though it is a failure, and stops short. Only when it is placed against the other novels can it be understood. Love plays a minor part, but is present. Self-criticism, in contrast, reaches almost demented proportions.

Initially, Galsworthy's attitude to insanity is clear. It is that of the social critic, for whom anybody who fails to respect conventional ways of thinking is considered insane. He exploits the comic aspect of the hasty judgements made on Lavender. But he feels that the reader will begin to find him too idiotic. Thereupon, he asserts that Lavender is not mad. In the third stage, things go wrong. Lavender becomes actually insane, showing signs of mental confusion, hallucinations, and goes through increasingly frequent periods of delirium or comatose inactivity. His pathological hatreds and obsessions about the war and the role of the press (which are more relevant to Galsworthy himself) are described. There are few occurrences of anxiety, or at least they are flatly presented, with a single, commonplace nightmare. But pathological episodes abound. The end is farcical, but more melancholy than dramatic. It confirms Lavender's impotence, plunging the book into the realms of abnormal psychology.

### Saint's Progress (1919)

A Church of England clergyman, Edward Pierson, will not allow his daughter Nollie to marry a young officer, Cyril Morland, who shortly afterwards is killed in battle. Nollie is expecting a child. She reveals this to her father, challenging him to condemn her. He exhorts her to expiate what she has done. But when his parishioners' disapproval is voiced publicly, his pride as a father is wounded. He resigns and leaves England, to become an army chaplain. Against his will, Nollie marries an atheist, Jimmy Fort.

Galsworthy had had the idea for such story nearly fifteen years before. In working out the plan for his critical novels, he had included a story designed to show the disharmony between Christianity and the English character. This had not yet been written.

Galsworthy does not treat religion in *Saint's Progress* as a form of thought and inner life, but as a social, even political force. Yet — and this is the paradox of the novel — Pierson's religious attitudes are rooted in his psychology. He takes very little part in the discussions in the book. He is neither a thinker nor a scholar, much less a polemicist. His theology comes down to the idea of being submissive. He is occasionally depicted in the exercise of his ministry, but most of the story consists of his personal and family problems.

Galsworthy, however, has an argument which reintroduces religion, putting it in the centre of the book. He gives his clergyman the turn of mind he regards as unavoidable, imposed by determinism: 'He had been too long immune from criticism, too long in the position of one who may tell others what he thinks of them.'[29] Because of his social position, he identifies with authority, trying to maintain the principles of authority and conventional morality. He always wants to decide for his daughter. The character may owe something to Anthony Trollope, but is more likely to have been influenced by Samuel Butler. This is the central concept of the novel, although its psychology is quite different from that of *The Way of All Flesh*. Pierson does not have the same stifling power over Nollie as Theobald Pontifex has over Ernest when he is young, and Nollie loves her father without fearing him. This reflects the difference in the relationships of both authors with their parents.

Butler's name is not mentioned by Galsworthy in relation to *Saint's Progress*. But there is no doubt of the influence *The Way of All Flesh* (1903) had on him. In 1910, in a letter to Frank Lucas, he called it the best modern English novel. The influence of Trollope is far less evident. There is only one reference to his novels, underlining the parochialism of the author of *Barchester Towers*.

Galsworthy was anti-clerical, and should logically have made his clergyman a dangerous character. This was not so: his capacity for hating was too slight for it to be easy. In fact, he endowed Pierson with several of his own real or imagined characteristics, above all his inner distress about his personal role in the war. He made him sensitive, to beauty for example, and even weak. The story reveals

Pierson as a lonely, completely ineffectual man. He is a failure as a
man, a father and a priest, and knows it.

The character is unsatisfactory because of a certain inconsistency. Galsworthy does use Pierson's asceticism to launch a very
pertinent attack on puritanism. 'He doesn't mind making people
unhappy, because the more they are repressed, the saintlier they'll
be.'[30] But it is hard to imagine somebody so inept being dangerous.
Pierson is also too much like heroes of several other Galsworthy
novels, particularly Hilary in *Fraternity*. Finally, he is an
illustration of an exaggerated generalisation, and one that is ill-
founded: Galsworthy admits that he is not representative. If he
had wanted to denounce the Church and its ministers, he should
have depicted a genuine clergyman.

Nollie is a passionate and impulsive creature, like Gyp in
*Beyond*. But she does not exert the same charm, for her personality is less powerful. There is a subplot concerning Leila Lynch, an
ageing adventuress, whose lover Nollie steals. The story resembles
the first and third episodes of *The Dark Flower*, but without any of
their poetic beauty and intensity. Two other characters, George
and Lavendie, act mainly as mentors.

The themes are the same as in *The Burning Spear*, handled in a
different, non-satirical, more realistic style. The disturbing effect
of the war on new generations, and the headlong changes in moral
behaviour, are described. The idea of 'modernity' is mentioned,
and the symbol of *The White Monkey* is foreshadowed.[31]

How does Galsworthy illustrate the three themes of the novel,
religion, love, war? The idea of a clergyman's daughter dis-
honoured by her illegitimate child was a promising one. Examining religion in war-time was also an adept combination. And the
circumstances were favourable to the blossoming of love as Galsworthy imagined it. But despite this, it is not very successful. On
several occasions the story is swamped in sentimentality, even
though the style is realistic: conclusive evidence of Galsworthy's
lack of balance and inventiveness at this troubled period of his life.
The best parts of the novel are those describing how the scandal
burst in Pierson's parish.

Galsworthy was not familiar enough with clergymen to depict
them convincingly. *Saint's Progress* contains only a faint echo of
the biting and subtle satire displayed by Butler in *The Way of All
Flesh*. Nearly fifty years separated the two works, and Butler's
themes had lost some of their virulence over the years.

## THE FORSYTE CHRONICLES (1920–8)

*In Chancery* was published on 22 October 1920. But the origin of the event goes back to the spring of 1917. As has already been said, it was then that Galsworthy thought of *Indian Summer of a Forsyte*, an essential prerequisite to continuation and completion of the Forsyte Chronicles. This was published on 25 July 1918, just three days before the 'inspired Sunday' at Manaton, described by Marrot, when Galsworthy so quickly, perhaps in a single flash, realised that *The Man of Property* could be a beginning, the first part of a vast literary opus. His words have already been quoted: 'This idea, if I can ever bring it to fruition, will make *The Forsyte Saga* a volume of half a million words nearly; and the most sustained and considerable piece of fiction of our generation at least.'

So there is some overlapping between the period of the lyrical novels, publication of which ended in 1919, and the period of the Chronicles, at least if the date on which these new novels were planned is taken into account. The date of 28 July is significant, like the year 1901, when Galsworthy planned his 'critical' novels. On that summer's day, in the peaceful setting of Manaton which he loved so much, he looked beyond the end of the First World War, and managed to overcome the depression that lay so heavy on him. His recovery coincided with the freeing of the creative spirit.

It was both a return to his old sources of inspiration, and a new start. His mind, so long troubled, found profound consolation in setting aside the present and going back to a past that, while far from ideal, was at least familiar, solid and understandable. And when he had taken the story to its end in *In Chancery*, he skipped right over the years from 20 August 1901 to 12 May 1920, when *To Let* begins. This enormous leap may be criticised, but in any case it showed his determination to have nothing more to do with war.

*In Chancery* was started in July 1918, and work continued in spring of the next year; its date of completion is not known. The interlude entitled *Awakening*, designed to provide a link with the following novel, *To Let*, was written either near the end of 1919 or in 1920. The only thing that is certain is that the period from the summer of 1918 to the autumn of 1920 was an extremely fertile time for Galsworthy.

His return to a period of the past that he had related twelve years earlier was done in complete freedom. The success of *In Chancery* cannot be explained simply as the result of the balance between the critical and the lyrical, defined by Galsworthy as the source of perfection in the last phase of his career. Clearly, it may be pointed out that beauty remains present, in the person of Irene, that the interludes are poems in prose, that the spectacle of the powerlessness of man and the victory of fate in the novel continue to show the critical attitude he had displayed in *The Man of Property*. I accept all this. But if *In Chancery* were only that, it would be no more than a tame sequel, using the same ingredients with an extra dash of the poetic. In fact the perfection of *In Chancery* arises not from an increase, but on the contrary from a purification of the over-abundant and disparate material found in *The Man of Property*.

It would be quite normal to find Galsworthy unaware of this fact. Creative artists are not always penetrating about their development. But in the thrust and parry of discussion with Edward Garnett, about *The Patrician* when it was being written, he alluded to past quarrels, with a remark in which he covered half the distance that was needed to grasp the qualities of *In Chancery*: 'The feeling that *The Man of Property* gives you, of not being able to see the wood for the trees, comes of my having known *too much*.'[32]

This pruning-down and enrichment in the second volume of *The Forsyte Saga* is not peculiar to the first trilogy, and is to be found in the others. Other favourable factors contribute to the success of *In Chancery*, however. The theme of *The Man of Property* remains; but it does not detract from character development, which enjoys what was until then lacking: time. This is why Galsworthy's claim in *The Creation of Character* always to have tried to write psychological novels is justified in the case of the Forsyte Chronicles. These works contain a remarkable flowering of the psychological novel as a character study, with unforgettable characters like Soames, Irene, Old Jolyon and Fleur, to mention only the protagonists. Soames is one of the great creations of English fiction in this century. What makes him live is his touching and universal side.

With the end of *In Chancery*, Galsworthy terminates his description of Victorian England, as he had known it during his childhood, adolescence and young adulthood, mainly through family experiences. The period is easy to identify and define in his works, because it ends simultaneously with the end of *In Chancery*.

The action of *The Man of Property* takes place in 1886; *In Chancery* begins in 1895 and ends with the birth of Fleur, in 1901, the year Queen Victoria died. The first two novels in *The Forsyte Saga* are therefore based on Galsworthy's knowledge of the Victorian age, acquired during thirty-four years of life under Victoria's reign. One essential fact is revealed by the publication dates of the two novels, 1906 and 1920: every page is written with the minimum lapse of time needed to gain perspective: twenty years for *The Man of Property* and nineteen years for *In Chancery*.

Many things change with *To Let*, and this detracts from the cohesion of the trilogy. Instead of arranging the novels in two trilogies, he could have added *To Let* to *A Modern Comedy*, and made it a 'quartet'. The book was written in 1921, and is set in 1920. Certainly, great novelists can write good novels about their own times, without needing to stand back like historians. Some of the Galsworthy novels already considered take place more or less contemporaneously with the period when they were written. But *To Let* represents a weakening in Galsworthy's skill, because the subject is presented differently.

He jumps from the Victorian age, over the whole Edwardian decade and the war, to the post-war age, nineteen years later. This might be unimportant, or even beneficial, for another author. But it was unfavourable for Galsworthy. His critical attitude remains, but it is gradually deflected from its original object, the late Victorian Forsytes, towards different characters, in an age that disconcerts and annoys him by its 'modernity'. The book has a certain charm, but is not so interesting as those that preceded it. Galsworthy lets himself be borne along by his impetus, without new inspiration.

As psychological novels, the other two trilogies are just as interesting as *The Forsyte Saga*. But as social novels they are inferior. The social analysis becomes more superficial or anachronistic.

Galsworthy starts off afresh in *The White Monkey*. The *Saga* is finished. He adopts a new technique to handle a new situation, imitating the way the new generation talks and parodying the style of its favourite authors. But well before the end of the book he seems to run out of steam, and, abandoning his attempt, gradually returns to the style and subject of *The Forsyte Saga*. *The Silver Spoon* thus becomes its continuation, and *Swan Song* its conclusion. As *A Modern Comedy* progresses, it shows the qualities that had made the first trilogy so powerful — except that the author becomes more and more indulgent towards his characters, young or old.

Discussion of this phase of Galsworthy's career cannot be ended without mentioning the malicious and dogmatic interpretation given to it by D. H. Lawrence, and the innumerable other critics who merely fell into step with Lawrence. The essay written by Lawrence in 1927 has greatly influenced all Galsworthy criticism, at least up to the present. And yet, although brilliant and fiery in style, it is not based on any detailed knowledge of Galsworthy and his works. It provides a perfect expression of a personal viewpoint, but not objective criticism.

I am referring only to the part of his essay where he outlines his opinion of Galsworthy's career. An initial allusion to *The Country House* would suggest that after this novel Galsworthy subsided into conventional attitudes. But a coherent judgement comes further on, when Lawrence writes:

> In the three early novels, *The Island Pharisees*, *The Man of Property*, *Fraternity*, it looked as if Mr Galsworthy might break through the blind end of the highway with the dynamite of satire, and help us out on to a new lap. But the sex ingredient of his dynamite was damp and muzzy, the explosion gradually fizzled off into sentimentality, and we are left in a worse state than before. The later novels are purely commercial . . . of no importance. . . . When you arrive at *To Let* . . . what have you? Just money![33]

Ironically enough, Lawrence's own dynamite gets damp precisely when he believes that Galsworthy's has fizzled out. He argues that satire in the Forsyte Chronicles falls flat because Soames' antagonists, Irene and Philip Bosinney, are asexual. The irony is that Lawrence, not appreciating Galsworthy's depiction of love, has drawn a completely mistaken conclusion on the insubstantiality of his passions. This was quite wrong, for there is every reason to believe that Galsworthy was a sensual man. An extremely sensual atmosphere pervades many pages of his writings, and anyone failing to notice them is missing one of the most striking features of his art. His sensuality will be discussed in the study of his themes below.

Since Lawrence issued his diatribe, many other critics have

repeated his arguments, or parts of them, quite arbitrarily concentrating on the single criterion of property. According to them, the concept weakened as the Chronicles went on. But there was no reason for Galsworthy to confine himself to the theme of *The Man of Property* right through the two trilogies. Indeed, even in *The Man of Property*, is it fair to say or suggest that the novel is restricted to a criticism of the idea of property?

There is undoubtedly a drop in quality in Galsworthy's novels during this phase. It is clear that he committed an error of political judgement at the same time, and this worsened matters. When he claims to have depicted, in *A Modern Comedy*, 'the new lurch' (to the left), as earlier he had described the 'deviation to the right', one cannot accept that it was because he was 'obeying his essential attraction for the middle of the road.'[34] It is astounding to find him so under-estimating the power of money and ignoring the survival of its privileges. The aristocracy had little need of him to defend it, and it is a pity to find his last three novels devoted to it, like *The Patrician*, but in a totally different spirit.

But does this prove that he had turned his coat? One has to be ill-intentioned, or ignorant of the man and his work, to believe it. To begin with, except in the early years of the century, when he approved the great Liberal reform bills, Galsworthy never identified himself with a political party. Next, the so-called reactionary tendencies of his last novels are not in the least confirmed by his later works in other *genres*, nor by his correspondence. Anyway, if the novels are themselves examined closely, his concern for the poor and his generosity of spirit towards them will be found to have persisted as before. His new interest in middle-class or upper-class virtues is added to his interest in ordinary people, without diminishing it in any way.

Finally, although his claim to be impartial may not be accepted, at least the desire to be so was not a mere literary formality. It was the constant and perfectly sincere preoccupation of a man whose very word and deed was accompanied by sometimes excessive scruples. He was even known to try and correct imaginary injustices. 'He is nothing if not judicial,' wrote Max Beerbohm, most perceptively, in 1909, in the caption to one of his caricatures of Galsworthy.[35] He provided a final example of his ever-conscientious method in *End of the Chapter*.

His critics were less bothered by scruples. It is surely hypocritical of them to clamour about scandal and betrayal, on the basis of the development of his feelings towards Soames. There are few instances of more credible character growth. Soames is thirty-one when the Forsyte Chronicles begin, and seventy-one when they end. It would be odd if a man's behaviour did not change in the forty years of his progress from being a recently married man to becoming a grandfather.

Galsworthy's ultimate indulgence towards the old rascal Soames was not symptomatic of any political turnabout. It was what happened with all his characters, whether they were rich or poor, young or old. He was the man who, with no dishonesty, could say that he was 'personally of a humane and peaceful and more or less contemplative composition'.[36] In other words, he was incapable of hating. He would probably have written better novels, full of scoundrels and wicked deeds, if he had been different. But we must be honest enough to take him as he was.

## *In Chancery* (1920)

In 1899, Soames Forsyte, who has been on his own for twelve years, wants a child to whom he can leave his fortune. He has to divorce first. He needs proof of Irene's adultery, and goes to see her. But once in her presence his old love reawakens. He offers to forgive her. But Irene is no longer the defenceless creature he had known. She resists him and appeals to Young Jolyon. Soames' rage brings them together. Soames obtains a divorce, and remarries with a young Frenchwoman, Annette. They have a daughter, Fleur. This part of the plot is accompanied by the story of Winifred Dartie, Soames' sister, and the ups and downs of her married life. Characters in another subplot are Winifred's son Val, Young Jolyon's daughter Holly and her brother Jolly.

Fourteen years elapsed between the publication of *The Man of Property* and *In Chancery*. Certain changes of viewpoint are apparent. History does not play much part in this new novel. It is concerned rather with depicting a social type that characterises an age. The theme of divorce is still present, but it is less important, whereas other aspects such as character studies are given more attention.

Soames is typical of the average middle-class man. His persistence in asking an unconsenting wife to give him a son reflects the national inability to admit defeat. He is a bit like a British bulldog. His hope of striking a bargain, and his insistence on the advantages of an agreement, are the habits of a businessman and lawyer. He lacks the generosity and loftiness of an aristocrat. But neither is he meanly vindictive or coarse. His sexuality, unsatisfied in marriage, is not given free rein in relationships that his fastidiousness makes him accept with repugnance. He finds ridiculous the idea of arming himself with a horsewhip or pistol before going to his cousin's.[37] And yet he neglects his interests to such a point that he appears less and less like a man of property and more and more like an individual with all his idiosyncrasies. His real temperament is revealed. He is a sad person, crippled by the failure of his one great love. When he finally takes action, he is seen to sacrifice his own values, or at least allow them to become warped. As the victim of a mirage, he is a very poor businessman in his private life. He spends some four hundred and fifty pounds, unreflectingly and unnecessarily, to have his wife shadowed. His dealings with Madame Lamotte and her daughter are more successful, but by no means strikingly so. He could have done better, and been less rash. But his judgement is disturbed, and he is in fact a beaten man.[38]

The action of *In Chancery*, as it proceeds, shows the cruel fate that is weighing on him. The image of a spider's web is used extensively. The very title of the novel has a double meaning: in wrestling jargon, it refers to being held round the neck.[39] However, unlike other Galsworthy heroes, Soames is in no way mentally disturbed (provided he is seen in his surroundings). However great his sufferings, his mental and nervous balance is never under threat. His whole consciousness is not affected. Apart from his errors of judgement on the two women he is involved with, neither his work nor his actions, nor even his dignity, are affected. He remains himself, limited but sound in mind, a prey to uneasiness, but safe from the gnawings of anxiety.

Galsworthy's psychological analysis of Soames does not rule out a moral verdict. It reveals Soames' non-violence as cautious hypocrisy. His one act of violence, through its consequences, makes him partly responsible for his first rival's death. It could be a legal crime. As in *Justice* and *The Silver Box*, he provides another example of one-sided use of the law, a law made by the privileged to defend their privileges. But this idea remains in the background.

There are fewer full-length portraits in *In Chancery* than in *The Man of Property*, for most of the characters from the first novel reappear in the second. Several of them take on a new importance, however: Winifred, her husband Montague Dartie, and Soames' father James Forsyte, all three splendidly characterised. With two deaths, two divorces, one of which misfires, two remarriages, two births and engagements, *In Chancery* is far more eventful than the first volume of the *Saga*. Yet the story is more straightforward, less fragmented. It has greater unity, because of the way the subplots are integrated into the whole.

The hasty judgements of *In Chancery* by Arnold Kettle, in *An Introduction to the English Novel*, and by other critics, are unacceptable. They seem to be influenced by Lawrence's resounding attack, in which the novel is not named. Contrary to their opinion, the first two books in *The Forsyte Saga* are of comparable quality in their range and diversity. The earlier volume is more tragic, and its ending more moving. But *In Chancery* is more polished, subtler, clearer. In short, it is more successful. And the satire is in no way inferior. In spite of what Lawrence asserts, it is in *In Chancery* that the verdict on Soames is the most severe.

## To Let (1921)

The cousins Jon and Fleur Forsyte have now grown up, and they meet by accident. Intrigued by their parents' attempts to keep them away from each other, they are determined to uncover the mystery, which increases their natural affection. They meet in secret. But Fleur, determined to make Jon her own, persuades her father to ask Irene to consent to the marriage. Jolyon intervenes, and reveals the past to his son who, for the sake of his mother, gives up Fleur.

With Soames and Irene irrevocably separated, Galsworthy felt terribly alone, felt the story emptied of all its substance. In an attempt to communicate this feeling of emptiness, as it were, he sweeps away the characters who, if not actors in the drama, had at least been witnesses to it. George, and the Forsyte aunts and uncles, vanish in a kind of hecatomb. Jolyon survives them, but only to die before the end of the novel.

While *In Chancery* is full of memories, *To Let* describes the present: in it Galsworthy leaps forward to 1920. But this is a misleading impression. In fact the whole drama arises from the weight of the past on Fleur and Jon. This is how Galsworthy manages to prolong the struggle between Irene and Soames. Once again he has put Soames in the dock, without any sense of repetitiveness. His old sufferings are stirred up again, in addition to the uneasiness he feels about his daughter's conduct. The mystery that once surrounded Irene is also skilfully recreated, thickened in the most cruel way by the progress of time. Knowing all that has happened, a reader is drawn into infinite compassion for the efforts of the two young people to discover the truth.

But there are some weak points in the story. In order to bring fresh sorrows down on Soames, Galsworthy has indulged in certain improbabilities and some over-subtleties. And, as has already been said, in deflecting his critical judgement, to some extent he revises his opinion of his characters. It is quite legitimate to show Soames as an affectionate father, and entirely credible that with anyone but Irene he should be so indulgent. But he is credited with a capacity for abstract reflection, tact and fastidiousness which are not in character. Jolyon, previously the very embodiment of tolerance and non-interference, intervenes harshly in his son's life before dying. His body lies, as it were, across the stage. All these points make a reader ill at ease. The novel does not even bring the *Saga* to a conclusion, since neither Soames nor Irene dies, and Jon and Fleur will meet again. In other words, *To Let* is the beginning of *A Modern Comedy* as much as the end of the *Saga*. It is a transitional novel, lacking unity and cohesion. And yet it contains far more fine passages than such weaknesses might suggest. The lyrical, elegiac poet makes up for the inadequacies of the novelist and moralist. Within the dark and gloomy setting of *To Let*, like a jewel in the bottom of a casket, he has placed the tender, graceful love between Fleur and Jon, a tale filled with youthfulness and beauty. As it continues, the heroine takes on the stature of one of Galsworthy's best creations.

## The White Monkey (1924)[40]

Fleur, now married to Michael Mont, but disillusioned after the failure of her early love, is bored. She is tempted to have an affair with Wilfrid Desert, the aristocratic poet, but in the end holds back. Michael is told about Fleur's past by June, and forgives her. He is overjoyed when she bears him a son. There is a subplot about the unemployed Bicket and his wife Victorine. Soames also tracks down a dishonest director of an insurance company, before retiring from business.

Galsworthy seems to have set to work with the intention of writing a satire of contemporary literature and art, and of fashionable London society which, he felt, fawned too much on them. The dryness of tone, and the inane remarks quoted, leave no doubt as to the strength of his feelings. Substitution of imaginary names for real names suggests that the names of writers and artists in the book also conceal his contemporaries. For readers who were well-informed about the fashionable world, *The White Monkey* offered the fascinations of a *roman à clef*, of which almost nothing remains.[41] Galsworthy imitates the way the new generation talks, and parodies its favourite writers. This produces some chapters in a rather garish style and of uncertain significance. His portraits are mere outlines, and his judgements summary. The 'moderns', which he would have done better to call 'contemporaries', are humourless, incapable of serenity (a strange criticism coming from him!), and lacking in ideas. This satirical vein soon runs out.[42] Galsworthy's comic imagination tended towards the burlesque, impossible in Fleur's drawing-room.

This is why he soon turns to his real characters. But it is obvious that the main plot of *The White Monkey* is not very fertile. Once Fleur is married, it is hard to bring her to life. He wants to show that she is wounded and bewildered. But he could not conceive of beauty being pitiable or vicious. The result is that Fleur becomes unpleasant, or at least incomprehensible. Wilfrid Desert is the classic lover. Michael takes over from Jolyon. His humour and volubility help make the novel less dry, more good-humoured. He also supplies the only unity, for he is the only character to take part in all three plots.

Paradoxically, it is the least important story, the tribulations of Bicket and Victorine, that, despite some sentimentality, is the most successful. The most important fact, however, is the reappearance of Soames. After an icy entrance into Fleur's drawing-room, the 'man of property' accustoms himself to the atmosphere there, even finds it quite charming and pleasant, so that there is a marked lightening of mood. But it should be noted that the 'moderns' have by then disappeared. Aware of the failure of his satire and the inadequacy of the main plot, Galsworthy fills the gap by returning to his main character, on whom he can rely. Soames dominates the whole third part of the book, and with him clarity of style is restored.

While Galsworthy altered his themes and style during the novel, his narrative technique — once the first four chapters are finished — remains the same as in his other books: precise chronology, an intermittent narration reflecting multiple points of view, but leading to three successive crises. However, this technique, used so successfully by him elsewhere, has no inherent virtues. *The White Monkey* is not a good novel. It suffers from barrenness, over-complexity, obscurity, in the first chapters at least. But its most serious flaw is that, from start to finish, it remains superficial.

## *The Silver Spoon* (1926)

Michael, elected to Parliament, becomes spokesman for Sir James Foggart,[43] author of a plan for the social and economic trans-formation of England. Fleur is in her drawing-room. Soames, who watches over her, expels from it a young woman of noble birth and free morals, Marjorie Ferrar, who is guilty of making a libellous remark about Fleur in an evening paper. Most of the story consists of the scandal and its consequences. A libel suit takes place, despite Soames' efforts to avoid this. Fleur wins her case; but, enraged to find her rival more popular than ever, she decides to leave London.

The title is neither very accurate nor very felicitous. It would have done just as well for the first or third novel in the trilogy. Admittedly, this symbol of vanishing privileges takes on historical truth when Galsworthy, as an uneasy observer, extends it to the whole of England in 1926, at the time when her world supremacy had vanished. This provides a justification for his interest in the social and economic problems of the time. But it is tricky to bring such ideas into a novel. He manages it as best he can, as usual, by resorting to comedy and drama.

However, the idea of the silver spoon, as applied to Fleur's origins, is soon abandoned. And in fact Fleur no longer occupies the central position, as she did in *The White Monkey*. Her rival, Marjorie, is presented far more brilliantly. The duel actually takes place between Marjorie and Soames. A title such as *The Lawsuit* would have been more appropriate, reflecting the core of the plot more accurately. Once again, and better than ever before, Gals-worthy makes use of his intimate knowledge of lawyers and courts.

He analyses the preliminaries and consequences of the case in detail. But in particular he intensifies the excitement of the novel by creating a 'play within the play'. The effect of impartiality he

succeeds in giving recalls his play *Strife*. The issue is uncertain.
Marjorie's lack of strict morality has been revealed by her rival's
lawyer, and Marjorie has admitted it. Consequently, she does not
obtain the damages she expected. But she overcomes her handi-
cap, showing herself capable of overturning the situation and
winning the jury's sympathy. Whereas Fleur's lawyer oversteps the
limits agreed on with his clients. He pleads too well. He proves the
plaintiff's virtue to such effect that, in circles that affect to regard
morality as old-fashioned, it becomes embarrassing. Fleur loses
her case by winning it.

The lawsuit, then, is a kind of play inserted into the novel, far
more oratorical and vivid, subtler and richer in meaning, more
pungent, than any scenes of dialogue among ordinary men could
be. And yet there is nothing artificial about it. It forms part of the
novel, and contains some of Galsworthy's best writing. The discussion takes on a general character, and deals with moral
problems of the time, while retaining its dramatic quality.

The lawsuit determines the whole tone of the book. With its
wealth of intricate argument and subtlety, *The Silver Spoon*
succeeds as satire where *The White Monkey* had failed. From
morality Galsworthy moves on to literature, paying back in kind
those writers who are trying to oust him.[44]

### *Swan Song* (1928)

Fleur and Jon meet again during the General Strike of 1926, six
years after their separation. She cannot live without him. She
entices him into the woods at Robin Hill, where they had first
known each other. But although she believes that physical
intimacy will make him hers, she loses him. He runs away, and she
will never see him again. Fleur goes to hide her grief at Mapledurham, where her father has retired. Carelessly throwing away a
cigarette, she sets fire to Soames' picture gallery. He dies fighting
the fire and protecting his daughter.

Galsworthy uses the General Strike as a way of bringing together
his scattered characters. As in *The Forsyte Saga*, the Forsytes
gather instinctively, to face the crisis. *Swan Song* provides an
answer to the questions raised in *The White Monkey*. Under
difficult circumstances, the essential virtues of the English shine
out: the nation is not so decadent as might have been feared.

There is a certain complacency in his description of the reassuring sight offered to an observer by the English capital, countryside and character. But he soon loses interest in the current industrial situation, and it becomes clear that the Forsytes, all the surviving Forsytes, are the main subject, not the strike. Winifred's house is where they now meet, instead of Timothy's. This is the new 'Forsyte 'Change'. The book is the occasion of a farewell meeting, a final look back at the past.

Even more than a response to *The White Monkey*, *Swan Song* is a continuation of *The Forsyte Saga*, and could be regarded as part of it. There is a two-fold link, both temporal and fundamental: with *To Let*, on the one hand, and with *The Man of Property*, on the other. Fleur's love-affair, so harshly interrupted by Young Jolyon before his death, begins again, seven years later. She reawakens their memories, and at the same time tries once again to force the hand of destiny. But her tragic passion also fits into a larger picture, for it reaches its climax forty-six years after the conflict between her father and Irene and, *mutatis mutandis*, repeats the conflict. She violates Jon, fired with the same possessiveness that had driven Soames to carry out the rape of his wife. Such passionate love also has disastrous consequences. In the very act of winning she loses, in the same surroundings where she and Jon, but also Irene and Bosinney before them, had loved each other, in the enchanting setting of Robin Hill, where Soames had had the misfortune to have his house built.

All the pathos and poetry arising from the earlier stories are flawlessly recreated, blended and sublimated when, in a strange vision, Irene's face and Fleur's come to form a single image in the mind of Soames.[45] The saga, so to speak, has come full circle. Fleur's unhappiness spills over on to the past which lies at its source and, by demonstrating its consequences, makes it all even sadder. June's revelations to Michael bring back the action of *The Man of Property*, giving a new and immediate dramatic value to those old events. Despite himself, Soames is drawn into this new sequence of events, by instinct and memory. He finds himself back in his old role. Through love for his daughter, he remains silent, and allows himself to be destroyed by the distant consequences of his initial act. As in the finale of a great musical work, all the most beautiful and stirring effects are repeated and amplified, giving the long *dénouement* of *Swan Song* tremendous majesty and fullness.

These pages contain some of the best of Galsworthy's writing. However, this novel, which was long regarded in France as giving a

faithful picture of England, cannot be considered a perfect specimen of his art, despite what he himself said. The narrative is too
slow and too fragmented, in the first two parts.


## THE END: THE THIRD TRILOGY (1929–32)

The theme of *End of the Chapter* predisposed Galsworthy to
indulge in sentimentality. On 2 November 1930, he wrote to
André Chevrillon: 'I have started on another family, the Charwells
. . . representative of the older type of family, with more tradition
and sense of service than the Forsytes. . . . It's a stratum . . . that
has been much neglected.'[46] Galsworthy needed all his broad-
mindedness to uphold such a thesis without getting involved in
snobbery.

He was right in saying that the main achievement of *Maid in
Waiting* was the character of Dinny. It is easy to share Gilbert
Murray's opinion of her: 'I think Dinny is the most delightful of all
your heroines.'[47] Other characters are also well observed.

This final trilogy ends Galsworthy's career with no surprises,
and nothing new. The main characteristics of his novels are again
brought together, confirming the trend in the previous phase
towards giving less importance to the ideas behind the story, and
more to vivid characterisation of the main individuals involved.
They are psychological and lyrical works, extremely pleasant to
read, reflecting the author's familiarity with the world he is
describing, and his practice in depicting a family setting. But they
are written in a minor key, with nostalgia pervading everything,
and no longer have the vigour and high relief of his best books. As
social novels they are both accurate and anachronistic: they depict
a way of life and a way of thinking that still existed, but that were
rapidly diminishing and on the point of becoming extinct.


### *Maid in Waiting* (1931)

Hubert Charwell, a young British officer, from a family of the old
landed aristocracy, is implicated in the failure of a scientific expedition to Bolivia. His honour is wounded, his career and even his
life threatened. His sister Dinny, outraged by the indifference of
the British authorities, takes up his defence. She cannot prevent
his indictment and imprisonment. It is not until the very eve of his

extradition that she succeeds in reversing the situation. In so doing she deserves the title the author has invented for her, probably in an allusion to the chivalric tradition.[48]

In *End of the Chapter* Galsworthy argued that the aristocracy is treated unfairly in contemporary society. As an illustration he presented Hubert Charwell, a character so passive that he arouses very little sympathy. He is placed in circumstances where his rights are not self-evident, and may even be questioned. From the start it is a peculiar, unlikely, complicated situation, that recalls the melodramatic events of certain Galsworthy plays. The plot is narrated in numerous politico-judicial episodes, and reaches quite fantastic improbability with the plan for Hubert to escape inside an anthropologist's impedimenta, and then by plane.

This plan is worked out by his friends: Hubert takes no part. He is present only through his past. He lets himself be defended and wed. He is a strangely disappointing and lifeless character. And yet he must be seen as a fresh embodiment of the Galsworthian hero. He is so haughtily reserved that he scorns to defend himself. The whole affair rests on a lack of evidence, and can be settled only by believing or disbelieving Hubert's word. It is a matter of trust. Does England trust her aristocracy, her army, her navy, her ruling class?

But Hubert is an allegorical figure rather than a character seen in depth, and his ordeal is a pretext, somewhat outside the main action. He symbolises duty for the main character, Dinny, who is also involved in a subplot, the story of the mental illness and suicide of Ferse. It is easy to understand why so many English readers are attracted to Dinny. Without going too far inside her, they have sensed her, and recognised her as one of them. Her innocent charm, her fundamental rectitude, her general pragmatism, her occasional tricks, her sentimental fondness for the family estate, the English countryside, and her native country, all these have endeared her to the reading public. And after so many mysterious heroines, passionate to the point of selfishness, Galsworthy readers also appreciated the novelty of a reasonable, virtuous and yet very youthful heroine. Despite her social position, Dinny is one of the simplest and most accessible of his female characters. That is no doubt why she is so likeable.

And, yet, it must be admitted that she is not given any very dazzling role in *Maid in Waiting*. There is little doubt that Hubert will get out of his predicament, and the novel never attains any great dramatic intensity. It is rather a sad and painful story, with comedy reduced to a very small part.

## Flowering Wilderness (1932)

This is the love story of Dinny Charwell and Wilfrid Desert, the nobly born poet and traveller who had already appeared in *The White Monkey*. Love brings them together, but fails to unite them.

Like *In Chancery*, this novel has the advantage of being in the central position in a trilogy. After *Maid in Waiting*, most of the characters are already familiar to the reader, particularly Dinny, who has had people in love with her, but who has so far remained unattached herself. So it is intriguing to find her in love. She had already been the protagonist of the earlier book, and *Flowering Wilderness* is even more intimately her story. Among Galsworthian characters, only Soames, Gyp and perhaps Fleur are comparable in stature. Dinny reigns for a shorter time than Soames, but her reign is more absolute. There is no subplot, and the main plot is given wide scope. It provided Galsworthy with exceptional resources, and, anyway, his best inspiration always came from a love story.

There are probably other more personal reasons to explain his successful depiction of Dinny, but they are not known. It is hard to believe that she is pure invention. Unfortunately, there is no information at all to enable a distinction to be made between what comes from imagination and what from memory. The most original aspect of the novel is that the heroine is so limpid. This time, it is her partner who is plunged into mystery − a reversal of the situation Galsworthy had created in *The Forsyte Saga*.

Wilfrid's past weighs heavily on the plot. His haughty character, and a sensitivity embittered by the experience of the First World War, have made him misanthropic. And yet he possesses charm, so that it is quite credible for Dinny, with all her fine qualities, to fall in love with him. He returns her love. When she discovers his dreadful secret (he had been converted to Islam under threat of death), she accepts the situation. They share the same ideas in the religious field. But how could the Charwell family, where respect for tradition and the cult of Empire reign supreme, where the prestige of England is the most sacred thing in the world, accept such a marriage? By 1930, religious prejudices seem too undermined,

and beliefs too weakened, to stand in the way of individual freedom. Yet disturbing omens gather. Friends offer uniform opinions
of Wilfrid. He is 'disharmony personified', says Fleur.[49] Dinny's
belief that she can reconcile him to himself does not last, for when
the news of his conversion spreads, Wilfrid is seized by a kind of
scruple, the fear of being called a coward, the wish to prove that he
is not one.

*Flowering Wilderness* contains the same burning tension,
pitiless logic and classic rigour as *The Patrician*. In spite of the
exceptional circumstances under which it took place, Wilfrid's
conversion does raise the problem of freedom of conscience, which
is extensively depicted in its full human significance. Wilfrid is
entitled to free himself from a world that fails to understand him.
He does so, without any shamefulness, by going into exile. Here, as
so often in his novels, Galsworthy shows his legal turn of mind.
There is a kind of pre-trial investigation of the hero. But it is not
impartial. Galsworthy is capable of showing sympathy for the
rebel, but not of fully understanding and justifying him. It never
occurs to him that a man of 1930 is strictly entitled to doubt the
Empire, and that there is no vanity in not sharing the vanity of
those who still believe in it. Admittedly, he says that the believers
are only a small minority, thirty years behind the times. But
devoting his story to them, as he does, reduces it all to something
limited and clannish.

This restricted and even narrow framework is the setting for a
tormented and lonely lyricism. *Flowering Wilderness* is thrilling
and often poignant to read. It is more concrete than *The
Patrician*, and more descriptive than *Maid in Waiting*, because of
its many outdoor scenes — it contains one of the most beautiful
Galsworthy ever wrote.[50] But above all it is imbued with a spirit of
veneration and respectfulness. The cult of national values and
respect for the heroine come together, quite illogically but
intimately, to create the unity of the novel. It is not only the best
part of the final trilogy: it is a moving, almost unbelievable
reminder of past fulfilments.

*Over the River* (1933)

Dinny's sister, Clare, has just left her husband, Sir Gerald Corven,
whom she accuses of being sadistic. She permits a young man
without any money, Tony Croom, to pay court to her, and refuses

to give in when Corven tries to claim his rights over her. The next year, when he believes that he has sufficient evidence, he sues for divorce. Clare, who has not committed adultery, defends the case, but loses. She becomes Tony's mistress, without deciding on her future. Meanwhile, news has arrived of Wilfrid's death. Dinny falls ill. But she will marry the barrister Eustace Dornford.

Galsworthy's last novel was published posthumously. The title suggests his intentions. It was to be about Dinny again, her trials and final victory. The river in which Wilfrid drowns, probably recalling the end of *The Pilgrim's Progress*, symbolises the barrier she still has to cross. But her role is only to advise her sister and assist her parents. From this point of view, *Over the River* is a repetition of *Maid in Waiting*, in a minor key. And some end was needed. Perhaps in a final challenge to oblivion, as death approached, Galsworthy once again broke the rule that had made him avoid happy endings. So Dinny marries Dornford; but she remains more vivid amid the misfortunes of *Flowering Wilderness* than in her successes in the other two books.

In contrast, Clare, who appears to be a secondary character at the beginning of *Over the River*, soon becomes the protagonist. Her adventures, also, are not entirely convincing. Her inferiority to Dinny is too much emphasised not to diminish any interest in her and Galsworthy's thesis concerning aristocratic virtues. Her most unsatisfactory feature is the uncertainty that surrounds her feelings and intentions. Will she fall in love? Is she capable of falling in love? And yet she is recognisable as a Galsworthy heroine, with the pride that she so haughtily bears in her.

Although she is less endearing than others, Clare appears to be a very credible specimen of young Englishwomen of good family in 1932: athletic, indifferent to society life, lively, adventurous. She differs from other heroines by her character; but there is nothing novel about her situation. It is almost a repetition of the theme of *In Chancery*, except that Clare is not solemn enough for any tragic developments. But there is no lack of intensity. Her biting rejoinders during her defence are the most positive aspect of the novel. Because of this, the account of the cross-examination in the Divorce Court takes on a breadth attained nowhere else.[51] The case, with the various procedures it involves and the developments that make it comprehensible, fills three-quarters of the book. The plot is so exactly centred on the problem of the divorce that it reaches its culminating point in the court itself, with Clare's snorting exclamation about the fine she has to pay: 'A thousand pounds for speaking the truth!'[52]

## CONCLUSIONS ON GALSWORTHY'S CAREER AS A NOVELIST

A career of more than thirty-five years was marked by the production of a score of novels, at fairly regular intervals (except around 1900–5 and 1914–18).

Galsworthy himself saw two sources of forms of inspiration predominating alternately as his career progressed, one 'critical' and the other 'emotional'. There is quite a lot of truth in this distinction, for in itself it is very typical of Galsworthy's way of thinking. The theme of conflict pervades everything, from his conception of art to his conception of life. Contrast, conflict, tension: for him, these are to be found at every level of reality, even in what may be called his metaphysical attitude: 'Existence is a limitless circle — swelling and shrinking. . . . Whether we are on the flood or on the ebb doesn't really matter, because the ebb leads into another flood.'[53]

This vision of the world, inspired by the German romantics, evolutionists, Hegel and Samuel Butler, is something of a patchwork, extremely personal, and he liked to think that he could find it in his own works. Similarly, he felt that his mind was the outcome of two opposing forces: a sense of form, which came from his mother, and a spirit of speculation, which came from his father. If one is to perceive the unity as well as the diversity of the works produced during his career, allowance must be made for these simple ideas, and their attraction for him.

However, there can be no question of stopping there. As time passed, circumstances began to complicate Galsworthy's life, and often invalidated his views. This is why his distinction between the two sources of his inspiration, which applied mainly to the beginning of his career, was less and less true later, particularly after the First World War, an event that overwhelmed both the writer and the man.

It is by no means certain, however, that without such an upheaval Galsworthy would have been a greater writer. Even if one tries to exclude, or at least reduce as much as possible, any valued judgements, it cannot be denied that his 'social' novels were leading him to a dead end. Admittedly, this phase produced two of his best novels, *The Man of Property* and *The Country House* — leaving aside another fine work, *The Patrician*, since it is marginal. But *Fraternity*, however odd and interesting for the scholar, was barely readable. An even less successful late return to this vein was *The Freelands*.

Despite its immediate paralysing effect on him, the war helped him to break fresh ground, by encouraging the poetic tendencies that had already appeared in *The Patrician*. This new trend produced several worthwhile novels, none of which, however, even *Beyond*, can be regarded as a masterpiece. After the success of *The Man of Property* and *The Country House*, Galsworthy's career was disappointing for many years. It was fourteen years after his first great success that he achieved another with *In Chancery*, and then the whole *Forsyte Saga*, the first trilogy. It was a return to his first sources, and, at the same time, different. For although every Galsworthy novel presents a thesis, its importance was gradually to diminish, giving way to character depiction. So the old family setting was the scene of a completely new development, at any rate as regards the villain turned hero, Soames.

Although Galsworthy had 'evolutionary' ideas,[54] he had little belief in changing human nature. This explains why the original drama of the Forsyte Chronicles tends to repeat itself, and the narrative to turn back on itself, like the lines on a seashell, once the artificiality of 'modernism' has been trounced. His career came to an end without producing any surprises and any renewal of inspiration, with an extended, nostalgic meditation on those things in the present that recalled the very best of the past. This romantic, not to say sentimental, ending was in no way an abjuration, but it showed how his inspiration was declining and wearing out.

If Galsworthy's career is compared with that of his German contemporary Thomas Mann — and there could be no more appropriate comparison — it is precisely the lack of any novelty in the last ten years of his life that is so striking. While Galsworthy seemed to be getting into a rut in his last books, Mann, with *The Magic Mountain* (1927) and *Joseph and his Brothers* (1933–44), was demonstrating his capacity to equal, perhaps even surpass, his masterpiece of the beginning of the century, by moving out along completely new paths.

# 7　The Galsworthian Novel

## THEMES

The constantly recurring themes of Galsworthy's novels are, in order of importance, beauty, love and suffering, divorce, honour, art and the law. Family and money will be discussed separately. Beauty comes first, because in every case it coincides with love: the beloved woman is always very beautiful; but not only women: the natural setting for the action is also unfailingly lovely. The beauty of a woman and the beauty of nature are of the same kind.

Every novel contains a love story and, with the exception of *The Island Pharisees* and *The Burning Spear*, it is always important. Its moments of greatest exaltation always occur amid the beauty of the fields, the woods, the Thames, with the light of day or the charms of night. This is why beauty is the most enduring theme of his fiction. Its predominance may also be explained by the fact that love is usually seen and experienced from the man's viewpoint. Even when the main character is a woman, like Gyp in *Beyond*, or Dinny in *End of the Chapter*, and however vivid, they are still seen with a male eye.

One original feature of the theme of beauty in Galsworthy's novels is that it cannot be dissociated from a feeling of sadness and dissatisfaction. This is expressed in the closing words of *The Forsyte Saga*. Soames is alone: 'And only one thing really troubled him, sitting there − the melancholy craving in his heart. . . . He might wish and wish and never get it − the beauty and the loving in the world.'[1]

Recounting his problems as a writer, Galsworthy wrote in 1927: 'The beauty of the world is the novelist's real despair; the heartache that he feels in the presence of Nature in flower.'[2]

The sensuousness of Keats, perhaps transmuted through the Pre-Raphaelites, is to be found in him, but less epicurean and more imbued with pessimism.

Some comment must be made on sex and sensuality in Galsworthy's novels. Contrary to what D. H. Lawrence claimed in the article already mentioned,[3] the case of Soames and Irene has nothing revolting about it. It is a clear case of sexual antipathy, and in making this the initiating factor in the drama, and stating that it was an insurmountable obstacle, Galsworthy was making a bold literary innovation.[4]

About *Fraternity*, he wrote:

> The whole point of *Fraternity* . . . is the satire on people whose epidermises are so fastidious and thin that even the greatest of all physical pleasures can barely be indulged in. . . . Irene and Clare are both women with plenty of capacity for love and sex . . . I am by no means deficient in appreciation of sense.[5]

Among other things, Galsworthy demanded the same right to physical pleasure for women as for men. Some brief quotations will show the absurdity of describing his characters as 'asexual'. In *The Country House*, he writes of George Pendyce: 'With the eye of his mind he saw a long procession of turf triumphs, a long vista of days and nights, and in them, round them, of them – Helen Bellew.'[6] In *The Dark Flower*, Anna Sturmer refers to her sexual maturity, and how much more pleasure she could give Mark than an inexperienced young girl: 'Let him but once taste the rapture she could give him! And at this thought she ceased clutching at the bracken stalks. . . . And all feeling, except just a sort of quivering deserted her – as if she had fallen into a trance.'[7] This was a daringly realistic passage. In *Saint's Progress*, Galsworthy criticises the ill effects of Pierson's widowerhood: 'No one had told him . . . that he should have married again, that to stay unmarried was bad for him, physically and spiritually.'[8] The most significant case is perhaps Miltoun in *The Patrician*, with his combination of an ardent temperament and great nobility of feeling:

> His spirit and senses were both on fire – for that was the quality of this woman, she suffered no part of him to sleep. . . . He lay down in a scoop of the stones. The sun entered there. . . . That warmth and perfume crept through the shield of his spirit, and stole into his blood; ardent images rose before him, the vision of an unending embrace. . . . And then there broke on him one of those delirious waves of natural desire.[9]

The instability of feelings in Galsworthy's love stories has already been mentioned. Inconstancy is perhaps too dogmatic and moralising a word to use. But there is no doubt that, in love as in everything else, he believed in perpetual change. He is constantly showing it happening, heroes agonizingly discovering it in their partners, or even in themselves.

The other form of constant uneasiness in the novels is another painful discovery — of the sufferings of society's victims.

This emphasis on beauty, love and sadness, sometimes at the cost of realism, explains, though it does not justify, the importance Galsworthy attaches to divorce — or rather to the theme of the woman in an unhappy or loveless marriage, who gets divorced or not, depending on whether her husband agrees. Irene divorces in the *Saga*; more frequently, the husband refuses his consent. But in fact the problem of married love is raised fairly explicitly in all the novels, and in the same terms: a woman who no longer loves her husband, or has never loved him, like Irene and Gyp, has the right to another man's love. The man who does not love a woman, and knows that she does not love him, is right to put an end to their life together, like Hilary in *Fraternity*, or not marry if there is still time, like Shelton in *The Island Pharisees*. This situation is to be found in the first two episodes of *The Dark Flower*, and in *Beyond*. Fleur's case is simply a poignant variant, in that she has never loved Michael. It is appropriate to examine this theme separately from the theme of the family, since the right to love, its arousal and its decline, reflects the indifference of Galsworthy's heroes and heroines to any family considerations.

In his way of handling the theme of the woman in a loveless marriage, it so happens that he draws attention to the physical shackles, and the material nature of the sexual act. But this does not make his approach in any way realistic. He ignores the vitally important sociological aspects of divorce, and the question of children. Throughout his life he remained haunted by the example of his own wife's unhappy first marriage. He was also writing in an age when female emancipation was the order of the day. Ibsen's play *A Doll's House* (1879) had been seen as a defence of the most extreme feminist arguments, and had aroused much controversy. It might have been thought that every woman saw her husband as a tyrant.

Although he disapproved of the militant suffragette movement, as was pointed out in the discussion of *The Patrician*, Galsworthy saw women as more defenceless than they really were: he exaggerated, just as the Swedish dramatist August Strindberg exaggerated in the opposite direction, from misogyny, and in reaction against Ibsen's influence. The psychology and the plots of Galsworthy's novels suffer from his prejudices on this matter.

And yet his subjectivity in relating a love story did not take him to the most romantic extremes. He was twenty-eight when his liaison with Ada began, and ten years older when they married. She was a few months older than him. Several of his most seductive heroines are mature women.

It would also be wrong to attack Galsworthy for his severity towards young people in *A Modern Comedy*. What he is satirising is modern behaviour, and the artistic and literary fashions in vogue, which he holds to be ephemeral. Nothing essential has changed, and for him love is essential.

The theme of honour is reserved exclusively for his male characters. He emphasises the indifference of his heroines to what is conventionally referred to as their 'honour'.[10] This theme of a man's honour re-invigorates some of his male characters who might otherwise seem pale. A sense of honour may appear old-fashioned today, and it probably is to some extent. The Galsworthian character's concern for his honour cannot be appreciated unless it is seen against the society in which he lived: a static, closed society that it is difficult for people nowadays to imagine. So when theft, or a lawsuit, or adultery is involved, and rumours about it run rife at the manor, or on 'Forsyte 'change', the hero is horrified. He is terror-struck at the thought that his name may be dragged in the mud by 'Society', and his misfortunes recounted in the papers. Many novels virulently satirise the gutter press, particularly *The Patrician*, *The Burning Spear* and *The Silver Spoon*. This reflects Galsworthy's phobia about publicity and his horror of vulgarity. Every effort is made to avoid scandal. It is typical that Soames should offer money to try and hush matters up. This is a vestige of the pride of the privileged classes.

Like divorce, this theme is handled both intensely and narrowly. Where his honour is involved, the Galsworthian hero is as racked with emotion as when he is in love. Sometimes even more so, and the emotion turns into rage and indignation. Wilfrid Desert in *Flowering Wilderness* leaves Dinny because her family has accused him of wanting her money. He sacrifices his love, a sacrifice that will cost him his life, in order to clear himself of this despicable accusation. Something of the same may be said of Lord Miltoun.

All of this shows how subjectively Galsworthy handles the

themes of his novels. It is not through oversight that no long list of social problems is included here. Galsworthy's social consciousness does not express itself mainly through his themes. It is reflected in his general uneasiness, and also partly through his rather pitiable poor characters.

The most striking exclusion of many social themes is Galsworthy's decision never to make two people of widely differing classes fall in love. Although love was his most important theme, and although he had such an acute sense of the tragic, he eliminated the most typical case of tragic love, the kind impeded by difference in wealth and culture. The 'little model' in *Fraternity* is the exception that proves the rule. Hilary is quite incapable of abolishing, by means of true love, the gap that separates them.

It is impossible not to be struck by the paradoxical position in which Galsworthy, the painter of love, finds himself imprisoned. It is not a matter of criticising him for narrow-mindedness: that would mean ignoring the age in which he lived, and his own origins. But his artistic field is correspondingly narrowed.

His open-mindedness about the social aspects of love in his novels is no greater than that of Jane Austen, and might be argued to be even less. The situations are sometimes similar. For example, Audrey, the heroine of *The Patrician*, is a minister's wife. But her social situation compared with her aristocratic lover's is ignored by Galsworthy, who is interested only in her position as an unhappily married woman. Galsworthy's heroines illustrate his indifference to social standing even more clearly than his heroes do. Unlike Jane Austen's heroines, they do not care about marriage. In *Beyond*, Gyp is even afraid that she might lose Summerhay's love if she consents to wed him.

Galsworthy very often uses art as a theme, separate from that of beauty. But it produces far less wealth of development. The over-frequent use of artists as fictional characters even sometimes gives an air of insipidity to the novels. There is sometimes an impression of an enclosed atmosphere, and of living by proxy. There are many kinds of artists in the novels, most of them painters. This may be explained simply by Galsworthy's family circumstances. There are also several writers and one or two musicians. This choice of professions should be interpreted empirically. Because of the more practical aspect of his activity, a painter suited Galsworthy best, whereas he was slightly embarrassed by introducing a writer, in case the character were taken for himself. His musical tastes contributed to his own sense of the poetic, but seldom led him to create characters. Only in *Beyond* and *Saint's Progress* does music play any considerable role.

He writes about painters rather than painting. This does not mean, however, that the artist is a clearly defined and studied social type. It is the artist's turn of mind that interests Galsworthy. And whenever he states and defines it, this turn of mind in fact proves to be a philosophy. 'The artistic theory of life', as he called it, almost makes art and philosophy merge: 'The real search for truth (at all events for those who follow the arts) consists in the searching of one's own spirit in contact with actual experience.'[11]

The Galsworthian concept of the artist has nothing to do with the definition of a social—occupational category. Yet it serves him as a basis on which to judge the rest of mankind. He can discern only one other type of person: the non-artist, non-creator, who is defined only negatively, in relation and with reference to the artist's creative act, seen as the only way of fashioning the future and ensuring progress. Probably under Pater's influence, he wrote:

> To the artist we look for those pictures of life as it really is, those correlations of sectional life to the whole, essential to the organic moral growth of human society. Moralists, preachers, judges, business men are all by nature or occupation advocates of the status quo; radicals and reformers are all professional partisans of the millennium.[12]

This over-simplification is a further indication of the goals Galsworthy was aiming at.

The supreme value he places on art is not reflected in his opinion of artists themselves. There is no idealisation. The portrait of Fiorsen in *Beyond* is as cruel as that of Hilary in *Fraternity*.

The law, and its implementation by the legal system, are another theme adopted with gusto by Galsworthy, and with great talent in the handling of dialogue. Although he had barely practised law, his legal studies had given him many opportunities to become familiar with legal procedure, and observe lawyers.

There is a discussion about Shelton's marriage contract in *The Island Pharisees*. Soames sues Bosinney in *The Man of Property*, and at the end of the novel Bosinney's body is identified by the Forsytes. In *Fraternity*, Hughs is interrogated briefly, and there is comment on the pointlessness of the sentence when he leaves gaol. One of the lengthiest developments arises from Soames' divorce, later in the *Chronicles*. In *The White Monkey*, Soames is presented in a more praiseworthy way as a lawyer, in his dealings with the swindler who runs the PPRF. *The Silver Spoon* contains the gripping libel case between Fleur and Marjorie. Dinny's brother is wrongly accused in *Maid in Waiting*, and is in danger of extradition. Finally, Clare's divorce case in *Over the River* gives Galsworthy a last opportunity to present a fascinating cross-examination, full of his typical humour and sense of comedy.

## FAMILY

Except for *Jocelyn*, where there is only a minor character who is the heroine's aunt, and *The Burning Spear*, all Galsworthy's novels take place against a family background. Family is just as important in those not forming part of the three trilogies, and if the Forsytes are treated on a vaster and more detailed scale than other families, this is due to the size of the work, and the time-scale involved, not to any difference in the author's viewpoint.

Galsworthy did not opt for any contrast and opposition between two families, as presented by E. M. Forster in *Howards End*, or Roger Martin du Gard in *The Thibaults*. This is hardly surprising, in view of the highly individual character of the heart searching he engages in. The family exists, it is a component of the situation, but not the aspect dealt with at greatest length. Indeed, it is not really a theme at all, or, if one, it is more material, less conscious than those already examined.

The hero sometimes does suffer because of his family, like Miltoun in *The Patrician*, or Jon and Fleur in *A Modern Comedy*. But they are mainly victims of their families' pasts. There is seldom any clash in the present between parents and children. Tensions may arise, but their effect is never decisive.

The role of the family is usually even slighter. Parental pressure has nothing to do with Helen Bellew leaving George Pendyce, or Miltoun leaving Audrey. The family does not intervene, or else does so with the utmost caution and nervousness. Miltoun's mother is afraid of him, and his father is embarrassed. Pride is a stronger force than family authority or threats.

Here again, the essential characteristic of the problem is its inward-looking nature. Only to the extent that a character bears family habits and attitudes as inner character traits is he ever governed by them. He embodies and perpetuates the family, just as much as he is its victim. Yet Galsworthy's philosophical outlook is pessimistic, particularly as regards relationships between human beings, and it tends to show the individual as a slave. So, despite the absence of any direct family responsibility in the matter, the misfortunes of his characters cannot be dissociated from their membership of a family. Although the family is usually reduced to the role of an observer — which Galsworthy uses to supply the reader with information — it is one of the inherent causes of events. Almost without knowing, it becomes the accomplice of a cruel fate.

The responsibility is undefined, but Galsworthy does not share it out evenly among the whole family. Parents are regarded with some indulgence. Unlike many other novelists, he does not exalt the mother's role. There is nothing in his writings to compare with the absolute mother-love and self-denial that becomes a blind cult of the family myth, in Steinbeck's *The Grapes of Wrath*, or in Duhamel's *The Pasquier Chronicles*. Mrs Pendyce is as far as he goes along this path. Mothers in the novels sometimes show courage, or at least firmness, like Emily and Winifred in *The Forsyte Saga*, but nothing more. On the other hand, there are fine and generous fathers: Old Jolyon and, in the end, Soames in the Chronicles, or Winton in *Beyond*. Others are less admirable. But on the whole Galsworthy's own experience shows through — he was always much closer to his father than to his mother. The affection and respect which he felt for his father are shown in his portrait of Old Jolyon. The extended Forsyte family has little sense of rank, but Old Jolyon comes closest to being the head of the family. Yet he remains an eccentric.

Galsworthy's attitude towards parents is, perhaps, rather unfeeling. But at least it is low key, something that becomes very clear when it is compared with works by three other writers, two of them published during his lifetime: *The Ordeal of Richard Feverel* (1859) by George Meredith, *The Way of All Flesh* (1903) by Samuel Butler, and *Father and Son* (1907) by Edmund Gosse. Parental influence is far more pervasive in all three writers, far more severely judged, even condemned. Galsworthy had probably read all three books: it is not absolutely certain for *The Way of All Flesh*, as mentioned earlier, but he knew Gosse personally, and must have been aroused by his brief but splendid childhood memories.

Galsworthy's personal temperament, and his social origins, explain his moderation and broad-mindedness. In the upper middle classes from which he sprang, young children were entrusted to nannies and then governesses. Their parents saw them only when they visited the nursery. Mothers were as remote as fathers, for they had to run large houses with a large domestic staff, and fulfil their social duties.

The extremely liberal educational system that prevailed in the aristocracy and upper middle classes encouraged independence of mind; personal temperament also counted. Galsworthy boasted of having always been 'exceptionally independent in mind, and given to spiritual claustrophobia'.[13] Heroes in his novels, even if shy and silent, never let themselves be intimidated whenever their convictions or freedom of action are in question. They possess the decided advantage of being moneyed – a personal fortune for those who are of age, annual allowances for the others. This money makes them mobile. When their education is finished, they set up their own establishments, separate from their families. They never have to face the overcrowding and conflict that occur in the cramped accommodation of a lower middle-class family with ideas higher than its station. In every one of Galsworthy's plots, the hero adopts a very typical and, it must be admitted, disconcerting, but highly effective attitude when crossed: he departs, without a word. The 'scene' with his family never takes place.

Whom, then, does Galsworthy hold responsible for the evils he sees in families? It is not easy to say. There are, of course, the uncles, aunts, cousins and distant relatives on whom he sharpens his satirical knife. Others may be seen more sympathetically, being mere harmless chatterboxes. Yet in certain circumstances they can become malevolent figures. Is it really in their capacity as members of the family that Galsworthy depicts them thus? Rather they are convenient scapegoats. He is unfair to them in that he treats them as outsiders, with no positive family virtues. Indeed, he himself helps to strip them of any specifically family character, in extending the meaning of the word 'Forsyte' until it ends up signifying the whole upper middle class, or even half the population of England. He defines a Forsyte as someone to be recognised by his sense of property.[14]

There emerges from his novels the rather paradoxical image of a family which hardly acts as a family, for good or ill, but which gradually merges with the higher social unit. If Galsworthy had elsewhere given a more substantial and flattering image of the family, his coolness could be taken as a criticism. It would mean that the Forsytes are incapable of displaying any real family spirit.

But such an interpretation would be totally without foundation. The action is not played out between individual, family and society. The units involved are reduced to two: the individual, and the family seen as the whole social class to which it belongs, or even the whole of society. Obviously, the family loses its identity. By excluding from his conception of human relationships everything that he regards as inessential, Galsworthy brings them down to a single antagonism between the individual and 'the others', between hero and everyone else, related to him or not.

The hero is man in general, everyman, the real man, reduced to his human condition. Others can be middle-class, aristocratic, working-class, Victorian, Edwardian or contemporary; they can come from any place. For Galsworthy they represent only localised, particular interests, shifting, limited realities.

A letter he wrote to Garnett in 1907 shows clearly that his views on the development of the middle class arose from his observations of tendencies within his own family, without being in any way differentiated from them.

The Galsworthys rising into the middle-class for two generations with all its tenacity, and ability (of a sort), now seem in the third generation all abroad, as if melting away again into a more creative sphere or nothing at all, muddling out as architects, writers, painters, engineers, do nothing at all, a non-practising barrister, a musicianly solicitor, one doctor, and a curious dandified land agent, alone represent the truly middle-class element and very poorly at that. What will become of them in the fourth generation? Very few have any children.[15]

Already in 1907 the idea of middle-class decadence was in his mind.

The nature and role of the family in Galsworthy's novels are, then, complex, difficult to grasp, even contradictory, depending on whether they are regarded from a psychological, realistic angle, or from a philosophical angle. The image of the family is realistic, in that it gives a true account of the very liberal and highly evolved way of life that prevailed at that time in the privileged classes of English society. Social obligations had to take second place to jealously guarded individualism. But at the advanced stage of civilisation of the country, a gentleman would set his own limits, instinctive but certain, on his individualism, so that private and public life were, on the whole, tranquil.

Philosophically, the family is seen as a mere contingency, a matter of pure chance. Galsworthy readily reminds the privileged that they owe their privileges to sheer chance.[16] Consequently, he spends little time studying the family, meditating on it as on other subjects, observing the details of how it functions. In so doing, he rules out a huge area of experience and observation, impoverishing his fiction. Yet he excludes it unhesitatingly.

Similarly, although he was capable of friendship and had friends, he is very sparing in his depiction of friendship. His writing suffers from his pessimistic view of the human capacity to understand and be understood by other men.

The Galsworthy hero illustrates the privileges he enjoys and of which, in spite of all his scruples and critical sense, he is not fully aware. As a member of the upper middle class, he possesses the means of preserving his own independence, and an instinctive knack of making sure it is respected, without haughtiness, but with a certain lofty air. His individualism is victorious, but at the cost of withdrawing partly into an ivory tower.

This detachment from contingencies is embodied in the lack of importance accorded by heroes to motherhood, children and the problems they raise. Here again, this reflects an attitude representative of a certain class. In both English and French middle classes, rather empirical but quite effective methods of birth control were already being practised by the end of the 19th century.

There are nine instances of extramarital sex in the novels. None of them is preceded, accompanied or followed by any anxiety, or even apprehension, in either the woman or the man, concerning the effects of the intimacy. There is often anxiety, but it arises solely from the intensity of their feelings, or from material difficulties.

It is worth remembering that any apprehension would have been unnecessary, for with only two exceptions, illicit sex never leads to pregnancy. Gyp in *Beyond* is the illegitimate daughter of Winton and a squire's wife, who died in childbirth. Winton is distressed, but never feels any remorse. In *Saint's Progress*, Nollie becomes pregnant before she is able to marry. She shows no sign of regret. Galsworthy's main characters are often childless. It was this aspect of Mark Lennan in *The Dark Flower* that brought a bitter attack by Quiller-Couch down on Galsworthy's head. His review of the book accused Galsworthy of imitating Shelley in seeking refuge in sentimentality, free love and philandering: 'There is not a child in the book . . . no book about marriage in which the child is ignored can even begin to be a true book.'[17] This summary verdict on the novel would be unacceptable today, but it was the general opinion when the book came out. Quiller-Couch was quite arbitrary when he defined the novel as being devoted to marriage. Indeed, Galsworthy could be criticised for failing to examine the actual institution of marriage. But it must be admitted that there are very few young children in his writings, and they are not depicted in any depth. His personal experience of children was limited. His adopted son had no offspring, yet there is nothing in what he wrote to suggest that Galsworthy in any way regretted this lack of heirs. On the other hand, neither is there anything to prove that he did not experience such a feeling.

There is no clear evidence in what is known of Galsworthy to show what he thought of children in his novels. His sense of restraint held him back from any extreme opinion in this, as in any other field. Although most of his characters do reveal undoubted detachment from family problems, numbers are not conclusive proof, and three of his main characters most endowed with strong personalities, Soames, Gyp and Dinny, have a highly developed sense of family.

Soames may be a failure as a husband, but he is not only a good father, but also a dutiful son, and a devoted brother; he is ready to help and give advice to the many Forsytes in their hours of need. This was just as true of Galsworthy himself with his relatives, as numerous as the Forsytes, but less gifted in making money. Despite her unhappy experiences with men, Gyp is an affectionate daughter and good mother. Dinny is extremely fond of her brother, as is Barbara of hers.

## MONEY

Money is a theme in Galsworthy's novels, in the same sense of the word as the family. It exists, it is present, it provides the novels with one of their proportions, it is one of the factors, like time, space and family. But unlike time and space, it is little more than a concrete fact, even more practical, immediate and contingent than the family. Galsworthy never reflected on it — or, at least, there is no sign of such a reflection in his novels. And since it is never mentioned in either his letters or his diary, this silence is hardly likely to mean concealment.

It does not make the behaviour of his characters in relation to money any less interesting. In fact their behaviour is more significant for its very instinctiveness, reflecting habits acquired over one or more generations. When one has never been short of money, one mentions it no more than is necessary. This applies to all the main characters in the novels. They come from the upper middle class, landed gentry or nobility, or, as often happens, from inter-marriage among these privileged categories of the population, and they share the condition of being well-to-do, whether because of money made when they were younger, or through inherited wealth.

This is by far the commonest case. Only the first-generation Forsytes, Old Jolyon, James, Swithin, Roger and Timothy (who are known to have been based on Galsworthy's uncles), have made rather than come into their fortune. By 1886, when *The Man of Property* begins, all of them except James have retired from business. The youngest, Timothy, is sixty-five, and the eldest, Jolyon, is eighty. He is still a company director, but for his own pleasure rather than because he needs to. The novel could have gone back in time and showed how those older Forsytes made their money, but it does not do so. All that is known is what their occupations were. James is shown shuffling through papers in his study; Old Jolyon is seen handling a general meeting of shareholders, and it is known that he owed his success in the tea trade to his fine palate. That is all. Should this be a matter for surprise?

Surely Galsworthy, like Trollope, simply does not show the professional or public life of his characters, when they have one, but basically their private life. The depiction of social habits is far less wide-ranging than in Balzac. Galsworthy presents no bankers, or doctors or journalists (though he inveighs against the more sensational newspapers), or tradesmen.

This is a deliberate choice, perhaps regrettable, but which has to be accepted. It may not be a complete explanation, but it is perhaps worth mentioning that Galsworthy himself never practised any of the professions in which the older Forsytes had engaged. Never having been in business, he would have had considerable problems in writing about it.

Accordingly, the Forsytes are never seen in the process of money-making. It is not absolutely clear how they did make their fortune, and its size is not stated either. It was an age when wealth was gauged by a man's carriage and horses and the number of servants he had. Galsworthy gives no information about this point.[18] This silence is significant. The Forsytes are rather suspicious, and seldom mention the matter among themselves. But Galsworthy's own personality and inclinations must also be taken into account. He was better educated, more refined, nobler by birth than his own uncles, because of his mother's family.[19] His attitude towards money was certainly different from his father's. Inherited wealth — 'old money' — always permits greater detachment from the whole sordid business than does hard-earned money. It was his respect for his father, if not for his uncles, that made it out of the question to emphasise the speed with which the family had risen in the world. The reticence, pride and generosity that explain so many aspects of his personality contribute to his great discretion on the matter of money.

However, there is no question of this indifference arising naturally from his status as a rich man, or of his scorning the material details of life, or being unaware of what ordinary living involved. He knew about money: out of his extensive resources he cared for the needs of a host of people, friends, relatives, servants, poor people. His silence on this theme is deliberate, reflecting his intention to reduce the significance of money in life's drama, as he saw it. It remained shadowy, like some of his characters.

A systematic compilation of financial details in the novels, showing figures, produces quite a volume of extremely interesting information. But if even part of this information were reproduced, with the conclusions that can be drawn from it, this could give a distorted idea of the density and importance of such references. His figures are incomplete, rare and they provide only indications. They reflect Galsworthy's fondness for certain forms of precision when writing novels, particularly chronological accuracy, but they are always extremely parsimonious, providing light, neutral touches. Galsworthy will provide any information on a will, the value of a stolen object, the price of a house, only if the understanding of a character requires it. It is always very concise.

For example, when Old Jolyon makes it up with his son, he says: 'I'm settling a thousand a year on you at once. June will have fifty thousand at my death, and you the rest.'[20] He then goes on to talk about his dog.

On his death in 1892, the size of Old Jolyon's fortune is revealed. During his lifetime it was known only to be considerable. In *The Man of Property*, Galsworthy had aroused readers' curiosity by mentioning the middle-class fascination with reading *The Times* obituaries, which always end with the amount left by the deceased. A round figure of a hundred thousand pounds was given; at the beginning of *In Chancery*, the impressive figure of £145,304 is announced. This would need to be multiplied by fifteen or twenty to give the equivalent present-day value. But what the Forsytes are most taken aback by is not the size of the estate, but the provision in the will by which Irene, his niece by marriage, is left fifteen thousand pounds, in the form of an annuity.

These precise figures are the only such ones to be found in the Chronicles. And even they do not give a full picture of how rich the eldest Forsyte was. Details would also be needed of his income and expenditure. However, there is nothing unrealistic about the amount Galsworthy does quote.

Some fragments of information are given about Soames' financial standing:

> Soames was reserved about his affairs, but he must be getting a very warm man. He had a capital income from the business — for Soames, like his father, was a member of that well-known firm of solicitors, Forsyte, Bustard and Forsyte — and had always been very careful. He had done quite unusually well with some mortgages he had taken up, too — a little timely foreclosure — most lucky hits.[21]

There is no doubt that he is lucky when he accepts Bosinney's offer to build him a house at Robin Hill for eight thousand pounds, not including the cost of the site. 'He was very comfortably off, with an increasing income getting on for three thousand a year.'[22]

It might be supposed that, in the work in which Galsworthy is describing what he himself, in the opening lines of *The Man of Property*, calls 'an upper middle-class family', money would be a more important subject than in the others. Admittedly, the idea of property is the main — though not the only — theme of this first novel in the Chronicles. Market value is the criterion that the Forsytes apply to everything. Turning over in his hands a piece of china found in his brother's drawing-room, Soames' father, James, illustrates this obsession for looking at everything with an auctioneer's or antique-dealer's eye, the need to put the right market price on it. Being a solicitor, he is trying to estimate Old Jolyon's entire fortune by weighing the object in his hands. Nothing fascinates him so much as a will. His passionate interest in money combines with his highly developed sense of family to make him the most typical of all the Forsytes. He is one of the best-known portraits.

But although such a mentality is often alluded to, Galsworthy did not feel the need, in order to make it comprehensible, to go into the details of any particular deals.

Money is only the most immediate and grossest form of wealth. Irene's lack of fortune illustrates the fact that Soames, instead of being content with his own well-to-do connections, has to some extent turned his back on such considerations in marrying her. The possession of his wife's body is not even enough for him. He wants to own her very soul. In fact, this is what most people in love wish for. In the same way, Galsworthy writes of the Forsytes that 'of all forms of property their respective healths naturally concerned them most'.[23] This is by no means peculiar to the Forsytes; indeed, a proper concern for one's health is surely a sign of intelligence.

In other words, Galsworthy uses the theme of property in such a way as to transcend it. This is why it may be argued that the importance of this theme in *The Forsyte Saga* has been exaggerated.

In both *The Patrician* and *The Country House*, the family estate shows a slight deficit: 'in spite of his strong prejudice in favour of country-house life, he [Squire Pendyce] was not a rich man, his income barely exceeding ten thousand a year.'[24]

The remark does not seem to be ironical. It is not for his wealth that Galsworthy attacks the Squire. His son George's debts are quoted in pitiless detail, covering more than a page, and showing that he owes £3295. He later loses £4000 on a single race.

Lord Valleys, Miltoun's father, has a budget of quite a different order from the Squire's. Galsworthy probably scorned to satisfy the idle curiosity of certain readers, and dazzle them with huge figures. He says nothing about either the estate finances or the nature of the personal fortune that enables it to be run at a loss (and even additional land acquired when the opportunity arises).

Here again, Galsworthy enjoys merely hinting, with the idea that those of his readers familiar with the world he is describing will need no lengthy explanations. It is for them that he is shaping the narrative.

The sole industrialist in the novels is Stanley Freeland, the only brother to have lowered family dignity in this way: on their mother's side the brothers are descended from the rural gentry of Worcestershire, whose origins date back to the Conquest. Stanley runs a prosperous plough factory inherited from an 18th-century ancestor, which exports all its output. In this situation, Galsworthy is quite open about money. Stanley has an income of fifteen thousand pounds, on which he lives in great style. He plays the squire without being one, employing a staff of twenty on a fifteen-hundred acre estate. As Galsworthy points out, this renegade earns more than his three brothers put together. One of them is a writer, another a civil servant and the third the family 'social reformer'.

Little attention has been given to the analogy between the history of the Freeland family and what is known of Galsworthy's ancestors on his mother's side. The Christian name of the 'reformer', Morton, even comes from Castle Morton, home of one of the branches of the Bartleet or Bartlet family.

Stanley's success in business is untypical of the Bartleet family. As Galsworthy wrote to Garnett, comparing his paternal and maternal forebears: 'The Bartlets have got a sort of crystallized, dried out, almost mummified energy; utterly unpractical, incapable of making or keeping money.'[25]

In the portrait of Stanley he departed from the historical parallel, withdrawing from the local and family context to offer an example of adaptability to economic facts in a family of noble origin. The youngest son turns to industry or business.

This historical phenomenon, already long-established in England, is accompanied by another, with special significance for the country's social and political stability. In the 19th century, businessmen who had made their fortune frequently used it to purchase large estates, thereby to some extent resurrecting the ancient functions of a squire. Edward VII, who mixed with the business middle classes and financial circles, opened up the ranks of the aristocracy to these postulants. Galsworthy accepted this policy, but does not seem to have shown much enthusiasm for the way it was implemented. None of the novels contains any complimentary allusions to Edward, before or after his accession.

It is mainly when there is a shortage of cash that the subject is talked about in Galsworthy's novels. For instance, when Soames starts to wonder about his wife's fidelity, he reassures himself by thinking that 'luckily, she had no money — a beggarly fifty pounds a year'.[26] Her lover is equally impecunious. Soames is well aware that Bosinney is little concerned with money. It is one of the reasons why he takes him on as his architect. It is also why, when he wants to take revenge, he sues him: he knows that it will be easy to beggar him.

In *Fraternity*, old Sylvanus Stone, the disembodied theoretician of universal brotherhood, keeps body and soul together on cups of cocoa at his daughter's. He has three hundred pounds a year, but lives on ninety and distributes the rest.[27]

Galsworthy sometimes provides figures for the earnings and money troubles of the poor, but never at length or systematically. In fact, he is as discreet about poverty as he is about wealth.

What is certain is that the Galsworthian hero is born to wealth. Giles Legard in *Jocelyn*, or Dick Shelton in *The Island Pharisees*, for example, do not even need to work. Even though his hero is in his thirties, there is very little question of getting a job. If he does have one, it is never very demanding, and does not prevent him from departing on long journeys abroad. The remedy often suggested for boredom is a trip round the world. Hilary in *Fraternity*, Mark Lennan in *The Dark Flower* and Felix in *The Freelands* take the fullest advantage of their exceptional freedom of movement.

A passage in *The Island Pharisees* helps to define the income range in this world. Passing through Kensington, Shelton sees the houses he is passing as the shells of owners with incomes of three to five thousand pounds. He makes the houses speak: 'The person who lives in me has only four thousand two hundred and fifty-five pounds each year, after allowing for the income tax.'[28]

Women have less money. Mrs Pendyce, although she comes of an aristocratic family, has only three hundred pounds a year. Gyp, as the sole heiress of her father-in-law, the Squire, is richer. On coming of age she has twenty thousand pounds, eight thousand of which comes from her mother, apart from the undisclosed amount which her father gives her.[29] This makes her financially independent of both Fiorsen and Summerhay.

Money plays a totally different role in Balzac's and Galsworthy's novels. All Galsworthy's rich characters keep their money and take advantage of it. But they have no cult of wealth. A few, like Young Jolyon, Hilary, Shelton, are even shamefaced about it. The others, the army of Forsytes, Pendyces, Valleys, use it to preserve their own comfort, position and advantages. They do not try to turn it into an instrument to serve their ambitions, or to acquire new political power. They are never miserly. This moderate attitude among the privileged reflects the political stability of England at the time.

No character ever rails against money. This illustrates Galsworthy's incapacity to realise or imagine how corrupting it could be within a liberal economic system. In *Addresses in America* and in his play *The Forest* he denounced the commercialism of the century. But it was its vulgarity, ugliness, inadequacies and excesses that he was condemning, rather than its inherent tyranny and viciousness. His sense of social injustice extended only a short distance into the economic area.

## CHARACTER TYPES AND INDIVIDUALS

A lecture that Galsworthy gave at Oxford University in 1931, entitled 'The Creation of Character in Literature', contains one of those paradoxes so common when he turns to the subject of literary criticism. He does not reply to the question raised by his title, and concludes that the character is an unfathomable mystery:

> Speaking as one who has been trying to write novels of character over a period of more than thirty years, the lecturer can make no real contribution to precision. . . . I sink into my morning chair, a blotter on my knee, the last words or deed of some character in ink before my eyes, a pen in my hand, a pipe in my mouth, and nothing in my head. I sit, I don't intend; I don't expect; I don't even hope. . . . Gradually my mind seems to leave the chair, and be where my character is acting or speaking. . . . Suddenly, my pen jots down a movement or remark. . . . Those pages, adding tissue to character, have been supplied from the store-cupboard of the subconscious, in response to the appeal of one's conscious directive sense.[30]

There is a polemical tone in these pronouncements, even more obvious when one remembers the hostile criticism of Galsworthy for producing characters who are types, not individuals. It is an old argument, to be found in the first book on Galsworthy, published in 1916 by the novelist Sheila Kaye-Smith, in which she wrote that he dealt 'with types rather than individuals'.[31]

Galsworthy was therefore familiar with a criticism that had never been very lenient. He counters it by speaking of his psychological novels. And the word 'type' is employed by him in a very loose sense. When he is thinking of the precise concept of type, Galsworthy often uses the word 'idea'.

Speaking of Miltoun, Sheila Kaye-Smith touches, without knowing it, on the difficulty that has tripped up so many critics. Imprisoned in the conventional view of Galsworthy as a petty-minded sentimental conformist, they have failed to follow the path of his thinking, which is quite straightforward. Miltoun is a 'type' by birth, but a rebel by nature and temperament; circumstances are responsible for revealing his own antinomy to him. In the same way, Soames possesses the outlook and typical behaviour inherited from the Forsytes, until the day when Irene reveals his true nature to him. His sensitivity is not sufficiently deadened for him to remain unaware of the cruelty of his fate.

Despite his sense of the complexity of things, Galsworthy was unable to define the situation of his leading characters: a state of semi-revolt. This irregular, confused, in-between position is common among them. It contradicts the type they represent, individualises them, leaving them in a supremely uncomfortable posture, like all false positions. It mirrors the condition Galsworthy himself knew, as someone who despite himself had remained typical of his class, while departing from it by temperament, forced into this by his seriousness and perpetual unease.

Squire Pendyce is an exception to the rule: a leading character who is a type, as Galsworthy admitted.[32]

Apart from the personal equation, another complicating variation is not pointed out by Galsworthy: not all the social circles he presents are equally constricting. The miniature world over which the Squire rules is the most rigid; that of the upper middle classes at the end of the Victorian age less so; that of the nobility still less; as for the world of intellectuals and artists at the end of the Edwardian age, in which the Dallisons move, it shows signs of disintegration. Such signs are more and more frequent in the same circles fifteen years later, in the post-war period, when Galsworthy wrote *A Modern Comedy*.

## GALSWORTHY'S PSYCHOLOGICAL INSIGHT

Sheila Kaye-Smith was right to emphasise the excellence of Galsworthy's fictional situations, and the way he exploits them.[33] But she failed to describe these situations correctly. In fact, they constitute a single situation. She wrongly identified it with a social and moral problem. The social problem is often only a pretext, an opportunity, and is only one aspect of reality. Neither does the word 'moral', in the narrow sense of conventional morality, define the basic preoccupation.

The essential factor is what Galsworthy tried to define as a 'spiritual examination'. Occasionally, aware of his inability to find the right term, he hesitated, and left readers to hesitate, between 'passionately spiritual' and 'spiritually passionate'. But he left no doubt as to the fact that it is a highly individual, even lonely experience.

This is very clear in the violent argument with Garnett about *The Patrician*. Galsworthy wrote to him: 'It's not a piece of social criticism — they none of them are. If it's anything it's a bit of spiritual examination. . . . I've neither the method nor the qualities of the social critic.'[34]

Twelve years later, in the preface to the Manaton Edition of *The Forsyte Saga*, he went even further: 'This long tale is no scientific study of a period.'[35]

In 1910, Garnett had already answered that the inner conflict Galsworthy felt and described did correspond to antagonisms existing in English society, which gave his writing great significance as social criticism.[36]

Clearly, Garnett's opinion was very largely right. However, Galsworthy's own analysis was quite perceptive. The description of special cases, the study of what may be called an 'outsider psychology', does of course still mean defining a social relationship or relationships. So he is, vaguely, a social novelist. But it does not mean only or even essentially describing class relationships, or confining oneself to a study of collective psychology. It is on this important point that the view advanced here differs from the classic interpretation of Galsworthy's fiction. His approach to society comprises two opposing movements. On the one hand, he composes the attributes of the group (couple, family, organisation, profession, class or nation). On the other hand, he shows how the individual, despite inevitable membership of his group, is not fully integrated in it.

What Galsworthy is constantly describing, with the myriad variations introduced by the temperament of each character, is the emotional rather than the intellectual repercussions of this situation. It involves three forms of relationship: with the loved one, with the family, and with strangers; and all possible combinations of these.

The outsider mentality is difficult to detect in the works, without first being recognised in their author. This is what explains the tardiness and slightness of most Galsworthy criticism. The concept gives a coherence which no other interpretation is capable of providing. It reduces Lawrence's argument that the Forsytes are not human beings but only social beings to begging the question. Galsworthy's extrapolation from personal situation was not just an over-generalisation. It engendered monotony, and detracted from the quality of his writing. Not content with choosing 'outsiders' in his own social class, where he could make them credible, he widened the formula to the 'masses'. *The Freelands* contains a drunken boor who is distinguished from his type by being, on top of everything else, epileptic. The character becomes pathological.

On the other hand, the outsider mentality fits in very well with Galsworthy's particular lyricism, and is to be found in what have been called his lyrical novels. This is in the nature of things. Is romanticism not always some kind of a revolt of the individual against certain social conventions, and the affirmation of his right to dispose of himself as he sees fit? The outsider sooner or later walks alone. Failure to adapt to the institution of marriage imposed by current legislation is the form the condition takes in these novels.

*The Dark Flower* also presents the 'Galsworthian' situation with striking clarity, although in a completely unaccustomed context. The novel could be understood when it came out, although it is clearer now that the episode in Galsworthy's life related by Margaret Morris is known. However, it is, above all, the change in attitudes and in relations between the sexes since 1913 that has made the novel more credible. At the time it was published, the hero, Mark Lennan, 'the amorist' as certain readers called him, was unconvincing. He either shocked people (though not enough to fascinate), or bored them with his listlessness. In either case, Galsworthy's intentions were misunderstood. It is now known that the third episode, Mark's third romantic adventure, is autobiographical. Galsworthy was forty-three when he met Margaret, who was nineteen.

Literary use of this episode is perfectly consistent with the logic of his whole fictional prose output. The type is indeed an amorist, although Galsworthy appears to be denying it in the preface for the Manaton Edition, when he writes that he chose the three love affairs in his hero's life, and left out everything else in his life. Galsworthy must be allowed the right to select. But it is hard to believe that the rest, what he has not told, would give a very different idea of the character — who is no debauchee, however, or even a Don Juan.

So the amorist is not true to type either. Like Miltoun, like Soames, like Pierson, he is a special case. The second episode emphasises his shyness and timidity at his first meeting alone with Olive Cramier. One day, he is seized by an anxiety that is not only, or even essentially, a matter of conscience. Listlessly, and without quite knowing why, he reacts against his usual tendencies, and drops his amorist's role for good.

*Beyond*, which mirrors *The Dark Flower* in that it relates the love life of a woman, presents the same situation, with equal clarity, but with yet another variation. Here, it is not the author who has chosen. He excludes nothing, which explains why the book is so long. It is the heroine who chooses, by caring for nothing in life except her passions. Her personality is as developed as Mark Lennan's is restricted; however, the depiction of this strong personality[37] is not the only subject of the story. Because of her temperament she is very much an outsider, quite unable to adapt to social institutions.

Gyp is the most completely passionate creature in all the novels; Mark is more emotional. Together, they mark the precise boundaries of Galsworthy's particular psychological field. In *The Dark Flower* and *Beyond*, as has been seen, he deliberately casts aside any preoccupations other than psychological ones. It does not alter his psychological views, but reduces them to essentials.

His favourite area is not character study — which interests him, but mainly as a means to an end — but the psychology of the instinct, analysis of emotion, feelings, daydreams, and also conscious thought, but not very practical or intellectual. In all these forms of psychological life, it is movement, change, evolution that he is seeking and describing. The states he describes show a quality of fluidity, which coexists strangely with the habitually static nature of character; Galsworthy sees no contradiction there; quite the contrary.

By instinct, the first word used above, is meant mainly romantic love. The other instincts, such as mother love, father love, filial love, or the instinct of self-preservation, are rather neglected. Although physical love is suggested rather than described, and is seen as a movement of the soul, it must be said that passion is more charged with instinct and emotion than rich in feelings. Its very intensity and self-centredness deprive it, not of delicacy, but of a certain disinterestedness, which reduces communicability.

The calm, mute nobility of passionate love is exalted in *The Patrician*: 'They parted with another tranquil look, which seemed to say: "It is well with us — we have drunk of happiness." '[38]

It is passion, far more than sentiment, that is sacred.[39] His heroes are more passionate, less emotional, than he was himself.

This lyricism gives plenty of room to dreaming. 'His thoughts were dreams, his dreams thoughts — all precious unreal,' he writes of Mark Lennan.[40] Of Audrey's mood in *The Patrician*, he writes that 'she wanted to be told of things that were not, yet might be'.[41]

Unfortunately, Galsworthy had a weakness for the allegorical dream, illustrating a deep tendency in the personality or emotional state. He shows no signs of having been familiar with or having understood Freudian dream analysis. He uses the term 'subsonscious', which had become common, but has no clear idea of what it implies.

Conventional moral feelings and judgements have no place here. Why should he try to weigh characters in the balance, judge vices and virtues, since he is amoral? He told an unidentified correspondent that he was surprised at the importance attached by readers to the virtues and vices of his characters. For him what mattered was whether they were 'badly or well made'.[42]

The priority given by critics to the Forsyte Chronicles has helped distort opinions of his psychological insight. Because of Soames' tenacity in trying to keep possession of Irene, it has not been noticed that such constancy is unusual among Galsworthy's characters. There is no moral judgement, but absolute pragmatism, simple observation of the fluidity of moods and the permanence of change in the human heart, as in everything else.

Galsworthy's psychology is mainly confined to the emotions, or a mixture of emotion and intellect, but it plunges deep, with nothing to stop it except the lack of scientific and philosophical training. It lies between normal and depth psychology, which explains the frequency of pathological cases, or at least pathological states, among his characters.

In his lecture on the creation of character in fiction, Galsworthy rightly says: 'This is . . . the least trammelled and most subconsciously inspired form of character creation.'[43] A few sentences later he exalts 'the novelist's introspective and luxurious method, almost wholly controlled by the subconscious mind ministering to the creator's dominant mood at the moment'.

Ultimately, Galsworthy did answer the question about the creation of character. But few of his listeners could understand the answer properly. It is not surprising today, and Galsworthy must be recognised as a Freudian — even if an unconscious one. The moody behaviour of several characters, Hilary in *Fraternity* or Young Jolyon in *The Forsyte Saga*, is revealing. The plots show the considerable part played by oversights and slips.

Asking Galsworthy whether he was a moralist or an artist, and claiming that *Fraternity* annihilated any moral doctrine, Conrad went very far in the analysis of Hilary Dallison as a pathological case. It is a lucid and restrained study.[44] He never guessed (understandably) that Hilary was Galsworthy himself, stylised, deliberately and masochistically blackened, with the same frantic sincerity that makes *Fraternity* or *The Burning Spear* further examples of spiritual examination.

Galsworthy used psychoanalytical concepts without quite knowing it. He seemed unaware of what a pathological case even was. His correspondence contains a reply to the daughter of an eminent Victorian statesman, who complained that his characters were 'not normal or healthy'. His answer was completely beside the point.[45]

The exchange dates from 1915. A glance backwards may help to throw light on Galsworthy's attitude, and explain his reticence when the idea of health is forced to his attention. In 1904, in the polemical *The Island Pharisees*, his rhetoric was based on denouncing health as a false value. In the midst of his crisis of conscience, Shelton writes to his fiancée: 'There's something about human nature that is awfully repulsive, and the healthier people are, the more repulsive they seem to me to be.'[46] Antonia replies: 'I don't think I understand what you mean. One must be healthy to be perfect. I don't like unhealthy people.'[47] Shelton is irritated by these words. In them he finds the explanation of everything he sees and hears in those circles. It is as if he had found the chemical formula for rich people.

Health was taken rather more seriously in *Fraternity* in 1909. It is a scientific fact, which can be explained. Thyme, the daughter of the happy Dallison couple, and whose very name evokes nature, symbolises their success: 'Thyme, that healthy product of them both . . . had never given them a single moment of uneasiness.'[48] This is no doubt why Thyme is loved by young Doctor Martin Stone, who has made health an article of faith and a programme. The ideas of 'the Sanitist', as Stephen Dallison ironically dubs him, are recounted in terms that reflect the influence of Darwinian ideas at the turn of the century: 'This young man had come into the social scheme at a moment when the conception of existence as a present life corrected by a life to come was tottering; and the conception of the world as an upper-class preserve somewhat seriously disturbed.'[49] Although it is rational and generous, Galsworthy does not approve of Stone's programme, which he sees as involving the abandonment of 'all abstract speculation'.[50] For Galsworthy, this meant a lack of any humanity and sense of light and shade. The story shows Stone's interventions being followed in both cases by failure. As William Bellamy points out, Galsworthy believed that no treatment that neglects psychological problems can succeed.[51]

Yet it was his own insufficient knowledge in this field, then fast expanding, that prevented Galsworthy from perceiving exactly what constitutes mental health. This essential concept, implicit throughout his writings, is only partly and negatively defined: he was incapable of formulating several of the conditions necessary for nervous balance. Like many writers of the time, he denounced the excesses of urbanisation and mechanisation. But he was sensitive mainly to the physical dangers, and threats to a way of life. He failed to see that even someone living as securely as himself was under threat. His compassion for the mentally ill was only to be expected from a foe of violence and cruelty, in the age of the pioneers of modern psychiatry. But he did not understand the therapeutic reasons for humanising the conditions under which patients were forced to live.

Is any overall judgement of Galsworthy as a psychologist possible? His sensitivity, his hypersensitivity, meant that he was able to go very far in his exploration of the area of the emotions. His delicacy and analytical mind enabled him to deploy and organise these important resources, blended with a certain intellectuality. His limits as a psychologist appear in several directions.

He created characters without asking himself whether they were virtuous, pleasant, normal or disturbed. Many are difficult people, depressing, even insufferable. They more often inspire compassion than sympathy. Galsworthy does not seem quite aware of the reservations many of his readers have when introduced to such people. This is a weakness in his intellect, a lack of knowledge of normal and pathological psychology; a certain want of taste, combined with an absence of moral sense. There is no denying that his work is sometimes irritating. Yet his vague intuitions of how his characters are abnormal confer a modern psychological realism that is lacking in Bennett, and that points to the novelists of the next generation.

## THE GALSWORTHY HERO

It is now possible to draw a portrait of the Galsworthy hero. He is often mature in age. Several girls are given partners who are in their thirties, or approaching thirty. There are fewer younger men, and they are shy and sensitive.

Reserved, even taciturn, his hero is neither a real man of action nor a real man of thought. He has something of the amateur or the artist about him. He faces few practical problems. In most cases, his means relieve him of such considerations. Otherwise, his temperament allows him to over-ride or elude them. Jealous of his independence, he never lets himself be imposed upon. If importuned, he takes his leave. If he finds life tedious, he goes round the world. He acts little; his action is rare but impulsive, and sometimes dangerous when it does occur. He usually abstains from intervening, even if this causes him to suffer a feeling of impotence.

He is cultivated and sophisticated, rather than educated. His thinking is not very clear, and even less logical. He is fundamentally amoral — at least in matters of love. And it is mainly love that is involved. Throughout the novels there is not a single person governed and fired by moral preoccupations, just as there is not a single real criminal.

His pride, dignity, instinctive sense of decency and restraint protect him from any baseness, as they do from asceticism and sacrifice. He embodies the privileged gentleman of the period, a free and civilised being who places his own limits on his behaviour.

Several of the most attractive heroines are, as has been seen, mature women. Irene is only twenty when Soames marries her, but she is twenty-three or four when she takes Bosinney away from June, who is six years her junior, and thirty-eight when Soames entreats her to return home with him, thereby pushing her into the arms of Young Jolyon. Galsworthy continues to laud her beauty. Anna Stormer, married for twelve years, is nearly thirty-six when *The Dark Flower* begins. Olive Cramier is twenty-six. Helen Bellew is 'thirty or thirty-two',[52] and in full possession of her charms, in *The Country House*.

There are also young women. Fleur and Jon are both nineteen when they meet. Antonia and Barbara are the same age in *The Patrician*; Sylvia and Nell in *The Dark Flower*, and Nedda in *The Freelands*, are younger. In *Fraternity*, Thyme is seventeen and Ivy nineteen. They are all endowed with charm and freshness, whether because of their shyness or, on the contrary, because of their vivaciousness. But they have less personality than their elders. Audrey, Irene and Gyp hold a pre-eminent position among the heroines. There are of course Fleur and Dinny, but they both belong to another epoch, the post-war period, and each occupies a special position. It is Audrey, Irene and Gyp that best illustrate woman's pride in love.

Analysing Galsworthy's attitude to these heroines, W. L. George writes: 'His emotions tend to lead him to the excessive opposite of brutality. . . . I am always malcontented by his women. . . . All . . . appear weak in their loveliness. Mr Galsworthy seems to see women as such wretched prey. . . . This is true, but not so completely as he makes out.'[53] He could have added that, because of the weakness of many male characters, this is doubly unrealistic.

There is some truth in the remark. Even more clearly than Irene, Audrey is neither Victorian nor Ibsenian, because of her indifference to civil status and rights. But both of them, whether they like it or not, are in the position of Victorian women. They have almost no means of gaining independence, since they have no proper professional training. Galsworthy is optimistic in showing them on their own, and capable of making do, by using their musical knowledge and talents. In the Edwardian age, a growing number of women were beginning to seek training and work. This tendency is not illustrated in the novels.

Yet it can be argued that he had a prophetic vision of the evolution of society. The way his women throw off social protection, or even male protection, shows their remarkable self-confidence, even if it is obscurely motivated. It is a type that Galsworthy may have encountered, still rare, but which he perhaps realised would be less and less so in the future.

There is a strange yet significant contrast between the hero's situation and behaviour, and his preoccupations. Without any real reason, his worrying and 'spiritual examination' capture all his attention. One of the weaknesses and improbabilities of the novels is the failure to provide substantial enough motives for these heart-searchings. His heroes are less generous than he was himself, and far less committed to social action. Since they are so amoral in their private lives, it is hard to believe that they should be so set on defining a new social morality. Some part of the novels become verbose. The observers and moralists that appear throughout the novels, Shelton, Young Jolyon, Gregory Vigil, Courtier, Felix Freeland, act as intermediaries, but they are also screens against reality.

The Forsytes are the only members of the middle classes whose wealth comes from trade, the property market or banking. The novels as a whole show that, in society as depicted by Galsworthy, the middle classes do occupy a very important place, but not a predominant one. Alongside the six novels in the first two trilogies, there are four others devoted to the aristocracy (*The Patrician* and the *End of the Chapter* trilogy), one concerned with the landed gentry (*The Country House*), and four others in which both these social groups intermingle with the urban middle classes, professional people, intellectuals and artists (*The Island Pharisees, The Dark Flower, The Freelands, Beyond*). Finally, in five other novels, the social origin of the characters is not clear. They are always well-to-do, but may belong to one or other of the appropriate classes.

In a letter to Garnett in 1910, Galsworthy emphasised the difficulty of drawing the line of demarcation between the aristocracy and the landed gentry.[54] In most of his narratives, he illustrates the gradual interpenetration of the various sections of the middle classes and the two upper classes, a complex process of mutual influence and borrowings. Its very slowness is a guarantee of its success, and on the whole the country may gain from it. Though pessimistic when he looked at man in the family or social setting, he was quite confident in the future of the nation and the human race. Without knowing exactly in which direction they were heading, he had no doubt of their capacity to adapt.

It may be that the same society is presented in Galsworthy's plays and novels, and is equally outdated. However, the difference in viewpoint itself is important. Someone like Shelton or Young Jolyon, driven by disquiet, imagines or at least hopes for the future. This is why the novels, as seen through their eyes, underline the evolutionary aspect of the situation; whereas the need for dramatic effect in the plays leads Galsworthy to emphasise the grievances, oppositions, hatred, pride and toughness of the establishment, old and incapable of turning away from the past.

But not only the viewpoint differs. The plays display greater differences between rich and poor, and a different distribution of the classes. On the stage, clerks, workmen, domestic servants, the poor, victims and prostitutes appear as characters. There is almost nothing of this sort in the novels, once he had failed with the first version of *The Island Pharisees* (Ferrand even reappears eight years later, in the play *The Pigeon*). But, contrary to what might be expected in plays reputed to be 'social', the privileged classes, just as in the novels, form the most numerous and influential group.

However, the working classes are better represented in the plays than in the novels. The upper middle class is rather less well represented, landed gentry and aristocracy much better. The gap between the extremes is wide, the gulf apparently deeper. Two factors alter the relationship, however, both arising from the very nature of the dramatic *genre*. First, Galsworthy's plays give solid, material form to what is only virtual in the novels. Things that never come to much in Hilary, Shelton or Lennan, or that are neutralised by pride and caste spirit in Miltoun, are given freer rein in the drama. The most striking contrasts are between *The Eldest Son* and *The Country House* or *The Patrician*, between *The Show* and *Fraternity*. In two plays, characters take the step that Hilary drew back from in *Fraternity*.

Obviously, a very inaccurate image would be given if it were merely stated that Galsworthy's plays are more 'social' than his novels. In some ways they are less so, in others more. The impression of greater social concern is to some extent an illusion. It arises from the fact that social preoccupations predominate in the plays, though without excluding philosophical considerations. In the novels, various other types of inspiration compete with and contain one another.

It is hard to offer any judgement on the picture Galsworthy

draws of the upper middle class and the nobility. His conception of both these social groups can be seen to have evolved. Edwardian as he was, the First World War caused a profound upheaval in his attitudes.[55] His lessened severity towards the Forsytes as the Chronicles reach their end is attributable to the war and its consequences, not to any political turnabout.

His evolution was even more marked towards the nobility. There is a blatant contradiction between *The Patrician* and *The Country House* on the one hand, and *End of the Chapter* on the other. Which of the two images represents Galsworthy's real opinion? No absolute answer can be given: historical perspective is needed. The lack of any substantial interval between the fictional events and their date of writing detracts from the last two trilogies. It is the novels written earlier, before 1920, that have greater historical value. The picture they present of the upper middle classes is rather different from that of Dickens and Thackeray. But the differences can be explained by the time lapse. The same class is being described, but Dickens and Thackeray showed it in its maturity, and Galsworthy later in life, when its position was comfortably established, and its former inferiority complex had given way to Pharisaic self-congratulation. It was even hobnobbing with the aristocracy, and often marrying into it.

However, even in this historical perspective, Galsworthy's attitude suffered from serious inconsistency. He ended up by restoring some of their virtues to the middle classes, in particular their solidity. On the other hand, it cannot be forgotten that he announced the decline of the Forsytes, and the third generation of the family is indeed not notable for its capacities and achievements in any area. So the image of the upper middle class is historically accurate within the limits of a certain period, approximately 1880 to 1914, although it is rather vague. However, by widening the definition of 'Forsyte' to encompass half or even the whole of the nation, he reflects the fact that in this period the upper middle class reigned supreme.

The image of other social classes in the novels is far less accurate, and even vaguer. There is not a single important character who is of humble condition. The lower middle class is very sparsely represented. Poor people are poor before being human, as Frank Swinnerton accurately pointed out. But they are accorded less space in his novels than Swinnerton's and St John Ervine's criticism might suggest.[56] They are present less as themselves than through uneasiness about them. Strictly speaking, they are almost absent.

These remarks on the novel characters may be concluded with some words by Galsworthy himself, containing a caustic contrast between Conrad and Henry James: 'Henry James drank tea, Conrad wine. Henry James lived imaginatively in a world from which elemental nature and the primitive raw material of human nature were excluded.'[57]

Certain similarities between Galsworthian and Jamesian characters (both have time to think about themselves) make the verdict on James' tea-drinking somewhat rash. But enough attention has been given here to Galsworthy's analysis of instincts, passions and emotions, to show that, like Conrad, he was a wine drinker — though he did not have a very varied cellar.

## LOCATIONS OF ACTION IN THE NOVELS

It is hardly necessary to point out that Galsworthy did not make much use in his writings of his memories of travel. Particularly surprising is the complete absence of any trace of the long voyages he undertook as a young man.

These were followed by others which were entirely a matter of choice. Strikingly little of them appears in his novels. There are more echoes in the short stories, making their exclusion from the longer narratives all the more significant. He may be compared in this with Turgenev, who seldom described his places of exile, and usually evoked only memories of his homeland, offering thereby the example of a strict decision.

It is worth remembering Galsworthy's predilection for three different places: London, Devonshire and the South Tyrol. A division is already apparent in the third novel, *The Island Pharisees*: there are two main places for the action, London and the English countryside. The only subsequent exceptions to this rule are *Fraternity*, which takes place entirely in London, and *The Burning Spear*, near it. The main location of *Jocelyn* is the region of Menton. But even then a significant part of the action occurs in London, foreshadowing the division between the city and the country.

In each novel, either London or the country is the main location. From *The Island Pharisees* on, the country means somewhere in the English provinces, away from towns and cities, and usually near London. The remotest place is Devon.

One of the episodes of *The Island Pharisees* begins below the lowering walls of Dartmoor prison. The action of *The Patrician* takes place in the same region. 'Bucklandbury', the village near Lord Valleys' estate, may be Buckland-in-the-Moor, only five or six miles south of Manaton. Both these villages were and remain full of rural charm, with their surrounding hills and thatched cottages set amid the luxuriant greenery that the mild climate encourages. Galsworthy describes these landscapes. The two contrasting faces of the area, sombre or gay, depending on whether one goes up on to the moor or down to the sea, seem to have corresponded perfectly to his tastes and moods.

He may have found something similar in the more grandiose setting of the Italian Tyrol, which also shows contrast and harmony between the Dolomite mountains and the verdant valleys, with their gentle, civilised landscapes. The Italian Tyrol and Devon come together in the first episode of *The Dark Flower*. *Villa Rubein* is set precisely in an area where the Galsworthys were particularly fond of staying, Cortina d'Ampezzo and San Martino di Castrozza, in the heart of the Dolomites. The episode of the ascension of the Cimone della Pala by Stormer is based on an experience related by Ada Galsworthy.

Memories of the Dolomites are only briefly evoked in *The Dark Flower*, however, and Devon is even more summarily sketched in. The descriptions are lovely, but they reveal almost nothing peculiar to the region. Gyp's honeymoon trip in *Beyond* takes her to Torquay, and there are very brief references to the south coast of Devon and the sea. James and Soames visit Wembury in the Forsyte Chronicles, but Galsworthy sets it in Dorset. (In calling Soames' grandfather 'Superior Dosset', he is deliberately diverting attention, for it is of Devon that he is thinking.)

These are the only images of the South Tyrol and Devon to be found in his novels. It would be impossible for anyone reading only the novels to guess how much Galsworthy loved both these places, and how often he spent long periods in them. This is another instance of his extreme reserve and the economy of the means he employed. It is not only that the descriptions of actual places and their local colour are very limited: he is also always discreet, even secretive. No name of any existing place is given in *The Patrician*; he even prefers the sibylline word 'Moor' to the name Dartmoor.

More is told about the area in his short stories, such as 'A Man of Devon' and 'The Apple Tree'. But only in his poems is Galsworthy's love of his ancestral lands really revealed. It is almost as if the more he loved a place, the more difficult he made it for the reader of his novels to identify. But to those familiar with the area, he offers the pleasurable shock of recognition and rediscovery.

Most of the action of *The Freelands* takes place in the west of England, in Worcestershire, not far from the town of 'Transham', which has not been identified. Galsworthy's own maternal ancestors came from this county, and from Cambridgeshire. This second memory may well explain the choice of 'Mildenham', said to be thirty miles from the Wash, as the country home of Gyp's father, Winton, in *Beyond*. Mildenham is an imaginary name, but there are two Mildenhalls, one of them a small town twenty miles north-east of Cambridge, with a country mansion near it. Finally, the action of *Saint's Progress* begins at Kestrel, near Tintern in Monmouthshire.

Apart from these incursions into Devonshire and the west of England, East Anglia and the Welsh borders, Galsworthy does not move away from London and the Home Counties.

The Forsyte Chronicles take place mainly in London. All the Forsytes of Old Jolyon's generation live around Hyde Park. In the next generation, Soames, more sophisticated, begins the great Edwardian exodus to the suburbs. Chelsea, like Hampstead the favourite abode of artists and writers, is where Irene goes after leaving Soames. Helen Bellew, in *The Country House*, and Audrey Noel, in *The Patrician*, also live there, separated from their husbands, as does Mark Lennan as a young sculptor, in *The Dark Flower*. Those of humbler status, and poor people, do not live in the poorest districts of the capital: the East End is not mentioned in the novels.

Unlike the upper middle class, aristocratic families always have their house in the country and their London residence, like Lord Valleys in *The Patrician*. Galsworthy detects changes in the residential habits of the political class during the Edwardian age. Lady Casterley, Lord Valleys' mother-in-law, lives in the family house on the edge of Richmond Park. This has been so 'ever since it became usual to have a residence within easy driving reach of Westminster'.[58] After the war, Michael Mont, as a Member of Parliament, lives right in Westminster, near the House of Commons.

Soames goes round the world with Fleur, in the hope of making her forget Jon, but there is almost no comment on the voyage. There are other insigificant glimpses of the French Riviera, not to mention Soames' expensive Paris trip.

Galsworthy, then, accorded far less importance to travel in his novels than it had in his own life, and than it had for any well-to-do Englishman — at that time the English were still the world's great travellers. But a certain indifference to locality can be discerned even in the way he talks of London, which is where so much of the action of the novels takes place: at least part of all twenty novels is located there. It is described only succinctly and selectively. He was attracted by the London parks, and fascinated by the quaysides and the river, which are often described. But there is no general picture of the city. What is going on in London is known, the vast murmur of its many activities is heard, its crowds are to be glimpsed, its infinite life is sensed; but the image he provides is subjective and quite incomplete. Very occasionally, a monument, Saint Paul's, where Soames finds something to match his mood, finds a place in the urban scene.

No other English city is described. Scotland, Ireland and Wales are mentioned only as places for holidays. Galsworthy divided the first of his books in which he managed to expound his ideas, *The Island Pharisees*, into two roughly equal parts, the first called 'The Town', and the second 'The Country'. He gave no titles to the two parts of *The Patrician*, but the same two would do, in reverse order. This division and distinction express an essential contrast and duality. Here, as elsewhere, he was trying to get beyond appearances, and transient or formal reality. This reduction of geography to two fundamental and opposing principles is comparable to the division of time into three parts, as happens in most of the novels, in its clearest form in the three episodes of *The Dark Flower*: Spring, Summer, Autumn.

London is 'the Town', as Dartmoor or Robin Hill or Mapledurham are 'the Country', by virtue of the allegorical meaning attributed to each place. By deliberate simplification, Galsworthy goes beyond their individual features, and attains the general and universal. If he finds London a satisfactory symbol for every city, it is because of its immensity and infinite variety of aspect. He liked London the way he liked the novel form, for its malleability and the freedom it gave him. He created places in the same way as he created characters. They are ambivalent; they may be individual, but they are also typical, expressing some general concept.[59] Two major and compatible concerns underlie his presentation: economy of means, learnt in the school of Flaubert and Maupassant; and a search for places, which amount to subjects, that inspire deep enough emotions to allow him to transcend localised realities by making them poetic. His way of describing settings complies with his need for realism, but even more it contributes to the evocative poetic, lyrical, epic or cosmic power of his writing.

## TIME AND ITS LIMITED ROLE AS A FACTOR IN DEVELOPMENT

The Galsworthy novel is not only, nor even always basically, a character study. Development of the personalities of the main characters is therefore less necessary or fundamental than in a psychological novel. No one could know in 1906 that Soames would after many years be given time and opportunity to show the development of his character. This was the development, of course, for which Galsworthy was so criticised, and it arose from the fact that there was a sequel to *The Man of Property*. Soames and Mark Lennan of *The Dark Flower* are the only characters to be given a lifetime in which to grow and change.

One criticism may be made of the development of Soames, but it does not relate to his character. Galsworthy slightly over-intellectualised him in *A Modern Comedy*. This was probably inevitable once he made Soames one of his mouthpieces, after Young Jolyon's death. But it was a betrayal of psychological truth, for Soames, although his intelligence was not limited, was matter-of-fact and rather surly, and should have remained so.

Gyp, the heroine of *Beyond*, has a great deal of personality, but her single-minded, passionate nature rules out any profound changes in her character. Her life may be a series of romantic experiences, a kind of denial of the progression of time.

Remarks on static characterisation apply particularly to the first-generation Forsytes described in *The Man of Property*. When Galsworthy says that death does not enter into their calculations and expectations, it is a satirical way of saying that they are frozen, if not stuffed. But their longevity also has its positive sides.[60]

Galsworthy believed in evolution, but he had little faith in changing human nature, in the short term anyway. The obvious and conclusive reason for the static nature of the characters in his novels is that the plots span too short a time for any development to be visible. This matter of plot duration is examined below.

He did not rule out change in the longer term. An exchange of letters with Hardy contains the idea that a change might be perceptible in the human spirit during one life-span. Hardy wrote that he had 'almost despaired of civilisation making any big step Forward'. Galsworthy replied: 'Underneath the evidence of our barbarism I do cherish the thought that there is an undermining spirit of reason at work. There *has* been an advance even in my experience.'[61] Faced with the pessimism of the man who wrote *Jude the Obscure*, it is interesting to see Galsworthy expressing genuine confidence in progress, or at any rate rational evolution; no more can be asked of him, surely.

## DATING AND TIME-SPAN OF THE ACTION AND ITS CRISES

Galsworthy did not write historical novels. There are few references to historical events. There is the death of Queen Victoria, the First World War, the General Strike of 1926. It is unusual for such events to have any direct bearing on the action. They help place it in a context, but this context has no strict scientific or historical accuracy. It is easier to define negatively than positively. Galsworthy did not write political history, or even social history, but at most a highly selective history of habits and ideas; even here, reservations need to be made. Too much importance should not be attached to dates.

Discussion of dates must not give the impression that time indictions are frequent and always clear. Galsworthy adopted the same parsimonious attitude as with details of the wealth and spending of his characters. It is only on the penultimate page of *Beyond* that the period can be determined exactly as summer 1914: 'This was early in the fateful summer, before any as yet felt the world-tremors, or saw the darkness beginning to gather.'[62] Many such clues to time and date are likely to escape the average reader.

The period of the action is given, or can be deduced, in all novels save three: *Jocelyn, Villa Rubein* and *The Freelands*. The two extremes are 1 August 1880, when *The Dark Flower* starts, and 10 August 1933, when *Over the River* ends. Galsworthy's novels therefore encompass fifty-three years. The undatable novels probably lie within the same limits.

But of the novels, only five take place wholly or partly in the 19th century: *The Dark Flower* (1880–1908), *The Man of Property* (1886–7), *In Chancery* (1895–1901), *Jocelyn* (written in 1898) and *Villa Rubein* (written in 1900). *Fraternity* and *The Patrician* take place during the first decade of the 20th century, *Saint's Progress* and *The Burning Spear* towards the end of the First World War. *Beyond* ends in 1914. *The Freelands* would seem to ante-date the war. The post-war period is described in the last four novels of the Forsyte Chronicles (*To Let* and the second trilogy, *A Modern Comedy*), and in the third trilogy, *End of the Chapter*. In his last novel, *Over the River*, Galsworthy catches up with the present.

The periods of the action of the novels can be divided into three epochs: the end of the Victorian age (the *fin de siècle*), the Edwardian age and after, up to the First World War, and the post-war period. This division produces three groups of novels, with about the same number of each.

Like the period, the duration of the action is known for most novels. Apart from the special case of *The Dark Flower*, which spans twenty-eight years, and *Beyond*, which covers five years and a few months, it never exceeds two years. At the beginning of *In Chancery*, only four pages are devoted to the years 1895 to 1899. The most usual time-span is eight to sixteen months, although *The Island Pharisees* and *The Silver Spoon* last six months, and *To Let* five. The action of *Fraternity* lasts only a month and a day.

The actual duration is even shorter than these figures might suggest, for they are 'crisis' novels. During a crisis, the action may be described almost day by day, but such crises are separated by intervals of up to several months.

Crises often occur towards the end of the various parts. This division into two, four or most often three parts has already been likened to the acts of a play. The crises are of primary importance for the action. Each of them resolves a situation, a problem whose difficulty lay in its latency. It introduces the elements that will ultimately bring another crisis to a head. In general, one crisis erupts in the spring, another in the summer or autumn. The seasons play their part in the progress of love stories: or, at least, their progression corresponds to the phases of love, from its awakening to its decline.

Time, then, has an important function as a framework for the action, as a programming device for the novelist, to be distinguished from the role of time as an immediate element in characters' awareness, and as a factor in their development.

This distinction is not even enough when one begins to study the plot. The reverse of progression and progress prevails here. It is not enough to say that there is no progression. The fact that there is none, and that this is known, is one of the components of the situation, creating a feeling of despondency, dejection, impotence. Fatality weighs upon the protagonist. This is another influence of Greek drama, even more important than the influence noted earlier.

Indications of time vary in number, kind and precision. The largest number of dates is to be found in the Forsyte Chronicles. The year is given in *The Country House* as 1891, then 1892. *Fraternity* is less precise: it begins with the words, 'On the afternoon of the last day of April 190–'. Sometimes, there are clues to the period. For example, the action of *The Island Pharisees* takes place during the Boer War. Chronology is little in evidence in *The Patrician*, and it is only by deduction that the action can be situated in the closing years of Edward VII's reign, probably more or less contemporaneous with the writing of the book. There is talk of the danger of a European war, of aircraft and balloons. Very few dates are given, and they are always incomplete.

The kind of information usually supplied, which defines only the amount of time that has elapsed since an earlier, equally undated event, throws very little light on the matter. The reader has to employ his deductive faculties, his capacity for reconstitution and remain constantly alert, if he is to try and follow the chronology. The possible satisfaction is similar to that of a good detective story. But occasionally the investigation is doomed to failure, because items of information are missing. This may well be deliberate on Galsworthy's part, in order to leave things uncertain, and increase the impression of doubt, mystery and hazard. This effect – and the contrary effect of realism produced by accuracy of detail – may both be sought in turn. For instance, the chronology of *The Country House* is rather vague towards the middle of the narrative, but very precise in the first and third parts.

## PLOT AND INACTION

Galsworthy's plots are usually quite complicated and even, in places, confused. What makes them so is not the large number of facts and actions, but, on the contrary, the lack of any such evidence of day-to-day life. Characters are agitated by emotions and passions, but these are not followed by quick, clear, effectual public action. Quite the contrary: there are more accidents than actions.

The case of Soames, who is in some measure a practical, effective person, if not a man of action (he looks after the whole family's affairs), is once again deceptive. He tends to disguise the usual rift between plot and action. In the three novels that followed *The Man of Property*, namely *The Country House*, *Fraternity* and *The Patrician*, the paradoxical drama of inaction is presented. It is not just a material component of these novels, but the actual subject Galsworthy is pursuing, and out of which he intends to squeeze the last drop of meaning.

This idea and character trait might seem incompatible with the very idea of a fictional narrative. Yet in fact it is not surprising to find them in Galsworthy's novels. As has been seen, he was himself haunted by the spectre of impotence to act, and persistently described its forms, causes and effects, thereby demonstrating his integrity or masochism, or both.

However, the author's own character does not account fully for this theme. There are also intellectual, historical and literary influences. The analysis of *Fraternity* showed that it illustrates the *fin de siècle* atmosphere of decadence, with its indulgence in, or apprehension of 'hamletism' – a word that Galsworthy used in his preface to the Manaton edition of *The Country House*. These influences are strong in all the novels Galsworthy wrote in that period, and probably throughout his career. They have a perhaps regrettable but characteristic effect, mainly on the plots.

Another influence with the same effect is that of Russian literature. The unassuaged longings of the Slav soul were a constant element in the work of the great 19th-century Russian writers, including, in order of importance for their influence on Galsworthy, Turgenev, Tolstoy, Chekhov and Dostoyevsky. The blend of idealism and gloomy resignation so frequent in the Russian novel is of course transmuted by his English temperament and ways. His characters talk far less than their Russian counterparts. They are less lacking in practicality and restraint.

There is a close and special link between Galsworthy and his great Russian contemporaries. All, save Chekhov, were born into privileged sections of society. This creates a very important bond. More than any other English writer of his age, Galsworthy came from the nobility and the upper middle class. This made him eminently fitted to understand the deep-seated disquiet of the Russian élite, at a time when the world it had dominated was slowly collapsing under its feet.

In different ways, the protagonists of *The Country House*, *Fraternity* and *The Patrician* give proof of their powerlessness to act. George Pendyce in *The Country House* is typically unaware, a man whose mistress tells him, 'You and your sort are only half alive!', without his understanding, or even trying to understand, that she is leaving him because he has so quickly bored her. The perfect egoist, incapable of any altruistic, generous or even thoughtful feeling, George turns in on himself, in both happiness and unhappiness; he does nothing to ward off the blows that fall on him, to find friends, seek help from his parents or another member of the family. It is his mother, on her own initiative and almost against his will, who rescues him from the impasse in which he finds himself.

The hero of *Fraternity*, Hilary Dallison, is almost completely and utterly apathetic, incapable of love or hate, powerless to move towards either of the women between whom he is placed. Finally, he quits the country, leaving them both. It is obvious that he will be quite incapable of picking up the pieces of his life. This all-enveloping inertia seems to make him as remote from George Pendyce as from Miltoun. But they all share a trait which could be fundamental: impotence to act. Even Soames, for all his practicality and diversified activities as lawyer, loving father, dutiful son, attentive brother and collector, has a kind of, not impotence, but paralysis of the will, where Bosinney, Irene and later his second wife Annette are concerned.

The hero of the third novel, Miltoun, the dogmatic Patrician obsessed with the rigour of his sense of duty, would seem to be the opposite of George and Hilary. Whereas George, like the bulldog to which he is compared, will not let go of his wife, who no longer wants him, Miltoun is to put his very life in danger by sacrificing his love and his whole private life to his political duty. This sacrifice is the culmination of the plot, coming only after a lengthy period of anguish and uncertainty, which forms the substance of the plot. So, despite the difference of character and situation between George Pendyce and Miltoun, the plot of *The Patrician*, like those of *The Country House* and *Fraternity*, demonstrates its hero's impotence.

Like Galsworthy himself, his heroes tend to be taciturn, not because of any momentary or habitual ill-humour, but because of real isolation from their surroundings. British reserve, always so obvious to the French, for example, was particularly marked in the classes of society described by Galsworthy when he was writing his novels. Observation of this phlegmatic attitude provides an inexhaustible source of interest and sometimes amusement for French readers.

For Galsworthy, it is not just a character trait, but the determining factor in the way he organises the plot. From this point of view, *The Patrician* is the most revealing. It is neither the best, nor one of the worst. But, perhaps because of the milieu he chose, the aristocracy, and the hero's single-minded, exceptional character, the specific features of the plot are easier to discern. They are introduced only very gradually. The facts of the problem are set out coldly in a series of portraits, which give the reader the impression that he is visiting the family home, and looking at pictures of each of the ancestors on the walls of the portrait gallery. He leaves them, only to overhear snatches of conversation, during brief encounters. He feels lost in this huge house, where silence reigns and everyone seems to be avoiding everyone else. Mystery and incomprehension dominate the relationships among those living there. The hero's impotence and indecision are aggravated by ignorance of the real situation, an ignorance that both reader and characters share: 'that grand chasm which yawns between soul and soul remained unbridged,' says the author at the very end of the novel, confirming the inexorable, permanent nature of the situation.[63]

The family suspects that Miltoun is having an affair with a married woman, but no one knows who she is, or the exact situation. How can they find out? Question the person involved? Lady Valleys has always been afraid of her son. However, at her husband's request she takes action: 'Miltoun did not answer, and silence being that which Lady Valleys habitually most dreaded, she took refuge in further speech. . . . Miltoun heard her with his peculiar look, as of a man peering through a vizor. Then smiling, he said, "Thank you" and opened the door.'[64] Will his brother

Bertie do any better? 'Good friends always, they had never much to say to one another.'[65] Finally he does speak, but in vain. Worst of all, when Miltoun learns that he cannot marry Audrey, he leaves her without a word.

Audrey, questioned herself by Lady Casterley, Miltoun's grandmother, who believes she can impose her wishes on him, does not reply. The hero's sister, Barbara, who, in contrast, wants her brother to be happy, visits Audrey too, and asks whether she will not try to free herself from the husband she has left. Once again, Audrey says nothing.

While the action is dragging, and the plot becoming more complicated, a crisis suddenly erupts. Barbara, out of fondness for her brother and anxiety about his state, goes to look for him. Unable to find him, she decides to enter his bedroom, at nightfall. She knocks at the door, with a feeling that she is taking the ultimate risk. Hearing no reply, she enters, and calls out to no effect. 'Dared she now plunge in on this private agony? . . . Flinging away her fears, [she] said "It's me!" . . . Suddenly she felt him slip away from her, and getting up, stole out.'[66]

It is Barbara who later finds Miltoun ill and delirious, alone in London, and who warns Audrey. She hides what she has done from the family. When her bother is out of danger, she informs her mother who, in turn, keeps the secret. Miltoun, completely alone, bears 'in his friendless, proud heart all the burden of struggles which shallower or more genial natures shared with others'.[67]

Galsworthy's *tour de force* is to have used the least likely elements of a kind of hesitation waltz to create dramatic intensity. After slow preparation of the ground, this intensity arises out of the contradictory stages of thought, and the steady growth of feelings and passions, through a kind of unfathomable shift or mutation of circumstances. Miltoun first gives up the woman he loves, then, after his illness, makes her his, and finally leaves her.

All this may seem confused, and it is indeed so, from beginning to end. But it shows precisely how this unusual relation of action to plot emerges in the Galsworthy novel. The plot progresses so fleetingly, in chapters that are sometimes too brief and too numerous, that for a long time it is not clear whether it even exists, or will ever become gripping. Only a partial, fragmented view is ever obtained, as the light of a broken narrative is cast in turn on a character or group of characters, one problem or another, with disconcerting complicatedness. All is shifting. The hero does not

know who he is, he does not know the being with whom passion
brings him suddenly into such intimacy. Each person develops in
his own direction, unpredictably, as the play of circumstance and
chance dictates.

The plot is further complicated by the many relations, friends or
others who intervene, usually verbally. These interventions are, or
at least appear at first to be ineffectual. Someone will say that he
knows something, or believes something else. The rumour spreads,
but without any immediate direct consequence. However, the very
fact of it spreading alters the moods of the main characters, and
introduces a new balance of power. As a result, the drama, so long
contained, gathers and explodes. The unparalleled tension that
prevails in *The Patrician* is present mainly in the second half of the
book, reaching a paroxysm in the last sixty pages. It is only then,
with hindsight, that the reader, in possession of all the components
of the problem, manages to understand the progression of the
action, and realises the emotional and passionate romantic unity
of what had previously seemed so dispersed.

This confusion, obscurity and mystery are created deliberately.[68] Galsworthy was convinced that human life was governed
by the irony of fate. An act intended to obtain a given goal has a
quite different and even opposing result. His plots show the
irrationality of fate, just the action proves man's powerlessness.
Society is as much the realm of the irrational as life, but without its
living, natural beauty. It generates ugliness. Galsworthy sees it as
flawed, and social forms as transient phenomena. For him, the
plot is the meeting and conflict between eternal truths and passing
contingencies.

## THE NOVELIST'S ART[69]

When Galsworthy was writing his novels, he had to maintain the
sense of restraint and balance which his mentor, Edward Garnett,
rightly saw as one of his most outstanding and characteristic
qualities.[70] Given all that is to be found in his prose fiction and
absent from his drama, the plays may be seen as black and white,
and the novels in colour. Of course, the plays do have their own
complexity and divergences. An extreme subjectivity still pervades
them. But they are less multi-dimensional than the novels. They
are over-stated, in contrast with the novels, where an instinctive,

and at the same time deliberate, sense of restraint prevails, intended precisely to harmonise and blend his different inspirations. The difficulty of this task, and the lesser complexity of the plays, are illustrated by information that is available on the time he needed for each: writing a play required a few weeks, while a novel could take more than a year. His romanticism, his cult of beauty, particularly natural beauty, his observance of a liberal, considered and rigorous morality, his humour, his use of well-tried techniques are what gives his prose its plasticity and 'fluidity',[71] its delicacy, and veiled lyrical or sensuous reverberations, conferring a fullness and sureness of touch not to be found in the plays, which, although bold, hazardous attempts that sometimes come off, do not possess the unity of his novels. There is a gulf between his achievements in both these forms. Herman Ould, a man of the theatre, and a friend of Galsworthy who knew his complete dramatic works, puts the same idea in his own expressive terms:

> The reformer in Galsworthy is as evident in the plays as in the novels, but in little else do these two sides of his genius meet. There are a few passages in the novels which might, without alteration, be incorporated in some unwritten play – little scenes whose effectiveness on the stage can be visualised, pages of dialogue, particularly in the later novels, which only a dramatist could have written. From such indications his capacity for writing a play might have been deduced if he had never written one. But his novels could not be justly described, as Bernard Shaw's might have been, as a playwright's novels, nor his plays, as George Moore's might have been, as a novelist's plays. In both forms he wrote as to the manner born; the integrity of each art is perfectly preserved.[72]

Before examining the component features of his art as a novelist, it is worth looking at the overall effect obtained. In 1911, Galsworthy became impatient about the slowness of his breakthrough, and in a letter of complaint about his publisher's lack of vigour, he wrote: 'My own writing has this distinction . . . from the work, say, of James, Meredith, or Conrad – that it is absolutely clear in style, and not in the least exotic, and can be read by the average person without straining the intellect.'[73]

Earlier comments about the novel plots make it impossible to accept fully these claims to clarity. There are different ways of reading Galsworthy, and it is quite possible that some people read him without 'straining their intellect'. But how much of the meaning do they apprehend?

It is clear what Galsworthy means, however, and how it is justified. In opening himself to Meredith's influence, he was careful not to borrow his style. The argument of clarity is perhaps even more valid today than at the time. There is a marked contrast with the obscurity of some of his contemporaries, or of some present-day writers. His renewed popularity, in fact, may arise partly from the fact that his narratives are comprehensible, and form a coherent story. His novels are easier to read than Joyce's or Meredith's, or even Virginia Woolf's or Aldous Huxley's, and equivalent in difficulty to those of Lawrence or Forster.

One cause of difficulty or obscurity is, of course, the intermittent nature of the narrative thread. The main plot is usually flanked by one or more subplots. This multiple structure, which may owe something to Tolstoy's influence, is no guarantee of success, being found even in a mediocre work like *The White Monkey*. Galsworthy offers slices of narration. Retrospection and anticipation are neither frequent nor lengthy, and cause no more complication than in Conrad.[74] However, they do mean that the story has to be pieced together like a jigsaw puzzle.

Even when there is hardly any subplot, the narrative is not continuous, for Galsworthy, influenced without admitting it by Henry James, usually adopts the multiple-viewpoint technique. There is no single narrator. In fact, it might even be said that there are no narrators, for observers such as Young Jolyon, Felix Freeland and Courtier provide very little genuine narration. They are merely witnesses on their own account.

The point of view changes from one chapter to the next, sometimes within the same chapter. Events are related from the point of view of one character, then of another. Each of the main characters can almost be said to have his own chapter or chapters. The self-contained nature of the chapter is sometimes so perfect that it could be likened to a short story, although an extremely brief one. Galsworthy leaves it to the reader to situate the components of the narrative in relation to one another, and link them together. As has already been said, indications of time also make for greater textual difficulty, while increasing interest by their precision. They are often given after the event, irrationally and have to be interpreted.

On the other hand, Galsworthy sometimes makes the reader's task easier by providing an all-embracing view of his subject, right at the beginning of the novel. This is how *The Man of Property* begins. The Forsyte family tree is described and the Forsyte character set forth. *Maid in Waiting* also offers an initial overall view, although it is less expansive. Like the Forsytes, the Charwell family is shown gathered together. The opening lines of *The Country House* contain an especially dense, skilful and lively exposition of circumstances, period, time, place, essential character of the action (the word 'feudal' is used), and an indirect presentation of the main character (through the description of one of his servants):

> The year was 1891, the month October, the day Monday. In the dark outside the railway-station at Worsted Skeynes Mr Horace Pendyce's omnibus, his brougham, his luggage-cart, monopolised space. The face of Mr Horace Pendyce's coachman monopolised the light of the solitary station lantern. Rosy-gilled, with fat close-clipped whiskers and inscrutably pursed lips, it presided high up in the easterly air like an emblem of the feudal system.[75]

These panoramic introductions are brief, never as much as a page. An equally traditional technique is used for individual portraits, which are also limited in length. Galsworthy provides a physical and psychological portrait of each character, usually on his first appearance. They may be extremely short, fewer than six lines, sometimes longer and accompanied by a résumé of the character's past, but even these passages hardly go beyond two pages. They are always written from the omniscient author's point of view. The second part of *Swan Song* begins thus:

> Whether or not the character of Englishmen in general is based on chalk, it is undeniably present in the systems of our jockeys and trainers. Living for the most part on Downs, drinking a good deal of water, and concerned with the joints of horses, they are almost professionally calcareous, and at times distinguished by bony noses and chins.
> The chin of Greenwater, the retired jockey in charge of Val Dartie's stable, projected, as if in years of race-riding it had been bent on prolonging the efforts of his mounts and catching the

judge's eye. His thin, commanding nose dominated a mask of brown skin and bone, his narrow brown eyes glowed slightly, his dark hair was smooth and brushed back; he was five feet seven inches in height, and long seasons, during which he had been afraid to eat, had laid a look of austerity over such natural liveliness, as may be observed in — say — a water-wagtail. A married man with two children, he was endeared to his family by the taciturnity of one who had been intimate with horses for thirty-five years. In his leisure hours he played the piccolo. No one in England was more reliable.[76]

The best portraits are not the most factual ones, but those which, like the one just quoted, create a solid and simple bond between physical and psychological. The portrait of Soames is very soberly executed, with no colouring whatsoever. But it provides a perfect evocation of the man of property. The American critic W. L. Myers perspicaciously points out the sureness, vigour and rapidity with which Galsworthy selects the one trait that will individualise a character: Soames' scornful sniff, Swithin's broad chest, James' rounded shoulders, June and her flaming hair, Cramier's animal-like neck. His skill as a dramatist sometimes emboldens him to add a few expressions to these visual details: James' 'Nobody tells me anything', or Aunt Juley's inevitable gaffes. They add the final touch that brings the character to life. As Myers says, Galsworthy observes traditional methods, while making them evolve: he equals and even surpasses George Eliot in the art of the literary portrait, and shows greater skill than either Wells or Bennett.[77]

However, not all his portraits are so successful. There are some brief physical descriptions that have little point to them. One reason for their weakness is that, even when he wants to make fun of a character, Galsworthy never caricatures him. He cannot bring himself to give someone an uncomely body, deformities or even over-accentuated features. This lack of realism arises from his own feeling of repulsion for ugliness. It reduces his evocative power, and makes it impossible for him to sketch characters with the same ferocious force as Dickens.

Certain psychological portraits confined to a one-line or even one-word definition are also unsatisfactory. At the beginning of *Saint's Progress*, for instance, Nollie is described as 'a darling, but rather a desperate character',[78] while Hilary, the hero of *Fraternity*, is defined in the abstract as 'an intellectual'. Such superficial comments, undramatic presentation and arbitrary statements, to be taken or left, betray occasional flaws in his art as a portraitist.

But what a contrast there is between these moments of stiffness and the portrait of Margery Pendyce, a model of delicacy, a kind of pastel portrait that, in its elegance and clarity, recalls the French 18th century. Another originality is that it forms an integral part of the narrative, and is found, not at the beginning, but towards the end of the novel:

> The first morning song ceased, and at the silence the sun smiled out in golden irony, and everything was shot with colour. A wan glow fell on Mrs Pendyce's spirit, that for so many hours had been heavy and grey in lonely resolution. For to her gentle soul, unused to action, shrinking from violence, whose strength was the gift of the ages, passed into it against her very nature, the resolution she had formed was full of pain. Yet painful, even terrible in its demand for action, it did not waver, but shone like a star behind the dark and heavy clouds. In Margery Pendyce (who had been a Totteridge) there was no irascible and acrid 'people's blood', no fierce misgivings, no ill-digested beer and cider — it was pure claret in her veins — she had nothing thick and angry in her soul to help her; that which she had resolved she must carry out, by virtue of a thin, fine flame, breathing far down in her — so far that nothing could extinguish it, so far that it had little warmth. It was not 'I will not be overridden' that her spirit felt, but 'I must not be overridden, for if I am overridden, I, and in me something beyond me, more important than myself, is all undone.' And though she was far from knowing this, that *something* was her country's civilisation, its very soul, the meaning of its all-gentleness, balance.[79]

Although sometimes subject to criticism in itself, the brevity of his portraits is one of the most general features of his art as a novelist. They could never be taxed with cumbersomeness. It was Henry James, in 1914, who defined this selective skill, putting Galsworthy together with Maurice Hewlett and Edith Wharton among the partisans of choice and intention, and setting this method against the saturation treatment of Bennett and Wells[80] — who indeed do retain far more of the Victorian heaviness.

The lightness and variety of Galsworthy's style can perhaps best be illustrated by examining in detail a passage from *The Man of Property*, in which numbers have been inserted to indicate the different techniques he uses, and how he switches or moves from one to another:

(1) James wiped his napkin all over his mouth.

'You don't know the value of money,' he said, avoiding her eye.

'No! And I hope I never shall!' and, biting her lip with inexpressible mortification, poor June was silent.

(2) Why were her own relations so rich, and Phil never knew where the money was coming from for to-morrow's tobacco. Why couldn't they do something for him? But they were so selfish. Why couldn't they build country houses? (3) She had all that naïve dogmatism which is so pathetic, and sometimes achieves such great results. (4) Bosinney, to whom she turned in her discomfiture, was talking to Irene, and a chill fell on June's spirit. Her eyes grew steady with anger, like old Jolyon's when his will was crossed.

(5) James, too, was much disturbed. He felt as though someone had threatened his right to invest his money at five per cent. Jolyon had spoiled her. None of *his* girls would have said such a thing. James had always been exceedingly liberal to his children, and the consciousness of this made him feel it all the more deeply. (6) He trifled moodily with his strawberries, then, deluging them with cream, he ate them quickly; (7) they, at all events, should not escape him.

(8) No wonder he was upset. Engaged for fifty-four years (he had been admitted a solicitor on the earliest day sanctioned by the law) in arranging mortgages, preserving investments at a dead level of high and safe interest, conducting negotiations on the principle of securing the utmost possible out of other people compatible with safety to his clients and himself, in calculations as to the exact pecuniary possibilities of all the relations of life, he had come at last to think purely in terms of money. Money was now his light, his medium for seeing, that without which he was really unable to see, really not cognisant of phenomena; (9) and to have this thing, 'I hope I never shall know the value of money!' said to his face, saddened and exasperated him. He knew it to be nonsense, or it would have frightened him. What was the world coming to? Suddenly recollecting the story of

young Jolyon, however, he felt a little comforted, for what could you expect with a father like that! This turned his thoughts into a channel still less pleasant. What was all this talk about Soames and Irene?[81]

(1) Scenic, with a mixture of description and dialogue.
(2) An interior monologue by June, in which the dramatic element dominates.
(3) Panoramic: a comment by the author on June, followed by a more general opinion.
(4) Scenic: a conversation is indicated, but not quoted; June's mood is defined, and a slight change in her physical appearance described.
(5) An interior monologue by James, but which tends to turn into a panoramic analysis of his flow of consciousness.
(6) Scenic, describing James' action.
(7) Eight words of interior monologue, expressing a pure state of mind.
(8) Entirely panoramic: the author's eye embraces nearly the whole of James' life and describes it, using this knowledge to explain his present state, then penetrating more deeply, and finally returning to the present, but this time with a general explanation of his mentality.
(9) A gradual transformation of the panoramic view into an interior monologue: these lines repeat the fragment of conversation and give James' reaction to it, then a series of questions that assail his mind, all giving a dramatic character to the interior monologue, which ends with a twinge of his greatest anxiety, as Soames' father.

A single page contains eight modifications of literary technique. Dialogue is confined to two half-lines, which go on echoing throughout the passage. The dramatic tension they express persists and even increases. Visible action is minimal: June is silent, and only her eyes betray her anger; James does not even notice this, engrossed as he is in his own worries. Yet the whole passage, with all its gradations of style, is predominantly dramatic, with the symptomatic reverberations of June's exclamation in James' mind. Everything goes to intensify the crescendo leading to the climax, which is also internal. The dramatic interior monologue is the most significant form of expression, alternating with all the other forms, which contribute to its effect.

This technique is used to greatest effect in passages where Soames is present, often alone. They can cover four or five pages,[82] without ever becoming tiresome. Michael Mont, who also thinks silently on occasion in *Swan Song*, realises how difficult the situation with regard to Fleur is, for both him and Soames: they have chosen the 'hardest of all courses because least active'.[83] To remain silent, take no action, whatever happens: that is what makes the interior monologue dramatic, particularly since the temptation to act has to be surmounted at any moment.

This indirect narration has its psychological justifications. By its continuity, lack of exclamations and hyperbole of any kind, it reflects the thoughtful, reserved, solitary and uneasy character of the protagonists. In particular, it comes very naturally to people who talk little. Galsworthy's heroes are not loquacious. This was typical of the period when they lived, in the class to which they belonged. But it is especially marked in them, as it was in Galsworthy himself. It distinguishes them from Meredith's characters. There are very few chatterboxes, apart from Aunt Juley and Michael Mont.

What could be more vivid than the kind of mute dialogue established between Old Jolyon and his butler, when the butler comes into the dining-room to serve the meal, and finds him apparently asleep? The thoughts of each one about the other are described.[84] The butler's reflections occupy only a few lines. When he felt it suitable, Galsworthy could move into the mind of a minor character, even one who makes only a fleeing appearance. After Soames' death, the thoughts of his faithful employee, old Gradman, are reported in the same way.

The influence of the interior monologue may explain quite a common practice of Galsworthy's: dialogue reported indirectly in the past tense: 'The future — according to Annette — was dark. Were skirts to be longer or shorter by the autumn? If shorter, she herself would pay no attention; it might be all very well for Fleur, but she had reached the limit herself — at her age she would *not* go above the knee.'[85]

Galsworthy may have taken the idea of the interior monologue from Samuel Butler. However, despite the frequency and skill with which he uses it, and the number of characters revealed through his form of expression, not all of them main characters, it does seem that, unless certain conditions exist, Galsworthy does not use it. Is it his violent hostility to Squire Pendyce that explains its absence from *The Country House*, the feeling that no stream of consciousness could be attributed to a man so bereft of ideas, or merely the wish to achieve the greatest possible concision? It is not known. But although the narrative is of a high artistic level, there are a few awkwardnesses of detail in the style, precisely whenever the interior monologue is being avoided.

It is sparingly used in *The Patrician*, and very little in *Fraternity*. Some familiarity seems to be needed between the author and his character (not necessarily sympathy) to make the use of this form of expression possible.

It is not only in the opening pages or in portraits that Galsworthy takes a panoramic view of his subject. He adopts the method whenever he feels like it: hardly surprising on the part of a writer who, while abstaining from any preaching, yet claims to be a philosopher and moralist, and proposes his vision of the world. This is why he sometimes steps back from the character in whom he best managed to express himself. In a startlingly brief and dense sentence, he interrupts Soames' meditations, during a visit to the area his family had sprung from, shortly before his death: 'For a moment he seemed to understand even himself.'[86]

His opinions are expounded with less restraint in *Fraternity*. But even there, he is careful not to over-expatiate:

Like flies caught among the impalpable and smoky threads of cobwebs, so men struggle in the webs of their own natures, giving here a start, there a pitiful small jerking, long sustained, and failing into stillness. Enmeshed they were born, enmeshed they die, fighting according to their strength to the end; to fight in the hope of freedom, their joy; to die, not knowing they are beaten, their reward. Nothing, too, is more to be remarked than the manner in which Life devises for each man the particular dilemmas most suited to his nature; that which to the man of gross, decided, or fanatic turn of mind appears a simple sum, to the man of delicate and speculative temper seems to have no answer.

So it was with Hilary. . . . Inclination, and the circumstances of a life which had never forced him to grips with either men or women, had detached him from the necessity for giving or taking orders. He had almost lost the faculty.[87]

The variety of his talents is further illustrated in the last page of the chapter in *The Country House* entitled 'Mrs Bellew Squares her Accounts', already mentioned for its concision. It shows Galsworthy excelling in a purely scenic, narrative style, without the least personal intrusion:

> Mrs Bellew walked fast down a street till, turning a corner, she came suddenly on a small garden with three poplar trees in a row. She opened its green gate without pausing, went down a path, and stopped at the first of three green doors. A young man with a beard, resembling an artist, who was standing behind the last of the three doors, watched her with a knowing smile on his face. She took out a latch-key, put it in the lock, opened the door, and passed in.
>
> The sight of her face seemed to have given the artist an idea. Propping his door open, he brought an easel and canvas, and setting them so that he could see the corner where she had gone in, began to sketch. . . .
>
> Mrs Bellew came out soon after he was gone. She closed the door behind her, and stood still. Taking from her pocket the bulky envelope, she slipped it into the letter-box; then bending down, picked up a twig, and placed it in the slit, to prevent the lid falling with a rattle. Having done this, she swept her hands down her face and breasts as though to brush something from her, and walked away. Beyond the outer gate she turned to the left, and took the same street back to the river. She walked slowly, luxuriously, looking about her. Once or twice she stopped, and drew a deep breath, as though she could not have enough of the air. She went as far as the Embankment, and stood leaning her elbows on the parapet. Between the finger and thumb of one hand she held a small object on which the sun was shining. It was a key. Slowly, luxuriously, she stretched her hand out over the water, parted her thumb and finger, and let it fall.[88]

Long private discussions are rare. They hardly ever touch on personal problems, but involve exchanges of ideas on subjects of general interest. They are held between the moralist, when there is one, and other characters. Such moralists and observers include Gregory Vigil, Martin Stone, Courtier, Felix Freeland, George Laird and Young Jolyon. Their remarks are sometimes less interesting than other parts of the narrative, for lack of direct connection with the plot. And it is not only in such discussions that the intellectual substance of the novels is to be found.

It is significant that the only long passages of dialogue occur in courtroom scenes. The characters speak under constraint or in the performance of their functions. The following passage from *Over the River* illustrates this kind of dialogue. Scenic comments are reduced to four words, and Clare's responses to her husband's counsel are extremely laconic. The scene could be taken from one of his plays, except that it has nothing tragic about it:

'You saw your husband alone on that occasion?'
'Yes.'
'How did you receive him?'
'Coldly.'
'Having just parted from the co-respondent?'
'That had nothing to do with it.'
'Did your husband ask you to go back to him?'
'Yes.'
'And you refused?'
'Yes.'
'And that had nothing to do with the co-respondent?'
'No.'
'Do you seriously tell the jury, Lady Corven, that your relations with the co-respondent, or if you like it better, your feelings for the co-respondent, played no part in your refusal to go back to your husband?'
'None.'
'I'll put it at your own valuation: You had spent three weeks in the close company of this young man. You had allowed him to kiss you, and felt better for it. You had just parted from him. You knew of his feelings for you. And you tell the jury that he counted for nothing in the equation?'
Clare bowed her head.
'Answer please.'
'I don't think he did.'
'Not very human, was it?'
'I don't know what you mean by that.'
'I mean, Lady Corven, that it's going to be a little difficult for the jury to believe you.'
'I can't help what they believe, I can only speak the truth.'
'Very well! When did you next see the co-respondent?'
'On the following evening, and the evening after that he came

to the furnished rooms I was going into and helped me to dis-
temper the walls.'

'Oh! A little unusual, wasn't it?'

'Perhaps. I had no money to spare, and he had done his own
bungalow in Ceylon.'

'I see. Just a friendly office on his part. And during the hours
he spent with you there no passages took place between you?'

'No passages have ever taken place between us.'

'At what time did he leave?'

'We left together both evenings about nine o'clock and went
and had some food.'

'And after that?'[89]

Galsworthy, though less brilliant and witty than several of his
contemporaries, could handle dialogue most impressively. Professor Gilbert Murray told me that, without ever having been comparable to Shaw as a conversationalist, Galsworthy could write
more natural and realistic conversation than anything to be found
in *Plays Pleasant and Unpleasant*. But he never misused his gift.[90]

In studying Galsworthy's descriptive style, a distinction needs to
be made between indoor and outdoor scenes. His outdoor scenes
are immeasurably more important than the indoor ones. The
novels contain descriptions of interior decoration, furniture,
costumes, hair-styles and jewellery. But they are far from being as
meticulous and extensive as Robert Liddell claims in *A Treatise on
the Novel*, where he quotes Galsworthy's style as an example of
what not to do in this respect.[91] Arnold Kettle shows Liddell's
misapprehension, and rightly points out how Galsworthy enriches
his characterisation of the Forsytes by describing their furniture
and their favourite dish, saddle of mutton.[92]

But he does not properly discuss the actual technique of description. Galsworthy's settings are evoked far more than described.
That was enough for his contemporary readers. Nowadays, the
illustrations of Anthony Gross for *The Forsyte Saga* or, even better,
Donald Wilson's television film are needed to recreate the world of
the novels. To grasp the full richness of the text without such aids
requires imagination and thorough knowledge of the period.

Here is the description of the drawing-room when the Forsytes
meet. Old Jolyon enters:

> He found the front drawing-room full. It was full enough at
> the best of times — without visitors — without any one in it — for

Timothy and his sisters, following the tradition of their generation, considered that a room was not quite 'nice' unless it was 'properly' furnished. It held, therefore, eleven chairs, a sofa, three tables, two cabinets, innumerable knicknacks, and part of a large grand piano.[93]

It would hardly be possible to write more deftly. Far from becoming bogged down in details, Galsworthy sketches in the characteristic overburdening of Victorian decoration.

The same lightness of touch is to be found in outdoor descriptions; and no visual aids are needed to perceive all their shades and detail. One needs only to share Galsworthy's vivid feeling for nature, and his sense of the poetic. The setting nearly always plays an important role. Even *Fraternity*, the most urban of the novels, evokes nature, greenery, spring, with its glimpses of Hilary's garden and the London parks. Perhaps because of the rage that fills it, *The Island Pharisees* contains fewest factual or poetic elements of this kind. Galsworthy was temporarily blinded to what informed his love of nature. The bitterness and satire of *The Burning Spear* have the same effect. All the other novels reflect these feelings. They are most intense in novels like *The Dark Flower*, *The Patrician* and *The Freelands*.

Another distinction has to be made: what Galsworthy loves and describes is nature rather than the countryside. And those familiar with the London skies and its river, who stroll in its parks and appreciate the nocturnal spectacle of the city, know that nature is continually present. Galsworthy was such a person.

There are limitations on his vision of the rural or urban landscape, however. He describes the seasons, in which he sees the forces of nature revealed, except for winter, which he did not like. He normally left England before the bad weather, and did not return until the spring. He was not fond of the sea either, and there are little more than occasional glimpses of it in the background of a novel. Despite the importance he attached to farming, and his work in the fields at harvest time, his vision of the country is not entirely realistic. He sees it from the point of view of a rambler and poet, not as a farmer, even a gentleman farmer. Only gardeners were ever under his orders, and he never ran an estate. He talks very little of the soil, not saying whether it is good or bad, heavy or light, never notices weeds, nettles, thistles or briars. Farms, villages, country houses seldom appear in his narratives.

(The house built by Bosinney at Robin Hill is the only one to be described in detail.) But he often describes wild or cultivated flowers, gardens, meadows, streams, heathland, shrubberies, orchards, and above all the great trees that add such majesty to English woodland scenery. Like Turgenev, he loved woods, and described them wonderfully.[94] He was also aware of hills.

His landscapes are inhabited by domestic animals, dogs and horses, and cattle, and by wild animals, mainly birds. There are also bees, and sometimes moths.

The dominant component of his descriptions is light, rather than colour. He likes to follow its constantly shifting play and effects, as sun, moon and stars come and go. Night holds a fascination for him. The scents and smells that are so redolent in moments of great passion enrich the perception of the world. Noises are less appreciated, and he often makes an almost religious silence reign.

The Galsworthian landscape is not a fixed composition; it is a changing vision rather than a picture. Its outlines are shifting, its appearance ephemeral. It is usually evoked in ten to twenty lines, seldom more than a page. Only the great scene in the second part of *The Dark Flower*, immediately before the death of Olive, consists of a succession of admirable images and episodes.

The vision has lyrical and dramatic, rather than plastic, unity, for it is never a mere setting, a décor. It blends with a state of mind, a situation, although it is never possible to say whether it is man who loses himself in nature, or nature which reflects human thought. Without there being firm evidence, this probably shows the influence of Hardy. Like the plot, the landscape is full of mystery. Nature is in turn indifferent, cruel, smiling, divine, feminine, in voluptuous collusion with the scene. But it always offers a spectacle of extraordinary beauty — thereby distinguishing Galsworthy from Hardy.

A few passages will illustrate the great charm of his descriptions and the components that contribute to it:

A misty radiance clung over the grass as the sun dried the heavy dew; the thrushes hopped and ran and hid themselves, the rooks cawed peacefully in the old elms. . . .
George lagged behind, his hands deep in his pockets, drinking in the joy of the tranquil day, the soft bird sounds, so clear and friendly, that chorus of wild life. The scent of the coverts stole to him, and he thought:

'What a ripping day for shooting!'

The Squire, wearing a hat carefully coloured so that no bird should see him, leather leggings, and a cloth helmet of his own devising, ventilated by many little holes, came up to his son; and the spaniel John, who had a passion for the collection of birds almost equal to his master's, came up too.

'You're end gun, George,' he said; 'you'll get a nice high bird!'

George felt the ground with his feet, and blew a speck of dust off his barrels, and the smell of the oil sent a delicious tremor darting through him. Everything, even Helen Bellew, was forgotten. Then in the silence rose a far-off clamour; a cock pheasant, skimming low, his plumage silken in the sun, dived out of the green and golden spinney, curled to the right, and was lost in undergrowth. Some pigeons passed over at a great height. The tap-tap of sticks beating against trees began; then with a fitful rushing noise a pheasant came straight out. George threw up his gun and pulled. The bird stopped in mid-air, jerked forward, and fell headlong into the grass sods with a thud. In the sunlight the dead bird lay, and a smirk of triumph played on George's lips. He was feeling the joy of life.[95]

After this passage from *The Country House* comes another from *The Forsyte Saga*:

It was that famous summer when extravagance was fashionable, when the very earth was extravagant, chestnut-trees spread with blossom, and flowers drenched in perfume, as they had never been before; when roses blew in every garden; and for the swarming stars the nights had hardly space; when every day and all day long the sun, in full armour, swung his brazen shield above the Park, and people did strange things, lunching and dining in the open air. Unprecedented was the tale of cabs and carriages that streamed across the bridges of the shining river, bearing the upper-middle class in thousands to the green glories of Bushey, Richmond, Kew, and Hampton Court. Almost every family with any pretensions to be of the carriage-class paid one visit that year to the horse-chestnuts at Bushey, or took one drive amongst the Spanish chestnuts of Richmond Park. Bowling smoothly, if dustily, along, in a cloud of their own creation, they would stare fashionably at the antlered heads which the great slow deer raised out of a forest of bracken that promised to autumn lovers such cover as was never seen before. And now and again, as the amorous perfume of chestnut flowers and fern was drifted too near, one would say to the other: 'My dear! What a peculiar scent!'[96]

The other two passages are more purely descriptive, although they fit into the narrative, particularly the second. First, here is the end of a day's shooting spent by Squire Pendyce's guests, showing an apparently Keatsian influence:

> The sun had fallen well behind the home wood when the guns stood waiting for the last drive of the day. From the keeper's cottage in the hollow, where late threads of crimson clung in the brown network of Virginia creeper, rose a mist of wood smoke, dispersed upon the breeze. Sound there was none, only that faint stir — the far, far callings of men and beasts and birds — that never quite dies of a country evening. . . . But a gleam of sunlight stole down the side of the covert and laid a burnish on the turned leaves till the whole wood seemed quivering with magic.[97]

Finally, there is another evocation of night-fall, as Mark Lennan awaits Olive, the whole of nature seeming also to be hushed and waiting:

> All wind had failed, and the day was fallen into a wonderful still evening. Gnats were dancing in the sparse strips of sunlight that slanted across the dark water, now that the sun was low. From the fields, bereft of workers, came the scent of hay and the heavy scent of meadow-sweet; the musky odour of the backwater was confused with them into one brooding perfume. No one passed. And sounds were few and far to that wistful listener, for birds did not sing just there. How still and warm was the air, yet seemed to vibrate against his cheeks as though about to break into flame. That fancy came to him vividly while he stood waiting — a vision of heat simmering in little pale red flames.[98]

The flames that pass through Mark's imagination fuse two elements in the novelist's art, description and poetry. By its descriptiveness and poetic inspiration, *The Dark Flower* is predominantly a lyrical novel. It is regrettable that the American critic Ralph Freedman omitted to mention it in his remarkable study of the *genre*; whereas the poet and novelist Richard Church was more penetrating when he wrote:

Galsworthy . . . was an artist of sombre, almost feline sensuousness beneath his austere stoicism. His prose is like warm burgundy, poured into a glass of irony that instantly clouds at the contact. His *Dark Flower* (1913) is a novel written in a romantic intensity comparable to the poetic fervour which inspired Edith Wharton's *Ethan Frome* and Compton Mackenzie's *Guy and Pauline*. Here are three novels permanent in our literature, as single as perfect lyrics.[99]

*The Dark Flower* is Galsworthy's longest prose poem, and one of his finest, but there are shorter ones that are even more purely lyrical. These are brief sketches in which narrative tends to disappear. It is a pity that they were not included in the collection entitled *Caravan*, and can be found only in old editions inaccessible to the general public. Galsworthy was wrong to abandon them to their fate. They are among the most delightful, original and modern texts he ever wrote, and would serve well as a counterweight to over-simplified opinions of his art or lack of it.[100]

Symbolism is important. The flames seen and felt by Mark are the symbol of his destructive love for Olive. The tree he climbs with Sylvia, and where they spend some idyllic moments, is symbolic of their union and future happiness. The silver spoon that makes Fleur such a privileged child symbolises the ancient fortune of England, which is being dissipated, despite the country's reluctance to admit it. As Myers points out, Robin Hill is also a symbol, offering a dozen different interpretations, which combine in the word 'beauty'. Certain aspects of nature become symbols, to be found throughout Galsworthy's writings, thus becoming a kind of language, creating an atmosphere. Woods and orchards in bloom lend their own magic to the love scenes that take place there.

Symbols lose their artistic force when they are over-explicit, and become tiresomely over-simplified allegories. This is the case of the spaniel John in *The Country House*. Every appearance of the creature illustrates faithfulness to his master. The storms that accompany or presage unhappy events are also overdone.

It is not in accordance with the conventional image of Galsworthy to recognise an element of the supernatural in his work. It exists, particularly in some of the sketches already mentioned, describing trance-like states.[101] Such effects are sometimes found in the novels. Soames' mind is haunted for some time by the face of his dead rival Bosinney. Irene returns to Robin Hill, probably to seek a mystic contact with her lover's shade. However, Galsworthy rightly shows circumspection in introducing such elements into his long narratives. In all the descriptive and poetic passages, in fact, he shows the restraint and deftness that pervade all his work. Despite his great admiration for the work of W. H. Hudson, he does not adopt his descriptive style. *Green Mansions* is continuously or at least consistently descriptive; this is quite unlike Galsworthy's method. It is Hudson's vivid feeling for nature that influences him, however different the landscapes described by the two writers.

Finally, there is the comic aspect of Galsworthy's art. The very existence of such a vein is contested by Swinnerton, while Ould devotes only a few pages to it.[102] It is being considered here as something that is not of major importance. Analysis of the novels has shown that the plots are by no means comic. Comedy seems marginal and almost paradoxical, in view of Galsworthy's own disquiet and the tensions that prevail in his narratives. It does exist, however, and systematic investigation reveals many examples. It is one of the hidden aspects of this strange and Protean writer. Here too, there is a great contrast between plays and novels, which offer far more comic shades of meaning. None of the twenty-seven plays is an outright comedy, despite the Wildean and Shavian influences apparent in them.

His commonest forms of comedy are devoid of any gaiety. They involve satire and dramatic irony. Satire plays a negligible or slight role in the first two novels, but appears in its most virulent forms in the following ones: *The Island Pharisees*, *The Man of Property* and *The Country House*. It is found again in *In Chancery*, but from *To Let* on, it becomes steadily milder. Its role is reduced, though still significant, in the five 'lyrical' novels. It predominates in *The Burning Spear*.

This satire is itself complex. Humour is combined with it in varying proportions. The portraits of heroes, as has been seen, all contain something autobiographical. When he is speaking of himself in this way, Galsworthy is humorous, and keeps his emotions in check. This is particularly noticeable in Young Jolyon, Felix Freeland, then Michael Mont, who display a gentle, kindly irony, inspired by their creator's own sense of restraint and

measure. Soames is not the object of the fiercest satire. Even in
*The Man of Property*, he is not systematically blackened. In contrast, Squire Pendyce and the Reverend Barter, his friend and
ally, are treated ferociously, though Galsworthy never becomes
peevish in his condemnation. Here is the Squire's creed, which
some might well regard as blasphemous:

> I believe in my father, and his father, and his father's father,
> the makers and keepers of my estate; and I believe in myself and
> my son and my son's son. And I believe that we have made the
> country, and shall keep the country what it is. And I believe in
> the Public Schools, and especially the Public School that I was
> at. And I believe in my social equals and the country house, and
> in things as they are, for ever and ever. Amen.[103]

The mediocrity of the Reverend Barter's oratorical gifts and
intellectual faculties is more cruelly depicted:

> God — he said — wished men to be fruitful, intended them to
> be fruitful, commanded them to be fruitful. God — he said —
> made men, and made the earth; He made man to be fruitful in
> the earth; He made man neither to question nor answer nor
> argue; He made him to be fruitful and possess the land. . . .
> God had set bounds, the bounds of marriage, within which man
> should multiply, and that exceedingly — even as Abraham
> multiplied. In these days dangers, pitfalls, snares, were rife; in
> these days men went about and openly, unashamedly advocated
> shameful doctrines. Let them beware. It would be his sacred
> duty to exclude such men from within the precincts of that
> parish entrusted to his care by God. . . . They were not brought
> into this world to follow sinful inclination, to obey their mortal
> reason. God demanded sacrifices of men. Patriotism demanded
> sacrifices of men, it demanded that they should curb their in-
> clinations and desires. It demanded of them their first duty as
> men and Christians, the duty of being fruitful and multiplying,
> in order that they might till this fruitful earth, not selfishly, not
> for themselves alone. It demanded of them the duty of multiply-
> ing in order that they and their children might be equipped to
> smite the enemies of their Queen and country, and uphold the
> name of England in whatever quarrel, against all who rashly
> sought to drag her flag in the dust.[104]

Although satire is less violent in *The Forsyte Saga*, it appears there in more varied, concrete and numerous forms. It contains an unparalleled number of comic characters: Aunt Juley, James and (except at the beginning) June, with their fads and oddities; George, a wag and buffoon; Montague Dartie, a gay Lothario always short of the ready; Timothy, who keeps out of sight to avoid infection; and Swithin, the least cultivated of the Forsytes.

The most comic work after the Saga is *A Modern Comedy*, but the inspiration is different. The endless chatter of Michael Mont and his father, Sir Lawrence, who are more sophisticated than the Forsytes, more aristocratically dashing, gives it lightness and joviality. But only the second novel, *The Silver Spoon*, justifies calling the whole trilogy 'a modern comedy'. The theme of the novel is not comic, particularly when the image of the silver spoon, which Fleur is assumed to have been born with, is widened to apply to the whole English nation, unaware that its age of supremacy is gone, and that it is living beyond its means. The threats are not imminent, however, and in the meantime people enjoy themselves to the full. The quarrel between Fleur and Marjorie, Soames' intervention, the libel suit, the squabble between Michael and Sir Alexander MacGowan, are all related in a facetious tone, unusual for Galsworthy. Marjorie, her uncle the Marquess of Shropshire, and the theoretician Sir James Foggart are presented largely in a humorous way. But before the end of the novel it is learnt that a fresh crisis in Fleur's life is gathering, and the tone changes. *The Silver Spoon* is a long interlude between two more sombre narratives.

Finally, the main inspiration of *The Burning Spear* is satirical. But its humour is so weighed down with bitterness that it becomes absurd.

Galsworthy uses the device of dramatic irony in his satirical passages. Under the influence of Greek drama, he likes to show the vanity of men's efforts. In trying to regain possession of Irene, Soames pushes her into Jolyon's arms. He spends huge amounts to have her shadowed, only to be taken for her lover himself, because of the way he keeps following her. Finally, having sacrificed everything to have a son, he is presented with a daughter.

Galsworthy is also fond of parody, particularly to mock the press, lawyers and politicians. Word play and wit are less common. He possesses a certain gift for describing a comic situation, such as the collision between Swithin's phaeton and a costermonger's cart,

Soames' conversation with a hitch-hiker, the mosquito hunt in *The Dark Flower*, and the sight of Fiorsen falling into a trap in *Beyond*. Occasionally, Galsworthy is quite ready to indulge in action comedy.

Restraint, delicacy, lightness, variety and lyricism are Galsworthy's essential qualities as a novelist, and contribute to the mellowness and soft charm of his novels. They were not accidental, but were deliberately cultivated by him. So it is not surprising to find a description by him of the novel *genre* containing not the slightest trace of the 'materialism' Virginia Woolf so bitterly attacked in him: 'The novel is the most pliant and far-reaching medium of communication between minds. . . . The novel supplies revelation in, I think, the most secret, thorough, and subtle form.'[105]

The most striking, and certainly the most penetrating of Galsworthy's verdicts on his own writing was entered in his diary on Christmas Day 1910:

> [*The Patrician*] discloses me . . . as an impressionist working with a realistic or naturalistic technique, whereas Wells is a realist with an impressionistic technique, Bennett a realist with a realistic technique, Conrad an impressionist with a semi-impressionistic, semi-naturalistic technique, and Forster an impressionist with a realistically impressionistic technique.[106]

His use of the word 'naturalistic' could lead to misapprehension of the extent of French influence, which I have been at pains not to exaggerate. Realism also has its limits, which have been pointed out in various areas. But it does exist, particularly if one admits, as Galsworthy here himself does, that it is a *means*. The word 'impressionism' can, of course, be criticised when it is used in the context of literature. However, in this case, it is accurate. It reflects his constant quest for beauty, and the highly personal character of his works, a 'spiritual examination', an immediate vision, even where the most general and objective problems are involved.

But however accurate, it is inadequate as a definition of Galsworthy's complex art, which blends traditionalism with a modernism that is only beginning to be appreciated. It is an imperfect but original combination. In his symbolism, he is perhaps closer to the Pre-Raphaelites than to the Impressionists. However, the pervading sense of restraint in his narratives is somehow reconciled with their romanticism. This rules out any exaggeration, the extravagances of Lawrence's vitalism, Virginia Woolf's creative but vacillating subjectivism, or James Joyce's abstruseness.

# 8 Galsworthy's Philosophy and Outlook

## THE INFLUENCE OF DARWIN AND FREUD ON GALSWORTHY'S NOVELS

Evolutionary theories had a deep-widespread and complex effect on Galsworthy's novels. There is no evidence that he had read Darwin. He is only known to have read Samuel Butler,[1] whose *God the Known and God the Unknown* reflects an extremely independent-minded Darwinism. Butler rejected the mechanistic concept of natural selection, believing it to be enlightened by an intuitive sense. Galsworthy had his own reservations about Butler, particularly his view of God. Despite the lack of evidence, it would be wrong to conclude that Galsworthy had not read a lot about Darwinism, one of the great controversies throughout the second half of the 19th century, and even later.

His evolutionary ideas were personal in several ways, but on the whole he appears to have adopted the main principle introduced by Darwin. The idea of change is omnipresent in his work, and is expressed with great frequency in the novels. The closing words of *The Freelands* are 'The world is changing . . .'. In the Forsyte Chronicles, the succession of generations is presented as marking stages in the process. In the contemporary world, as Soames observes in *A Modern Comedy*, England still shows her capacity for adaptation. The word 'evolution' is actually used as the title for a short story published in a collection in 1912.[2]

But although he hardly questioned evolution in the plant and animal world, and in the history of societies, he denied its validity for human nature. Yet his belief in the immutability of man was not absolute, as has been said. This reveals a certain contradiction in his ideas, which he did not try to gauge exactly, or lessen.

Although he observed an evolution in contemporary civilisation, he was uncertain about what direction it was taking, and

175

this was why he was so often severe in his judgements. Courtier denounces the crimes committed by the rich under the banner of natural selection. 'Evolution! It's the devil!' cries the hero of *Exiled*, who has suffered in this way.[3] The cabman in 'Evolution', ruined by the arrival of the motor-car, is another victim of 'progress'. In the two poems 'Pitiful' and 'Akin', man's cruelty to animals is shown to be unforgivable, since this new knowledge has brought the animal world so much closer to the human. It is in *Fraternity* that his thoughts on evolution, and the protest against some of its forms, are given widest scope. The old biologist Sylvanus Stone, who has become a prophet of fraternity, laments the way the human mind has destroyed the whole meaning of the evolutionary process, and turned the country into a butcher's shop.[4] These violent terms illustrate Galsworthy's rejection of a brutal Victorian conception of Darwinism. As W. E. Houghton points out, it was used to justify the crushing of the feeble by the strong.[5] The weakest went to the wall.

'I [am] an evolutionist, who fundamentally distrusts violence,' Galsworthy told an American audience.[6] In view of his political attitudes, it is clear that his idea of selection is itself selective and highly qualitative: 'Social and political growth is, in fact, a process of evolution, controlled, directed, spiritualised by the supreme principle of Equity.'[7]

This spiritual energy, called 'a need for justice' in *A Sheaf*, is in fact extremely ill-defined. Whatever its nature, Galsworthy's conception of it brings him closer to Lamarck, Butler, and perhaps even Bergson,[8] than to Darwin. The idea of progress is ultimately presented as possible, if not probable: 'The world has an incurable habit of going on, with possibly a tendency towards improvement in human life.'[9]

William Bellamy examines the influence of Darwinian theories on Galsworthy, from a historical rather than philosophical standpoint.[10] In the history of the ideas of the period he is examining, from 1890 to 1910, he distinguishes three stages through which he believes the three Edwardian novelists passed in their novels: the *fin de siècle*, the period of anguished awareness of the post-Darwinian predicament, both disturbing and liberating; the early years of the 20th century, a period of transition; and finally the full Edwardian period, 1905–10. The Edwardians overcame the feeling of decline of the end of the century, and began anew. By discovery of the vital force that animates the human spirit, they affirmed man's right to seek health and well-being as an end in itself, independent of both religious dogmas and social goals. After 'medicalisation' of the body came 'utopianisation' of thought.

From this point of view, the 'Georgian' interpretation of their 'Edwardian' predecessors is seen to be wrong. The interest shown by Wells, Bennett and Galsworthy in analysing facts and social problems does not signify any resigned acceptance of determinism. For them, such an analysis is not an end, but a means. Their assertion of man's right to live for himself, far from taking English literature into a blind alley, carried it forward. It opened up the way for those who, in the name of art and individual freedom of conscience, were to pour scorn on these pioneers.

Bellamy's thesis, itself evolutionary in spirit, leads him to reject the dogmatic verdict of the Georgians on Galsworthy. By replacing him in the history of ideas, he emphasises the very modern aspect of his writing. This thesis thus coincides with my own on a most important point. We also agree on the significance to be attached to Galsworthy's social concern.

The limitations of his study need to be stated, however. Two of the three 'Edwardians' wrote only one novel before 1900, in the very last years of the century. In the case of Galsworthy, the period Bellamy is studying encompasses only five of the twenty novels – and he concentrates his attention on only four of these. His remarks on *The Man of Property* and *Fraternity* are excellent. On *The Country House*, he is brief but penetrating. His grasp of *Jocelyn* is uncertain. In no case does he study every aspect of the novels, confining himself strictly to his own point of view.

He follows traditional views, in suggesting that Wells, Bennett and Galsworthy are essentially Edwardians, and claims that they have many points in common, resembling one another more than they differ. But his erudite history of the actual theory of this 'triadic grouping'[11] from 1902 to the present day does not prove its validity.

For Galsworthy, Bellamy's investigation is both more and less fruitful than when applied to Wells and Bennett. It is less so, to the extent that 'utopianisation' is less noticeable than in the case of the other two; and more so, because the 'post-Darwinian' and 'post-Freudian' upheaval affected him more deeply and brutally than his two contemporaries, who had less to lose than a member of the formerly privileged classes.

Bellamy's most interesting comments are to be found in his chapter on Galsworthy during the full Edwardian period. All the novels under examination, with their many indications of decline, would be more characteristic of the *fin de siècle*. In other words, Galsworthy's career as a whole confirms Bellamy's views, but not the detailed division into three periods. Bellamy finds the third, 'activist' period difficult to prove in his case.

Bellamy's dialectic goes deeply into the intellectual components and causes of the phenomenon. Galsworthy's philosophy is nearly always hidden in his novels. They contain none of the information about sources, authors' names, titles and many abstract terms that help the reader of Meredith, for example, to follow his reflections step by step. Yet the Galsworthian philosophy *is* available to anyone who looks for it. His letters and essays offer many illuminating insights, and the rest can be deduced from his fiction. On the problem under consideration, the existence, if not of an 'activist period', at any rate of an 'activist' or, to put it more simply, optimistic aspect in Galsworthy's outlook, resources are not lacking. Bellamy fails to use them. It is not enough to confine oneself to the novels, much less to only some of them.

Galsworthy admitted that he had not studied psychoanalysis, and had read very little of Freud. He reported the interest that the Freudian 'doctrine' aroused, but he was rather irritated himself with it, as he was by any system. This was his theoretical viewpoint. His character analyses show that he had assimilated a number of the simplest and most important Freudian concepts. It is this influence that is partly responsible for the predominant position he attributed to sexuality in psychological life. Although he does not describe the most external manifestations, this should not disguise the importance he attached to it. As already pointed out, he was particularly good at describing insurmountable sexual incompatibilities and states of frustration. The portrait of June, and the story entitled 'Spindleberries', give examples of eccentricity arising from such frustration. Mrs Pendyce illustrates the link between sexuality and maternal love, another compensatory phenomenon. He refers to George's surprise at seeing his mother half-undressed.

Finally, in view of his aversion for generalisations, and his own reticence in this particular area, it is most significant that he emphasised the bond between the aesthetic sense and sex.[12]

Going further than Houghton, who had already drawn attention to Freud's influence on scepticism at the beginning of the century, Bellamy interprets this influence, which he discerns in his three Edwardian novelists.[13] More concretely, the relative lack of respect for the family in *The Forsyte Saga* probably reflects the Freudian point of view, even more than any hold Samuel Butler may have had on Galsworthy's imagination.

## GALSWORTHY'S POLITICAL OUTLOOK

Galsworthy claimed that he was not a politician, and even that he had no political beliefs. Few men, he argued, were less concerned with politics than himself, and he said that he had never believed enough in any political remedies to belong to any party. He insisted that he was 'neither Tory, Liberal nor Socialist'.[14]

But beyond these statements and principles, the actual situation is less simple. In his childhood, as he admitted, the environment in which he lived had the influence on him that might be expected. Referring to his memories of a visit by the great Gladstone to Harrow, when he was a pupil there, he wrote: 'We were reactionaries almost to a boy.'[15]

Galsworthy gives no account of his emancipation from these conservative views. The novels contain a single allusion to the return of the Liberals to power in 1906. The importance of the event is underlined by the use of the word 'resurrection' to describe it. It was the social, not the political aspect of the event that he was referring to.[16] However, his correspondence shows how caught up he was in the passions that rocked Britain at the time, and even more so when the House of Lords was stripped of some of its power in 1911.

A rather comic episode is recalled in an undated letter addressed to a 'local clergyman'.[17] This was the minister of the parish of Manaton in 1910. The two men seem to have had little in common in their views about the House of Lords, as on many other problems. Several stormy discussions took place during visits to Wingstone. Finally, Galsworthy asked his adversary to end these exchanges, which were only upsetting them both.

Dudley Barker points out that the collection of short stories *A Commentary*, and the novel *Fraternity*, appeared at the time.[18] Reforms were in the air, and Socialism was becoming a threat, or at any rate an eventuality. The government was drawing up social measures, designed to attenuate the evils written about by Galsworthy. So he cannot have been too surprised to be the object of violent political attack, and to be counted among the 'rabid Liberals'. He even referred himself to his 'radical reputation'.[19] On 14 January 1910, he wrote from Manaton to the local newspaper to announce that, if his name had not by mistake been struck off the electoral register for the mid-Devon constituency, he would have voted Liberal and against the House of Lords.

Paradoxically, this was his only formal act of support for the Liberal Party. There are other signs. Can his attendance at the ceremony in 1921 to celebrate the centenary of the *Manchester Guardian*, the main Liberal paper, have been pure chance? A man as deliberate as he is hardly likely just to have turned up. He was opposed to the maintenance of British power in Ireland by force.[20] Already in 1904, he had roundly denounced imperialism in *The Island Pharisees*: 'Why should *we*, a small portion of the world's population, assume that our standards are the proper ones for every kind of race?'[21] He was to issue a far more sustained and open denunciation in his play *The Mob*, in 1914. The play recreates the atmosphere in which Britain entered the Boer War, though it is never named. More, the hero, sacrifices his political career, then his life, by refusing to be a party to the attack on a small country whose only crime is to want to preserve its independence.

He attacked imperialism for the third time in 1922, in the play *The Forest*. It is a particularly interesting play, marking as it does the extreme point reached by his political philosophy, using more contemporary terms. The play is an outright condemnation of large-scale capitalism. In his London office, the millionaire Adrian Bastaple, the most out-and-out scoundrel of all Galsworthian characters, decides the fate of an African territory which offers a chance of aggrandizing his personal empire. The Foreign Office is called in. Missionaries will be sent out. An expedition is dispatched to outsmart the Belgian rivals. All its members die — a regrettable oversight! Unfortunately, the play is no good. However, to make assurance doubly sure, part of the press trounced it.[22]

Galsworthy spoke out against militarism and arms dealers in more general terms during the First World War,[23] and in favour of internationalism. He was no late convert: in 1914 he had declared himself expressly in favour of a peaceful league of nations and an international armed force.[24]

In 1911, however, he was in disagreement with Liberal policy on the parliamentary bill to redefine the role of the House of Lords. Galsworthy was in favour of abolishing the hereditary principle, but was opposed to the government bill because, he felt, it simply removed the upper chamber. He wanted a second chamber, holding real though limited powers.

The idea he expounded from then until the end of his life was that political institutions should be designed to diminish party friction and acrimony. He supported this view in correspondence with Edward Garnett and Gilbert Murray, both of whom were more progressive, and who tried vainly to influence him.

Only too often, refusal of the party system has concealed something far more sinister. In Galsworthy's case, there was no ulterior motive: his opinion came from a kind of fatalism.[25]

His correspondence reveals that he applied philosophical and even metaphysical beliefs to political ideas. There is the same anti-intellectualism and fatalism already detected in the analysis of several of his novels. The discussion at the beginning of *The Patrician* between Miltoun, representing the spirit of authority, and Courtier, representing the liberal attitude,[26] ends with neither side victorious. Reason has failed. Galsworthy seems incapable of reaching a decision.

At the very least, he shows a striking lack of practical sense. He did not have the basic rationalism, or at any rate optimism, that seems to be a necessary condition for any firm belief in democracy. He had not been formed by the French writers of the Enlightenment — Voltaire is the only 18th-century French writer to be mentioned in his writings. What is more discernible is the influence, however indirect, of 19th-century German metaphysical thinkers, Hegel and perhaps Schopenhauer. But the intellectual element of his beliefs should not be exaggerated. It is worth remembering that, on his mother's side, Galsworthy was connected to the nobility. His play *Strife*, even more clearly than *The Patrician*, illustrates the spell that powerful personalities could cast on him. Like *The Mob*, it shows that he was not completely sure that he trusted ordinary people.

During the First World War, he recognised that centralised, absolute empires had to be swept away: only democracy could cure nations of their aggressiveness. But this did not prevent him feeling strong reservations about the democratic system, which he quite unjustifiably saw as equivalent to modern civilisation, what was much later to be called the consumer society.[27] In short, the ordinary people have no soul: 'Unless Democracy − government by the people − makes of itself Aristocracy − government by the best people − it is running steadily to seed. Democracy to be sound must utilise not only the ablest men of affairs, but the aristocracy of spirit.'[28]

This is a characteristically 19th-century argument. It was the view of Ernest Renan who, although of humble birth, celebrated the aristocratic nature of culture. It is to be found in Carlyle and Matthew Arnold. It may seem old-fashioned in Galsworthy, and can be explained only by some strong Victorian influence, probably that of Carlyle. There is only one precise reference, but it is evidence enough. 'Parliament seems to matter less and less', says Michael Mont; and Soames replies, 'Parliament always was a talking shop'. 'And with that unconscious quotation from Carlyle, he raised his eyes.'[29] Galsworthy's correspondence shows that Soames was his mouthpiece here.

It is distressing to find Galsworthy indulging in such primitive anti-parliamentarianism. But subsequent events have proved that he was, to some extent, far-sighted. The House of Commons has indeed lost some of its power, although it still exists as a vital guarantee of freedom, a platform where the affairs of the nation are debated.

Here again, too much importance must not be attached to Galsworthy's theoretical opinions. He was very severe on the press, yet attached great importance to it, and used it widely himself. Between 1907 and 1928, he wrote no fewer than forty-nine letters to *The Times*,[30] and fifteen to the *Daily Mail*. Whenever it was necessary, he could overcome his distaste for the popular press. Similarly, his private correspondence with Winston Churchill and Herbert Gladstone, although concerning a social matter, had a political side to it. Both men were in the Liberal government of the day. It is worth noting that Galsworthy engaged in political activities when the Liberals were in power. He took advantage of the esteem in which he was held to obtain a reduction in sentences of solitary confinement. So he participated in the democratic system, and helped its progress.

After the First World War, he disagreed with the Liberals on a series of far more important problems than the matter of political institutions. During the war, he had written two long articles entitled 'The Land', setting out a detailed plan for revitalising agriculture in England, and for a return to the land. Despite their vehemence, it was obvious that they would have little effect, yet he persisted, repelled by city slums and excessive urbanisation.

About 1923, he wrote that 'industrial life, as we carry it on, leads to nothing but the ashes of happiness. . . . The future of the land is with the owning farmer, his sons and daughters themselves working.'[31]

In *A Modern Comedy*, Val accordingly breeds horses, and Jon goes in for farming.   Galsworthy's post-war plan is widely expounded in this trilogy, particularly in *The Silver Spoon* and *Swan Song*. As a remedy for the post-war curse of unemployment, he urged that young people of modest condition should be sent out as settlers to British overseas territories. He pressed for the electrification of industry, to make cities and towns healthier places. To prevent war, he argued that military aircraft should be banned, while farming should be developed to supply the country with enough food, particularly cereals, to allow it to withstand a naval blockade.

His ideas were a mixture of utopian idealism and clear-sightedness. Once again, the strongest influence was that of Victorian thinkers, whose revolt against the excesses of the Industrial Revolution he shared. He was probably inspired by Ruskin, Kingsley, Arnold, Carlyle, but also Hardy, though he went further than they did. With his morbid sensitivity to smells and noise, he foresaw present-day environmental pollution, and the growing movement to combat it. But his plan to take poor children away from their families smacks of paternalism. And he was completely naïve about economic factors, and the essential problem of the creation of wealth. He did not realise the absurdity of his bucolic dream of an agricultural country, at a time when the percentage of national resources produced by farming was diminishing steadily. Aware only of the ugliness of factories, he saw British industry as still all-devouring, never suspecting its relative decline.

In the area of economics and population, he came to espouse some of the Imperialist arguments he had long rejected as a basis for any political programme. In 1931, at the end of his life, he was violently opposed to Free Trade, and fought for support for farm prices, which amounted to protectionism. He even seems to have hoped for some kind of Imperial self-sufficiency, for both moral and strategic reasons — the preservation of the English race.

This was a rejection of Liberal doctrines. It even called into question the foundations of British prosperity, the trading skills which the middle classes had developed to a fine art. In 1920, he wrote that 'modern civilisation . . . is camouflaged commercialism'.[32] What did this mean, from someone who had vaunted the merits and solidity of middle-class businessmen? It could be seen as final confirmation of the severe verdict he had pronounced on the Forsytes, despite the weakening satire of the later volumes of the Chronicles.

Ultimately, while not forgetting his independence of mind and his persistent refusal to make common cause with any party, Galsworthy may be seen as a liberal, a reluctant one. Faced with certain practical problems, he was capable of envisaging and even recommending state intervention: 'some sort of State check in the interests of health, beauty and happiness.'[33] When he asserted angrily that the Liberal Party had no future, except as a buffer between the other two parties, was this not his way of admitting his preference for it, and his disappointment and resentment? Did he not feel that the nation above all needed men who could reduce party antagonisms? What made him a liberal was his refusal of all ideologies, his respect for individual rights, which he regarded as essential. It is an attitude that demands respect, even if its adoption apparently means accepting one's impotence in public life.

## GALSWORTHY'S PHILOSOPHICAL OUTLOOK

Books seem to have been no more important in the Galsworthy family than in most English middle-class families. It was his elder sister Lilian who introduced the habit of discussion and respect for the intellect, apparently quite late on in their youth. So although the atmosphere was not ideal, as a young man he had at least the time and material opportunity to satisfy his lively interest in reading.

At neither Harrow nor Oxford did he show any particular brilliance. The education he received may have had something to do with his late development. Certainly, as an adult, he was very critical, though without bitterness, about his schooling. At Harrow, he explained, he was 'debarred from any real interest in philosophy, history, art, literature and music, or any advancing notions in social life or politics'.[34]

It may seem odd that such a sharp attack on the public-school system should occur only in an obscure collection of speeches, and that the novels should say so little on the subject. There is a satirical but uninspired chapter on Oxford in *The Island Pharisees*, and an ironical allusion in *The Country House*.[35] His customary restraint and considerateness probably prevented him from rounding on Harrow and Oxford, but he did denounce the English educational system as a whole, and the intellectual inadequacy of his fellow citizens. He was probably influenced by Arnold's *Culture and Anarchy*, when in 1917 he wrote: 'Far be it from this pen to libel the English, but a feverish mental activity has never been their vice.'[36]

In an article for a Dutch newspaper in 1915, reprinted in two collections, he wrote of the Englishman that 'want of imagination makes him, philosophically speaking, rather ludicrous'.[37]

But it was in 1908, in the preface to the Manaton Edition of *The Island Pharisees*, that he handed down his severest verdict, claiming that most English people were incapable of any speculative thought.[38] This opinion is hinted at in many satirical passages of his narratives, but in a deceptively mild form. About the same time, a letter to André Chevrillon contained an incredible overgeneralisation: 'We have no philosophy.[39] But he saw in this a sign that the English would be more formidable than the Germans, when challenged. This confidence in his country's strength is reminiscent of Macaulay.

He very briefly confessed his own shortcomings in two letters. He told Thomas Hardy that he was 'miserably read in Philosophy',[40] and H. W. Massingham that he had 'a mind that can see and respect ideas and yet is based on realism'.[41] His ability to philosophise is definite, but limited. As has been said, his approach to emancipating himself from conventional opinions was neither initially nor essentially philosophical. It did not come from his reading. Yet there was a philosophical aspect. His secretiveness about literary and intellectual influences on him (except for Maupassant and Turgenev) means that there are very few philosophical works, or works with a philosophical bent, that he is known to have read. Even a list of these, however, would refute the conventional view, repeated by Kettle, that Galsworthy was an unpretentious middle-brow author with no intellectual depth.[42]

But his novels do not provide sufficient evidence of his philosophical outlook. It is far more clearly expressed, although never in purely abstract or perfectly methodical terms, in his five volumes of essays,[43] his prefaces, correspondence and poems. In fact, no part of his output can be ignored, if any overall view is to be gained. The stories and plays also give useful insights. However, the subject has never previously been investigated properly, which makes it even harder to outline.

It is regrettable that so little is known of Galsworthy's readings in philosophy. It would have been especially interesting to know how familiar he was with Victorian authors. He seems to have known Carlyle, Ruskin and Arnold fairly well, to judge by their apparent influence on him, although there are few references, all vague. The names of Herbert Spencer and Thomas Huxley do not appear. Although there are divergences of view on science, and a difference in philosophical profundity, Huxley and Galsworthy show a striking similarity of thought and feeling. It would be interesting to be able to establish some link. Such a connection can be established with John Stuart Mill on a single but important point, the status of women, and it may well have been wider. Similarly, mention of a book by Havelock Ellis raises speculation as to whether Galsworthy knew anything of *Studies in the Psychology of Sex*.

On problems that he was personally interested in, the status of women, anthropology, criminology, he was ready to read specialised works. Otherwise, and in the absence of evidence to the contrary, it is wiser to assume that his philosophical knowledge came to him second-hand, though this does not mean that it was of secondary importance. Schopenhauer may have influenced him, perhaps through Conrad and Hardy, although John A. Lester points out that 'cosmic pessimism' was a common idea in the period 1880 to 1914.[44] He shows the confluence between Keats' and Schopenhauer's outlooks in several ways. And Keats clearly left his mark on Galsworthy's descriptive and lyrical style, even if it is difficult to prove.

The lack of information from Galsworthy himself, which makes such an investigation so arduous, is in itself most instructive. His family, childhood and education left him with a kind of indifference to knowledge, or at least detachment, which reveals itself here and there, in a faint hostility to 'teachers'. This early attitude never vanished entirely. He never aspired to appear as a learned scholar. Never having been deprived of the means of acquiring knowledge, he was not so set on it as were many of his contemporaries, like

H. G. Wells, for whom books and science were instruments of social emancipation.

The concept that lay behind all Galsworthy's 'critical' novels, and even his lyrical novels, the actual idea of 'critique', must be seen in the context of the history of 19th-century philosophy. Houghton shows that the concept originated in the 18th century, with Hume and Voltaire. Its immediate source in the Victorian age was in the work of Jeremy Bentham, not merely the founder of Utilitarianism, but the man who introduced into moral and political philosophy the idea of judgement based on reason. Mill and Huxley widened its application, and saw scepticism as the prime duty.[45]

The subsequent stage, complete acceptance of determinism, is also to be found in Galsworthy, mainly in his psychological analyses and plots, where the miraculous is excluded. The word 'determinism' is not used, except in a letter to Hardy, but he was fond of another which is equally significant: 'product'.[46]

*The Country House* quite logically defines the relationship between the Squire and his surroundings in strictly mechanistic terms: 'the machine of which he was himself a wheel'.[47]

How can this acceptance of determinism be reconciled with his lack of belief in science? The contradiction would be more blatant in a French context. While Galsworthy's reflections on man and his environment are strongly reminiscent of Taine, they contradict the ideas expressed in Renan's *The Future of Science*. For Galsworthy, who, let it be remembered, was writing half a century later, science had no future. Indeed, it had already failed. Admittedly, he was not concerned with science in itself, but with its practical applications, and the power it conferred. He barely differentiated between science and industry. As a true disciple of Carlyle, but perhaps even more of Ruskin, he condemned industrialisation and its effects, urban slums and money-grubbing. He even condemned its cause, which is nothing else than science.

Such scepticism about science was quite widespread at the turn of the century. Galsworthy was tempted by its anti-intellectualism, though he did not go all the way, and see it as grounds for despair. He forged a new scale of values, taking art as a model. The work of art restored intelligibility to existence. In so doing, he tacitly recognised the contribution of aestheticism to contemporary thought. But beauty was not a mere object of contemplation, as it was for Pater. As well as providing pleasure, it inspired men to action. Speaking of himself in *Castles in Spain*, he produces a remarkable synthesis of the Victorian belief in duty and the aesthetic cult of beauty: 'By the love and cult of beauty he means *a higher and wider conception of the dignity of human life*; the teaching of what beauty is, to all — not merely to the few.'[48]

A certain Utilitarianism seems to inform his definition of what is good and useful for all. But a Tolstoyan influence is equally likely. Despite what he said, Galsworthy was receptive to Tolstoy's ideas, and, above all, his ideals. The treatises in which Tolstoy expounds his religious and aesthetic theories include *What is Art?*, published in 1898, and translated into English the following year. It aroused considerable interest and was widely discussed. For Tolstoy, the purpose of art is to contribute to loving communion among all men: in a less mystical form, this idea is to be found at the very core of Galsworthy's convictions and message.

It is encouraging to find that he called himself a humanist, and expressed quite openly his belief in humanism as 'a faith which is becoming for modern man — perhaps — the only possible faith'.[49] This throws more light on his philosophical outlook, and allows him to be placed in the history of ideas. Humanism reflects and summarises his beliefs. It may seem old-fashioned, or vague, like his political liberalism. But it is a philosophical attitude, and a generous one. Despite the amorality of his love stories, and the absence of serious moral failings in his characters, or any punishment for such faults, Galsworthy can be termed a moralist. Man needs 'sympathy and understanding' in his relations with his fellows.[50] In his eyes, the two vital virtues are kindness and courage, by which he means stoicism.[51]

This study of his philosophical outlook will conclude with consideration of his religious opinions. It will start by dealing briefly with an aspect of the portrait of Galsworthy, deliberately passed over in Part I.

His mother was a practising Anglican. She brought him up in the same way, though without ever being tiresome or tyrannical, as he was careful to point out. Apart from his rebellion against her conventionalism, nothing is known to explain his loss or lack of religious belief. Marrot's silence on the matter of his marriage indicates that he and Ada were married in a registry office. And Rudolf Sauter's detailed account of his death is quite explicit. He wanted no clergyman to be called in, and no religious ceremony after his death. His body was to be cremated and his ashes scattered.

The Society of Authors suggested that his remains should be transferred to Westminster Abbey. The Abbey authorities refused, but held a solemn memorial service, at which the Dean of Westminster spoke.

Although Galsworthy did not record the development of his religious opinions during his youth, he stated his adult convictions clearly and distinctly. Although it is not in the novels that he expressed himself most explicitly on the subject, it is present in a number of plots and episodes. One chapter of *The Island Pharisees* reports the conversation between Shelton and a clergyman who has agreed to give him shelter, during his journeyings in the west of England. Much more important is the Reverend Hussell Barter in *The Country House*, who has at least three chapters devoted to him. The whole of *Saint's Progress*, the hero of which is the Reverend Edward Pierson, is given over to the subject. Finally, there is the Reverend Hilary Charwell in *Swan Song* and, in the same novel, the brief appearance of a clergyman who informs Soames about his origins, when he visits Devon. Apart from these passages, there are isolated remarks about religion in many of the novels.

The nameless clergyman in *The Island Pharisees* is in financial straits, but Shelton detects a tone of dictatorial and inhuman superiority in his voice. They are in total disagreement on birth control, England's imperial policy, the rights of women, marriage and morals.

Galsworthy's harsh treatment of Barter in *The Country House* has already been discussed. The case of Pierson in *Saint's Progress* is quite different. He is pitiable, not detestable. He is not a genuine churchman.

Hilary Charwell is different again. He is merry, very friendly and go-ahead, loved by his friends and parishioners. But this should not be taken as reflecting any change in Galsworthy's attitude to organised religion. Charwell could be any philanthropist engaged in social action. He is endowed with none of the specific attributes of an ecclesiastic, or even of a religious person.

Finally, the clergyman who appears at the end of *Swan Song* is described quite neutrally.

Galsworthy is not indulgent towards the clergy. In his eyes, they are ill-placed to preach acceptance of suffering, not being among those who suffer most. But he goes further in his criticism, making most of his clergyman narrow-minded, selfish, even malevolent.

He could not forgive the Church for its condemnation of divorce, and his attacks may have been stimulated by this personal grievance. Yet, on the whole, he is quite moderate in his novels, at least compared with Butler. Indeed, he never goes into the subject of religion at any length.

His attacks, like his praise, are aimed only at the Church of England. Non-conformists are more or less excluded from his picture of English society.

Religion plays a more limited role in the stories. Three short but virulent ones are 'A Fisher of Men' of 1908, 'Manna' of 1916, and 'Salta Pro Nobis' of 1922, all three reprinted in *Caravan*.

Like *Saint's Progress*, one of his plays has a clergyman hero. *A Bit o'Love*, of 1915, is in several ways similar to the novel. They both treat the theme of religion subjectively, and are both flawed by sentimentality. But the play is better, the ideas more novel and lively.

The situation is not entirely original: it is really a variant on *The Man of Property*. Michael Strangway, a young curate, loves his wife, but she does not love him. He cannot and will not impose his conjugal rights, and because of this he becomes the laughing-stock of the village; he also has to face the fury of Mrs Bradmere, his vicar's wife, who informs him that 'there are times when forgiveness is a sin'. This is where Galsworthy introduces a twist. Dismayed to find himself surrounded by so much ill-will and desire to wound, Strangway finds his faith deeply shaken. To Mrs Bradmere, who tells him, 'God punishes,' he replies ingenuously, 'Is there a God?' 'You must see a doctor', she cries.[52]

The idea of a young cleric wanting to hang himself was bound to shock and even outrage public opinion in 1915 — when suicide was still a crime. Galsworthy no doubt thoroughly enjoyed the controversy. The play ends with another twist. Strangway abandons his suicide attempt when a little girl comes into the barn where he is about to hang himself; he is also consoled by the friendship of a peasant as afflicted as himself.

The meaning is clear. Strangway is saved not by God, but by two fellow creatures, and the sentiments created between him and them.

Little would be known about Galsworthy's philosophical and religious opinions if he had not written his essays, prefaces and particularly his poems. Mottram was aware of the irony of the fate suffered by the poetry. Galsworthy, like many other prose writers, attached great importance to poetry, and continued to write it, but it has remained almost unknown to the general public and critics.

In his preface to the volume of the Manaton Edition that contained his poems, he wrote:

> Human realisation of a First Cause is to be inconceivable. I am left to acceptance of whatever it may be. Out of mystery we come, into mystery return; Life and Death, Ebb and Flow; Day and Night, world without end, is all I can grasp. But in such little certainty I see no cause for gloom. Life for those who still have vital instinct in them is good enough in itself even if it lead to nothing.[53]

The poems are mostly meditative and often nostalgic. They are brief, with the sole exception of 'A Dream', and even with its 248 lines it cannot be compared with the great Victorian epics. It is a genuine metaphysical poem, perhaps inspired by Matthew Arnold; in its sombre austerity, it is a challenge to the divine. There will be no Last Judgement:

> This then, O God! is all my creed:
> In the beginning there was still
> What there is now, no less, no more;
> And at the end of all there will
> Be just as much. There is no score
> Of final judgement. Wonder's tale
> Will never, never all be told.
> There will be none without the pale,
> No saint elect within the fold.[54]

Other poems also offer thoughts about religion. 'The Moor Grave' is inspired by a suicide's grave. The poet feels how some men will humiliate others, in the name of revealed truth. 'Courage' is probably inspired by Arnold's poem of the same name, but is quite different, expressing a proud stoicism and a refusal of prayer. In 'The Soul', 'Reminder', 'Acceptation' (to be compared with Arnold's 'Resignation'), the sense of the mystery of life leans towards an uneasy aspiration to pantheism.

But before this is discussed, Galsworthy's opinions must be situated in the history of ideas. First, there is a certain anticlericalism, something far less common in England than in France at the time. Apart from satirical portraits of clergymen in his novels and stories (frequent in English literature since the 18th century), there are several frontal attacks on Christianity in the essays and correspondence. Galsworthy accepted wholeheartedly the Sermon on the Mount; but he saw organised religion as something evil. More moderate than Butler in his attitude to churchmen, he went further in his criticism of religion, and withdrew a greater distance from religious people. In 1912, he wrote to a clergyman that religion was 'a line of least resistance'.[55]

Like many Edwardian writers, Galsworthy was an agnostic, and stated it openly: in other words, he did not deny the possibility of a divine force or essence — he was not an atheist — but could not believe in the God of existing religions.[56] Again, there is no evidence of what influence affected him, and led him to such a position. It is only to be expected that he should not mention David Hume, Sir William Hamilton, Henry Mansel or Herbert Spencer, but it is disappointing not to find the name of Leslie Stephen, most of whose works were available to him. There is a reference to John Morley.[57]

He did not feel saddened by his lack of certainty. This optimism may seem a surprising accompaniment to the gloomy and dejected atmosphere that prevails in many of the novels. But allowance must be made for rhetorical effect, and, although he would not admit it, the desire to convince readers, by giving a darker image of reality. His essays reveal, if not optimism, at least an unexpected idealism. He talks frequently of 'that spiritual quality, that devotion to an idea, which is our only hope'.[58]

The 'activist' aspect of Galsworthy's philosophy, which Bellamy had such difficulty in finding in his novels, is best illustrated in a note reprinted in Marrot's biography: 'The only efficient, the only decent prayer is *Action*.'[59]

To preserve his reputation, he understandably refrained from expressing too openly ideas that would have rendered his writing unacceptable to people with conventional moral opinions.

He was not very sensitive to religious emotion, unlike Renan, who retained his sense of worship even after losing his faith. Galsworthy felt no metaphysical disquiet. His pessimism was less profound than Hardy's. Like Edmund Gosse, he could be called a 'second-generation' agnostic, calmer, less pious than the Victorian agnostics.

Galsworthy rejected as absurd any 'faith in [a] personal outside

God' who took an interest in individuals.[60] He was sharply opposed to any anthropomorphism. These opinions led him naturally towards pantheism. This was encouraged by other influences, those of Carlyle, Meredith, the Romantic poets, particularly Shelley, Wordsworth, Keats, and of the East. India, which transformed British ways, also fired their imagination. Galsworthy was interested in the history of religions, and read about Buddhism. He described Felix Freeland in the library at night, a book on Eastern philosophy on his lap, lost in thought. Rudolf Sauter has told of discussions with his uncle on the transmigration of souls. Galsworthy was disposed to accept the idea of absorption of the individual into the universe after death.

Nothing is known of his knowledge of Eastern philosophies, but they clearly attracted him. They had at least one advantage over Christianity, in that they did not lend themselves to anthropomorphism. He does not use the actual term 'pantheism', but talks of 'animism'. In Switzerland once, he said: 'The Matterhorn . . . looks wonderful nearly always, and has the animistic quality we have learned to look for in Nature.'[61] He was, in fact, pantheistic rather than animistic. Although the subject is not discussed frequently or at length in his writings, it is perfectly identifiable. There is the following passage about Miltoun in *The Patrician*, for example:

> He . . . took a path up the Moor. . . . There, below him, around, and above, was a land and sky transcending even his exaltation. It was like a symphony of great music; or the nobility of a stupendous mind laid bare; it was God up there, in His many moods. Serenity was spread in the middle heavens, blue, illimitable; and along to the East, three huge clouds, like thoughts brooding over the destinies below. . . . It seemed to Miltoun as if his spirit had left his body, and become part of the solemnity of God.[62]

The terms he uses may seem rather ambiguous, but it is hard not to be sensitive to the meaning of this passage, as well as to its beauty. It may be seen as the ultimate state of a spirit that tended to be solitary and liked silence, but was capable of blending the inner and the outer worlds, in a vibrant, blissful contemplation, where mystical adoration is free of any servility.

He probably achieved such a state only fleetingly, but he was too

stoical to complain of its momentariness. The following poem was
found among his papers after he died. It offers another vision of
the world, from beyond the tomb:

> Scatter my ashes!
>> Let them be free to the air,
>> Soaked in the sunlight and rain,
>> Scatter, with never a care
>> Whether you find them again.
>
>> Let them be grey in the dawn,
>> Bright if the noontime be bright,
>> And when night's curtain is drawn
>> Starry and dark with the night.
>
>> Let the birds find them and take
>> Lime for their nests, and the beast
>> Nibbling the grizzled grass, make
>> Merry with salt to his feast.
>
> Scatter my ashes!
>> Hereby I make it a trust:
>> I in no grave be confined,
>> Mingle my dust with the dust
>> Give me in fee to the wind!
>>> Scatter my ashes![63]

The pantheism that pervades this poem leads the poet to hope
for dissolution of his being, to ensure his communion with the
whole of nature. Cremation and the scattering of ashes were long
regarded in the West as just punishment for ignominious deeds. If
chosen by the deceased, they were irreligious, since certain
Christian denominations believed that they deprived his soul of
any hope of resurrection on the day of judgement. Galsworthy had
freed himself from these superstitions, and adopted a practice that
has now become common.

Given that he was self-taught in the area of abstract thought,
Galsworthy succeeded, through a kind of sixth sense, in acquiring
a grasp of contemporary philosophy which, although incomplete
and limited, was on the whole remarkable. His philosophical

outlook was broader than Bennett's. It moved along paths too different from those followed by Wells to be comparable. Unlike Shaw, or Wells, he never went through a religious phase. In the area of religion, where Anatole France's influence, although unproved, is likely, he went further than most English writers, in his anti-clericalism and opposition to Christianity. On the other hand, despite his passionate defence of the rights of women and his efforts to bring about reform of the law on prostitution, he was more timid and unimaginative in his attitude to marriage than Meredith. Unlike Hardy, he never condemned it as an institution.

His ideas were generally in line with thought at the turn of the century and in the Edwardian age, at least those trends then being manifested under the influence of Hume, Mill, Darwin, Spencer, Thomas Huxley, J. A. Froude, Morley, Carlyle (in politics), Ruskin, Arnold and Butler. Galsworthy was a determinist and agnostic, or at least a free-thinker, like his predecessors or contemporaries Leslie Stephen, Hardy, George Gissing, Gosse, George Moore, Hudson, Bertrand Russell, Wells, Bennett and Forster. He was a pantheist, like the Romantic poets and Meredith, with something of Eastern mysticism in his attitude. Beyond the anti-intellectualism so widely apparent in his novels, he was metaphysically, and, through his poetic vision, in sympathy with spiritualism, even vitalism. His work reveals obvious tendencies similar to those given full expression in Bergson's *Creative Evolution* (1907), *Mind-Energy* (1919), and perhaps *The Two Sources of Morality and Religion* (1932).

If literary polemics had not obscured the issue, and despite differences in ways and style, certain themes could have been seen to be shared by Galsworthy and other authors who, in attacking him, believed that they were radically different from him. Virginia Woolf also knew Freud and Bergson without having read them, and was influenced by them. Someone like Mrs Pendyce could almost have appeared in one of her novels. D. H. Lawrence's anti-intellectualism, and his aversion for modern industrial civilisation, his cult of love and even of the sun, find echoes in Galsworthy. Despite appearances, he is a sensuous writer.

He was not a dialectical thinker, but a moralist. It was no doubt his legal training that gave him the capacity to observe the actions of people without judging them, and to see beyond to where real responsibilities lay. 'Solitary Confinement' contains some of his most original reflections.[64] He criticised the very idea of punishment,

denying it any legitimacy or deterrent power. He even propounded
the theory, advanced for the time, that criminal tendencies arise
from an over-assertive character and an unbalanced will. His
opinion of the virtuousness of the wealthy was close to Shaw's.
Although his approach was by no means scientific, his role in the
evolution of ideas was not unlike that of Havelock Ellis, in the
precise and limited area of sexology.

In concluding this examination of Galsworthy's philosophy and
outlook, certain peremptory verdicts on him demand reconsider-
ation. Did his 'philosophy' amount only to a transient rebellious-
ness, when he married a divorcee? Was it really fundamentally
conservative, and narrowly nationalistic? Was it superficial, over-
cautious, and ultimately empty of substance?

# Conclusion

A love story lies at the heart of nearly every Galsworthy novel. The hero's senses and temperament are completely involved, his mind and consciousness less so, or at any rate less immediately, less directly. The novels, then, offer several harmonics. But a lyrical poetic style, and a restless, nostalgic atmosphere predominate. The role Galsworthy attributes to woman, her beauty, the passions she arouses and experiences, is so great that it is even possible to talk of his romantic conception of life. Indeed, his various allusions to Don Quixote suggest the image of a knight errant, always ready to take up arms to defend the defenceless, and draw attention to the dreamlike element in his philosophical outlook.

His lyricism, which can be described as 'romantic' because of the lovely natural settings in which he places it, has nothing exotic, theatrical or gushing about it. There is no question of parading yearnings or conquests. There is never any posturing. It is a secretive, contemplative, delicate romanticism, almost religious, in that it turns love into a religion. This is when it is most genuine. When his inspiration falters, it can lapse into sentimentality.

He claimed to be realistic, in describing the arousal and growth of passion in reality, in other words in complete freedom. He was particularly fond of a definition of him put forward by a critic who called him 'a romantic realist'. He liked it because it suggested a distinction between what he regarded as his own realism and the vulgar materialism that he attacked in D. H. Lawrence's way of depicting love. He did not realise that his heroes required leisure and money for the way they loved. It never occurred to him that his way of drawing a veil over certain things would one day leave readers dissatisfied.

'Realism' does not seem to be the right term to define his work. This study has already shown how limited and relative Galsworthy's realism is in every area, psychological analysis, description or choice of situation. Admittedly, the French Realists taught him certain value precepts, concision, the discretion of the narrator, avoiding any intrusion, any asides, any accentuation. But he did not know Zola, owed little to Flaubert, and even Maupassant's influence on him was restricted. He rejected his themes and crudeness. For Galsworthy, realism was no more than a device, a technique, a method, not a philosophy. He did not exploit the resources offered by the French Naturalists, as George Moore did in *A Modern Lover* or *Mummer's Wife*. As might be expected, not the slightest Surrealist influence is to be detected in his works.

The most obvious form of realism is the precision with which he notes time and place, and his descriptions of attitudes and gestures. This precision is not systematic, but selective and deliberate. The straightforwardness with which he describes the layout of places where action takes place is reminiscent of stage directions.

In general, he displays that most typically English quality of pragmatism, rather than realism. It has already been seen in his political attitudes, and is what made them so regrettably ambiguous. For Galsworthy, value and durability were inseparable. Whatever lasted, whatever possessed the power of survival, was good. This is where the source of his interest in families, and especially their older members, surely lay. Some old people are described admiringly (and admirably), though not all. He was capable of admiration and respect, but he measured them out according to each individual case and its circumstances. It would be wrong to talk of any faith in the family or cult of the family.

The main evidence of his detachment from realism is his principal characters' indifference to the material difficulties of life, and the choice of characters of the same standing in life as himself.

Galsworthy's outlook was not centred on objects and their possession. This is why he was so well placed to write *The Man of Property*. He had that sophisticated detachment from earthly goods conferred by the very fact of being a man of property himself, who had never known need, and had never nurtured material, social or political ambitions. At home, he ate and drank well, and may be assumed to have had an epicurean enjoyment of anything attractive and of good quality. His novels describe the heavy mahogany tables, silverware, sweet peas and thick carpets that create the muffled charm of those large upper middle-class houses where life is so pleasant. His characters include several Epicureans: Old Jolyon, Swithin, despite his vulgarity, Heythorp in 'A Stoic'. But Galsworthy had a conscience, and his novels are, in his own words, 'conscience-stricken'.

They are the work of a gentleman, who did not write in order to make a living, but who lived in order to write. This is the basic argument: far from arising from the attitudes of a materialist, far from being encumbered with possessions, his novels above all evoke an inner world, the most complicated labyrinths and profoundest contradictions of which are painstakingly analysed. It was almost without his realising it that, in creating this world, he depicted the social class to which he belonged. Since this class held power and set the tone, his writings provide a glimpse of the whole of English society.

The essential question he asked himself was both personal and general. It related quite precisely to the 'gentleman', the man who continues to observe good form, whatever happens. Galsworthy was deeply attached to such an ideal, because only in self-respect did he hold any faith. For him, real moral force lay in a man's verdict on himself: social retributions represented an arbitrary usurpation of this force. Yet, seeing the injustices of a society run by gentlemen, he suspected the inadequacy of their ideals, and consequently of his own. This misgiving never led him to such a thorough critique as that of Ford Madox Ford in *The Good Soldier*. He never turned to any other belief. He rejected all religions and ideologies, and maintained firmly the primacy of individual judgement, in accordance with the liberal philosophy of John Stuart Mill, whose essay *On Liberty* probably influenced him. He was attacked from both sides for his obstinate attachment to independence. Yet his only response, using Young Jolyon as his mouthpiece, was to assert that what men lack above all else is imagination — not creative imagination or intelligence, but moral imagination, the capacity to feel compassion. The heroes of his early novels feel ill at ease because, without giving up their class privileges, they are incapable of enjoying them with a quiet mind. This is what makes them outsiders in their own world.

His strongest criticisms bear on the position of women in a society where laws are made by men, to justify and perpetuate male domination. Both his romanticism and his criticism thus share the same origin and object. In his conception of the role of woman in a man's life, he is in direct opposition to Balzac, and different from Meredith, Hardy, Conrad and Shaw. Far from regarding love as a deception, or a form of seduction fraught with perils, he regarded it, like a true romantic, as an enhancement of one's whole being, and one of the peaks of existence. If he had thrown off the other shackles of Victorian convention, his position would have been that of an extreme feminist. But all he demanded for women was equality with men in love, not full equality of social rights, particularly the right to work. His writings show him attached to the idea that above all a woman is beautiful and intended for love; at the most, she might play a little music and do charitable work. The Victorian conception of the family no longer holds sway, but the ambitions that women began to entertain in the Edwardian age are not yet reflected. Unlike several of his contemporaries, ultimately he was in favour of marriage, on the sole condition that divorce should be easier.

His attitude was a mixture of conservatism, reformism, and, on one or two points, such as religion and education, revolt against the prevailing state of affairs. With the passage of time, his criticisms of English society may seem timid, over-cautious, flimsy; like the humour of *Punch*, they are not really intended to hurt. But this interpretation of his work cannot really stand up to any examination of the early novels, and other forms of writing: plays, poetry, essays and articles. It is hard to avoid such an error of perspective, for the novels not belonging to the trilogies have always been neglected, and are likely to remain so. And even in his most successful books, Galsworthy does not succeed in expressing his ideas dynamically enough to make them properly reflect his philosophy. His discretion and reasonableness are appreciated by those primarily seeking honesty, as in Montaigne. But more often they are turned against him. He has been condemned for not offering a system, an all-embracing and coherent vision of the world. A few years ago, he was being compared most unfavourably with Graham Greene.

His most serious weakness as a writer may be seen as the inadequacy of his creative imagination, arising from a lack of exuberance, spontaneity, gaiety, or immediate contact with practical life and with people, an absence of fantasy and even, on occasion, of a sense of the ridiculous. There is nothing everyday or ordinary about the scenes he describes. It gives his effects great distinction, but they are also rather thin, and sometimes cloying. His characters have few vices but, except for stoical courage in the face of death, they also lack virtues.

Galsworthy does not lend himself to classifications, simplified, modish definitions. In his confidence in the good-heartedness of the middle classes, once their imagination is awakened, his reasoning is as optimistic as George Eliot's or Dickens'. He also belongs to the 19th century in his reservations about democracy, his doubts about its vulgarity. Yet the extreme sensitivity and generosity of his social consciousness make him the most modern of the Edwardians. David Daiches very accurately points out that 'Wells' scientific humanism was essentially late Victorian, and so too was Shaw's iconoclastic wit, but J. Galsworthy's humane worrying about society remained important for a decade at least after the first war'.[1]

E. M. Forster puts Galsworthy among those authors who 'got their impressions and formed their attitudes in an earlier period, before the first of the two world wars'.[2] This is also penetrating, and it is confirmed most strikingly in the letter to Garnett in which Galsworthy admitted that the First World War had deeply disturbed his beliefs.

The analysis of *A Modern Comedy* showed it to be more superficial than *The Forsyte Saga*. Yet there is a lot of truth in its image of an unstable generation, thrown off course by the First World War. In other words, Galsworthy did not feel in perfect sympathy with the Georgians, but neither was he a typical Edwardian nor a representative Victorian. His independence of mind has been emphasised. He was also sufficiently receptive to take something from every period in which he lived. His example suggests, incidentally, that the three periods involved should not be differentiated too dogmatically or arbitrarily.

His indifference, or even hostility, to trade and industry, his tendency to adopt an amoral attitude in matters of private life, his pessimism, scepticism and tolerance, distinguish him quite clearly from the Victorians. Yet his criticism of the Forsytes does not take the form of any virulent, all-embracing condemnation of the Victorian age. He seldom uses the adjective 'Victorian', indeed, and abstains from any criticism of the Queen.

His artistic and literary tastes, as has been seen, were rather those of an Edwardian. His preference for the Impressionists, his condemnation of modern art, his aversion for Dostoyevsky and his posthumous fame, his anger at the statue of Rima sculpted by the controversial artist Jacob Epstein in 1924, in memory of his friend W. H. Hudson, all go to show Galsworthy displaying rather orthodox tastes as the Edwardian age went on. The outline of his literary fortunes showed that it was in the first decade of the century that he was regarded as a spokesman and innovator.

Yet one must never forget that the most formative period of his mind began before Edward VII came to the throne. The decade of crisis in his personal life, which made him a writer, lay half in the 19th and half in the 20th century. Through an odd coincidence, the same was true of his life. He lived thirty-three years in the 19th century, and thirty-three in the 20th. If his position has to be defined in the history of art and ideas, the second half of the reign of Edward VII is probably the right choice.

It is no easier to situate him in the history of English literature. He believed that he had been little influenced by it. Consequently, he had no interest in establishing his precursors: in fact, he did the contrary. Leon Schalit, whom he knew personally and trusted, and who discussed the matter with him, wrote that 'except Dickens and perhaps Thackeray a little, no English writer has influenced him, unless it be Shakespeare'.[3] There is every reason to believe that this remark was inspired directly by Galsworthy himself. His statements on the decisive influence of Maupassant and Turgenev on his art reveal how he saw himself: a pure-blooded Englishman (he prided himself on the absence of any Scots, Irish or Welsh ancestry), using a foreign art to depict his country. But although this might have seemed true at the start of his career, in time Galsworthy recognised that England also boasted stylists and artists: Stevenson, whom he liked, Pater, whom he mistrusted, Jane Austen, for whom he had little liking.

However, he never admitted, and probably never perceived, the full influence of English literature on his work. His art is far more English than he thought, although the many diverse influences on it never stifled his originality. The names of Shakespeare, Keats and the Pre-Raphaelites, Thackeray, Dickens, Carlyle, Ruskin, Arnold, Meredith, Butler, Hardy, Hudson, Conrad and others have been mentioned. The English authors to whom Galsworthy owed most are perhaps Thackeray, Meredith, Hardy and Conrad. A parallel can be drawn, not only between *Beauchamp's Career* and *The Patrician*, but between *The Ordeal of Richard Feverel* and *The Country House*. However, there are as many differences as similarities, perhaps more, so that such comparisons are of limited value. Conrad's moral or philosophical themes were probably more influential, despite obvious contrasts between the two writers. Do they not share the same sense of moral obligation, a taste for the irrational, even sometimes the supernatural, in spite of a similar hostility to Christianity? However, no literary and human influence was so strong on Galsworthy as that of Turgenev, from whom he borrowed frequently and extensively, thereby enriching the whole of his work. He could have been accused of parody, if the social context in England and Russia had not been so different, and if, despite these differences, there had not been a very great spiritual affinity between him and his master. Turgenev was the man he would have liked more than anyone else in the world to meet.

It is hard to see any meaningful similarities among the three Edwardians whom Virginia Woolf equally reproved, Galsworthy, Bennett and Wells. The analysis of *Beyond* showed the profound divergences between the novel and *The Old Wives' Tale*. Louis Tillier has pointed out differences between Bennett and Wells.[4] There is an even wider gulf between Wells and Galsworthy, in temperament, taste, talent and ideas. At most, the stature of both writers is comparable. Wells long appeared the greater, no doubt because of the wider and more universal nature of his work; but his reputation has not re-emerged in the same way as those of his two contemporaries. Of the three, I consider Galsworthy the greatest artist.

However, other terms of reference must be sought. The name of Trollope is sometimes mentioned, but Galsworthy is a better stylist and a more profound thinker. In a more recent period, the 'Georgians', particularly the Bloomsbury Group, have not thrust the Edwardians into oblivion as they expected and indeed appeared to do for several decades. Virginia Woolf and E. M. Forster both possess charms that are lacking in Galsworthy, but their inspiration is narrower. Other writers, like J. D. Beresford, Compton Mackenzie, or Frank Swinnerton, so gifted in the twenties, failed to live up to their early promise.

This is why Galsworthy can no longer be depicted as the last executant of a dying *genre*. Other family novels or novel sequences have been published with success by other authors. J. D. Beresford published a trilogy between 1911 and 1915. The woman writer G. B. Stern described a family in *Children of No Man's Land* in 1919. R. H. Mottram's trilogy *The Spanish Farm* appeared from 1914 to 1926. Between 1924 and 1928, Ford Madox Ford published the quartet of 'Tietjens novels'. At the end of the Second World War, L. P. Hartley made his reputation with a trilogy.

J. B. Priestley's temperament and realism make him more a

descendant of Bennett, but C. P. Snow's novel sequence *Strangers and Brothers* recalls the Galsworthian novel in several ways.

Without possessing the power and genius of Hardy, Conrad or Lawrence, Galsworthy may well be recognised as one of the leading English authors of the century. It may be that the renewed popularity of the *Forsyte* trilogies will encourage readers to discover the other novels and stories that best illustrate his humane outlook on life.

Deceived by the apparent facility of his style, critics have so far not taken the trouble to examine the more personal and innovatory aspects of Galsworthy's art. This is hardly surprising. But his two triumphs among the general public, nearly fifty years apart, and under very different historical conditions, suggest that real treasures may still lie hidden in his novels.

# Appendix: Statistics Concerning Printings of Galsworthy's Novels in Britain, Germany, Austria and France

## UNITED KINGDOM

Mr Charles Pick, Managing Director, William Heinemann, and Mr R. Davies, Sales Manager, Penguin Books, provided the following information and figures. It is quite astonishing to note the number of copies of Galsworthy novels printed in recent years, compared with similar figures for other contemporary writers.

On 11 November 1970, Mr Pick wrote:

> We have always had *The Forsyte Saga*, *A Modern Comedy* and *End of the Chapter* (the Forsyte trilogies) in print. Up to the time of the first showing of the TV series we were selling a steady 2,000/2,500 copies a year of the *Forsyte Saga*. Since 1 January 1967 we have sold 107,000 copies and 42,000 copies of *A Modern Comedy* and 28,000 copies of *End of the Chapter*. In addition Penguin have sold 1.8 million copies of the nine individual titles (we did not give them the trilogy rights).
>
> As a result of the increase in the reading of the Forsyte Chronicles, we have now put back into print as single volumes the following titles: *Beyond*, *The Country House*, *The Dark Flower*, *Fraternity*, *The Island Pharisees*, *The Man of Property* and *Saint's Progress*.
>
> I understand in other countries where the TV films were being shown, sales of the Forsyte Chronicles have been just as dramatic and all publishers seem to comment on the fact that young people have taken to reading Galsworthy again.

*Penguin books (dates in brackets are those of the first Penguin editions)*

| Title | 1967 | 1968 | 1969 | 1970 |
|---|---|---|---|---|
| *Man of Property* (1951) | 103 679 | 126 237 | 39 407 | 22 836 |
| *In Chancery* (1962) | 85 373 | 103 365 | 22 959 | 13 983 |
| *To Let* (1967) | 84 241 | 85 490 | 18 462 | 13 326 |
| *The White Monkey* (1967) | 63 398 | 78 781 | 25 551 | 13 491 |
| *The Silver Spoon* (1967) | 62 245 | 74 808 | 20 867 | 12 615 |
| *Swan Song* (1967) | 61 141 | 71 834 | 23 241 | 12 806 |
| *Maid in Waiting* (1968) | | 88 870 | 21 619 | 11 364 |
| *Flowering Wilderness* (1968) | | 85 067 | 16 000 | 8 463 |
| *Over the River* (1968) | | 84 019 | 16 094 | 9 568 |
| Annual total | 460 077 | 808 471 | 204 200 | 118 407 |
| Packs containing all nine novels | | 15 000 | 10 000 | 6 000 |

## GERMANY AND AUSTRIA

Herr Hans W. Polak, Managing Director of Paul Zsolnay Verlag (Vienna and Hamburg) provided the following information in a letter of 6 July 1973:

> The total sales of *The Forsyte Saga* in the German language are 1,600,000 copies between 1925 and 1972. Approximately between 1955 and 1972 the average sales of the trade edition were 800 to 1,000 copies per year, but since September 1972 and June 1973 the sales of the new edition were, I am glad to say, approximately 940,000 copies.

## FRANCE

The publishers Calmann-Lévy sold approximately 400,000 copies of *La Dynastie des Forsytes*, between October and December 1970.

# Notes

Notes refer to the following editions of John Galsworthy's works:

*Jocelyn*, by John Sinjohn (London: Duckworth, 1898)
*The Forsyte Saga* (London: Heinemann, 1950)
*A Modern Comedy* (London: Heinemann, 1948)
*End of the Chapter* (London: Heinemann, 1948)
Grove Edition of the other novels (London: Heinemann, 1927–51)
*The Plays of John Galsworthy* (London: Duckworth, 1936)

For Galsworthy's short stories, essays and poems the standard Heinemann edition has been used.

The thirty-volume Manaton Edition of Galsworthy's works, published by Heinemann between 1923 and 1936, is referred to only for its prefaces.

The standard biography, *The Life and Letters of John Galsworthy* (London: Heinemann, 1935), by H. V. Marrot, will be referred to in the notes as 'Marrot', followed by the relevant page reference.

NOTES TO THE INTRODUCTION

1. Marrot, p. 136.
2. There were six editions of *The Country House* between 1907 and 1914, and four of *The Patrician* between 1911 and 1919. *Fraternity* seems to have been less widely read.
3. *The Forsyte Saga*, p. 1036.
4. Edward Garnett, *Letters from John Galsworthy 1900–1932* (London: Jonathan Cape, 1934; New York: Charles Scribner's Sons, 1934) pp. 210–11.
5. 'Mr Bennett and Mrs Brown' in *Collected Essays*, vol. I (London: Hogarth Press, 1966) pp. 320, 327–30.
6. The prefaces to the Manaton Edition of Galsworthy's works, which were important texts, were by then available, but Lawrence does not appear to have read them. Marrot's book, with its vital information on the man and his work, came out seven years later.
7. In *Scrutinies* (1928), reprinted in *Phoenix: The Posthumous Papers of D. H. Lawrence* (London: Heinemann, 1936) pp. 539–56. See D. H. Lawrence, *Selected Essays* (Harmondsworth: Penguin, 1966) pp. 217–30.
8. Ibid., p. 229.
9. J. Guiguet, *Virginia Woolf et son oeuvre* (Paris: Didier, 1967) p. 34.
10. F. R. Leavis, *The Common Pursuit* (Harmondsworth: Penguin, 1962) p. 233.

11. Good examples are to be found in *The Pelican Guide to English Literature*, vol. VI, pp. 99, 104; vol. VII, pp. 212, 216, 284, 372. In *The Concise Cambridge History of English Literature* (Cambridge University Press, 1967) R. C. Churchill does not say a word about Galsworthy's novels.
12. On the other hand, *The Times*, following his death, could not forgive him his independent attitude to religion and morality. W. R. Inge, in the preface to *The Post-Victorians* (London: Nicholson & Watson, 1933), denied him any spiritual life.
13. R. Church, *Growth of the English Novel* (London: Methuen, 1951); A. S. Collins, *English Literature of the Twentieth Century* (London: London University Tutorial Press, 1951); R. A. Scott-James, *Fifty Years of English Literature 1900–1950* (London: Longmans, 1951).

NOTES TO CHAPTER ONE: GALSWORTHY AND HIS FAMILY BACKGROUND

1. Marrot, p. 796.
2. Leon Schalit, *John Galsworthy: A Survey* (London: Heinemann, 1929) p. 20.
3. 'A Portrait' in *A Motley*, pp. 1–29; *Caravan*, pp. 135–50.
4. Marrot, p. 58.

NOTES TO CHAPTER TWO: GALSWORTHY'S LEGAL TRAINING AND BACKGROUND IN LITERATURE

1. Marrot, p. 181.
2. Marrot, pp. 33, 35, 45, 64, 65, 568. Raymond Las Vergnas, in his introduction to *The Book of Snobs*, by W. M. Thackeray (Paris: Aubier, 1945) p. 45, shows its influence on Galsworthy, emphasising how Thackeray's message was given confirmation in *The Silver Spoon*, ch. 13.
3. Marrot, pp. 83, 84, 88, 97, 116–17.
4. Ibid., p. 131.
5. Ibid., p. 61.
6. Ibid., p. 136. See also *Beyond*, Manaton Edition, pp. x, xi.
7. Marrot, p. 99.
8. Garnett, *Letters from John Galsworthy*, p. 51.
9. Ibid., pp. 5, 30, 36, 177.
10. *Addresses in America*, p. 1, and unpublished reading list recommended by Galsworthy to his cousin Frank. On Henry James, see Marrot, pp. 115, 130, 217, 317, 326, 772.
11. Garnett, *Letters from John Galsworthy*, p. 218. On D. H. Lawrence, see also ibid., p. 433.
12. Marrot, p. 779.
13. *Fraternity*, Manaton Edition, p. xi.
14. *Five Tales*, Manaton Edition, p. x. When he testified to the Parliamentary Commission on Censorship, Galsworthy gave a list of censored plays known to him (Marrot, p. 218).

NOTES TO CHAPTER THREE: ASPECTS OF GALSWORTHY'S LIFE

1. Rudolf Sauter, *Galsworthy the Man: An Intimate Portrait by his Nephew* (London: Peter Owen, 1967) p. 136.

2. Mabel E. Reynolds, *Memories of John Galsworthy by his Sister* (London: R. Hale, 1936) p. 18.
3. Marrot, p. 45.
4. Ibid., p. 63.
5. Sauter, *Galsworthy the Man*, p. 54.
6. Ada Galsworthy, *Over the Hills and Far Away* (1937) p. 14.
7. Sauter, *Galsworthy the Man*, pp. 20, 21, 45, 46.
8. Marrot, p. 63; Reynolds, *Memories of John Galsworthy*, pp. 28, 29.
9. *The Inn of Tranquillity*, November 1933 edition, pp. 148, 149.
10. Dudley Barker, *The Man of Principle: A View of John Galsworthy* (London: Heinemann, 1963) p. 64.
11. Reynolds, *Memories of John Galsworthy*, pp. 534–6.
12. Marrot, pp. 33, 35, 225, 416, 534–6, 562, 572.
13. Sauter, *Galsworthy the Man*, p. 25.
14. Reynolds, *Memories of John Galsworthy*, p. 14.
15. Marrot, p. 532.
16. Ibid., p. 585.
17. Sauter, *Galsworthy the Man*, p. 16.
18. Marrot, p. 100.
19. Ibid., p. 101.
20. Ibid., p. 101.
21. Ibid., pp. 215–16. There is no indication of date, but it is probably from the later years of his life.
22. Margaret Morris, *My Galsworthy Story* (London: Peter Owen, 1967).
23. Rudolf Sauter and R. H. Mottram confirmed to me Marrot's categorical assertions.
24. His dilemma, and the whole situation, are described with remarkable accuracy in the third episode of *The Dark Flower*.
25. Marrot, p. 408.
26. Ibid., pp. 411–12.
27. Ibid., photograph facing p. 426.
28. Ibid., p. 426.
29. Ibid., p. 427.
30. Ibid., p. 428.
31. In summer 1917, he wrote an article in the *Observer* defending 800 conscientious objectors.
32. Marrot, p. 443.
33. Ibid., p. 443.
34. Marrot, *Bibliography of the Works of John Galsworthy* (London: Elkin Mathews & Marrot, 1928; New York: Charles Scribner's Sons, 1928) p. 35.
35. Marrot, pp. 645–50, or Sauter, *Galsworthy the Man*, pp. 136–42.

NOTES TO CHAPTER FOUR: GALSWORTHY'S EMOTIONAL NATURE AND ARTISTIC TASTES

1. Sauter, *Galsworthy the Man*, p. 39.
2. Neither his heroes nor his heroines are renowned for their faithfulness.
3. Galsworthy's affection for his nephew did not prevent him from helping numerous distant relatives and the villagers of Manaton and later Bury.

He is like the Squire in *The Country House*, but without the desire to order people about. See Marrot, pp. 581, 591.
4. Morris, *My Galsworthy Story*, p. 26.
5. Herman Ould, *John Galsworthy* (Chapman & Hall, 1934) p. 111.

NOTES TO CHAPTER FIVE: GALSWORTHY'S WAY OF LIFE

1. Marrot, p. 604; Sauter, *Galsworthy the Man*, p. 54.
2. Marrot, pp. 215–16, 411. Individuals included, for example, Conrad, an extreme but far from isolated case. An unpublished MA thesis by D. C. Cross, 'Unpublished Letters from Joseph Conrad to John Galsworthy' (University of Birmingham, 1966), reveals the unexpected scale of the help Galsworthy gave his friend.

NOTES TO THE CONCLUSIONS TO PART ONE

1. In reply to St John Ervine; see Marrot, p. 531.
2. See ch. 8 below.

NOTES TO CHAPTER SIX: GALSWORTHY'S CAREER AS A NOVELIST

1. *Villa Rubein*, Manaton Edition, pp. xii–xiii.
2. The book was written three years after the start of their relationship, and seven years before they married. Everything is over in twelve or thirteen months in the novel: an obscure revenge on time! Another point to note is that Jocelyn is twenty-two, whereas Ada was ten months older than Galsworthy.
3. *Jocelyn*, p. 144 (1976 edn, p. 88).
4. Marrot, p. 154. There is an excellent comment on Garnett's critical opinions and idiosyncrasies by Scott-James, *50 Years of English Literature*, p. 85. Garnett's view of the novels written by Galsworthy after he had stopped advising him also seems somewhat hasty: see Garnett, *Letters from John Galsworthy*, pp. 14, 16.
5. Marrot, p. 120.
6. 'The Salvation of Swithin Forsyte', in the collection *A Man of Devon* (1901). There is mention of Nicholas Treffry in *The Man of Property* (*The Forsyte Saga*, p. 135).
7. Garnett, *Letters from John Galsworthy*, p. 84.
8. Ibid., pp. 84–5.
9. *Villa Rubein*, Manaton Edition, pp. xi–xii.
10. *The Island Pharisees*, p. 95. Ferrand actually existed. He died in poverty. Galsworthy had kept his letters.
11. 'Diagnosis of a Forsyte', in *The Forsyte Saga*, pp. 217–26.
12. *The Country House*, p. 127.
13. *Fraternity*, Manaton Edition, p. ix.
14. *The Country House*, Manaton Edition, p. xi. Hilary is indeed compared

to Hamlet in *Fraternity*, p. 124, and ch. 18 may be seen as an adaptation of the Shakespearian monologue to suit the period. Turgenev had presented several Hamlet-like figures: 'Prince Hamlet of Shchigrovo' in *A Sportsman's Sketches* (1852), and *J. Pasinkov* (1855).

15. Samuel Hynes, *The Edwardian Turn of Mind* (Princeton University Press, 1968; Oxford University Press, 1968) pp. 54–86.
16. *The Patrician*, Manaton Edition, p. xiii.
17. Marrot, p. 448.
18. *The Dark Flower*, Manaton Edition, pp. xii–xiii.
19. One of the few references to Meredith is to be found in *The Patrician*, p. 124. There are three rather vague allusions to Carlyle in the novels, one on the first page of *The Island Pharisees*, another in *The Dark Flower*, p. 82, and the third in *Swan Song* (*The Forsyte Saga*, p. 760).
20. The suffragette movement was at its height when the novel was being written. It was completed in 1910. In *The Edwardians* (London: Heinemann, 1970) J. B. Priestley says that the first part of the suffragette campaign reached its greatest intensity in 1909. In what appears to be a contemporary letter, Galsworthy writes: 'Greatly as I have the cause of the emancipation of Women at heart, I am not a believer in, or supporter of, the militant tactics' (Marrot, p. 671).
21. *The Dark Flower*, p. 271.
22. Marrot, p. 384.
23. Ibid., p. 41.
24. Galsworthy's mother, who died while he was writing the book, was the model for this character, in whom emotion and satire are blended with splendid subtlety.
25. Galsworthy shared the Edwardian relish for the works of Anatole France, with which he was familiar.
26. *The Burning Spear*, p. 32.
27. *The Burning Spear*, Manaton Edition, p. ix. In fact, writing the book brought Galsworthy only personal satisfaction. It was a public failure, being doubly unfortunate: the opinions expressed about the war were unpopular when it was first published; and when they ceased to annoy, no one was interested in the war any more. But at least Galsworthy managed to relieve his feelings.
28. Marrot, p. 442.
29. *Saint's Progress*, p. 247.
30. Ibid., p. 312.
31. Ibid., pp. 159–60.
32. Garnett, *Letters from John Galsworthy*, p. 191.
33. Lawrence, *Selected Essays*, pp. 228–9, and *Phoenix*.
34. Preface written by Galsworthy for the French edition of *The Man of Property*.
35. Marrot, facing p. 246.
36. Ibid., p. 729.
37. *The Forsyte Saga*, pp. 417, 665.
38. Ibid., p. 645.
39. Ibid., pp. 617, 647, 677.
40. 'The White Monkey' is the title of a painting given to Fleur by her father.

For Galsworthy, the vacant look in the monkey's eyes symbolises the contemporary state of mind: not knowing what one wants.

41. 'Snooks' stands for the Carlton Club, and 'Jack O'Lantern' for Lloyd George. The novel begins on the day the Conservatives ended the war-time coalition, 19 October 1922.

42. Aldous Huxley, with his greater erudition and intellectual density, and more dazzling wit, handled this kind of situation more brilliantly in *Point Counter Point* (1928).

43. The first syllable of the political theorist's name, Sir James Foggart (no doubt based on a real-life model, but it is not known whom), evokes the fog inside his head. Once again, Galsworthy is thinking of Don Quixote. Michael Mont's attempt to carry his theories into practice is a tragic fiasco.

44. The 'great novelist L. S. D.' probably refers to D. H. Lawrence. When Galsworthy talks of books that are a success because of the scandal they cause, his attitude is complex: he was opposed to censorship (*A Modern Comedy*, pp. 508, 530, 622, 641).

45. *The Forsyte Saga*, p. 1053.

46. Marrot, pp. 629–30.

47. Ibid., p. 644.

48. Consideration of the last trilogy inevitably suffers from lack of information. Marrot admits that the end of his biography of Galsworthy was rather perfunctory. The chapter 'The Last Years 1926–1933' is little more than a collection of letters. There are very few comments by Galsworthy himself on *End of the Chapter*, and no preface in the Manaton Edition.

49. *End of the Chapter*, p. 333.

50. Ibid., pp. 401–3.

51. Ibid., pp. 770–823.

52. Ibid., p. 822.

53. Undated letter to Thomas Hardy (see Marrot, pp. 752–3).

54. Letter of 1929 (see Marrot, p. 796).

NOTES TO CHAPTER SEVEN: THE GALSWORTHIAN NOVEL

1. *The Forsyte Saga*, p. 1042.

2. *Castles in Spain*, p. 189.

3. Lawrence, *Selected Essays*, pp. 224–5, and *Phoenix*, pp. 539–56.

4. '. . . the inexorable nature of sex antipathies' (*The Forsyte Saga*, pp. 121, 122, 384).

5. Marrot, pp. 717–18.

6. *The Country House*, p. 92.

7. *The Dark Flower*, pp. 86–7.

8. *Saint's Progress*, p. 235.

9. *The Patrician*, pp. 110–11.

10. *The Dark Flower*, Manaton Edition, pp. xii–xiii.

11. Marrot, p. 707.

12. 'Faith of a Novelist', in *Castles in Spain*, pp. 186–7.

13. Marrot, p. 58. Claustrophobia has become a rather dated concept. But the term was part of the vocabulary of any educated person in Galsworthy's formative years.

14. 'Diagnosis of a Forsyte', in *The Forsyte Saga*, pp. 221–2.
15. Garnett, *Letters from John Galsworthy*, p. 134.
16. '. . . to be well-bred is just a piece of good luck, by no means entitling to complacency' (*The Country House*, Manaton Edition, p. xi).
17. Marrot, p. 381.
18. *Human Documents of the Age of the Forsytes* (London: Allen & Unwin, 1969), by Royston Pike, contains an excellent selection of non-literary documents and texts (none by Galsworthy himself) on English life at that period, with an introduction by the compiler. The chapter entitled 'The £ s. d. of Living' (pp. 145–75) gives information on the standard of living, depending on whether one earned thirty shillings a week or ten thousand pounds a year, or something in between. But Pike does not say where the Forsytes come in this income range. Only texts in the first chapter, 'At Home with the Forsytes' (pp. 21–66), actually refer to the upper-middle classes, describing their interiors, dress and social habits.
19. It is interesting to compare the Forsyte family tree, as it appears at the beginning of *The Forsyte Saga* and *A Modern Comedy*, with that of the Galsworthy family, given at the beginning of Marrot's biography and in Sauter, *Galsworthy the Man*, pp. 168–9.
20. *The Forsyte Saga*, p. 291.
21. Ibid., pp. 51–2.
22. Ibid., p. 57.
23. Ibid., p. 14.
24. *The Country House*, p. 10.
25. Garnett, *Letters from John Galsworthy*, p. 134.
26. R. J. Minney, *The Edwardian Age* (London: Cassell, 1964) p. 129; *The Forsyte Saga*, p. 53.
27. *Fraternity*, p. 123.
28. *The Island Pharisees*, p. 96.
29. *The Country House*, p. 267; *Beyond*, p. 25.
30. 'The Creation of Character in Literature', Romanes Lecture (Oxford: Clarendon Press, 1931) p. 18; reprinted in *Candelabra*, pp. 272–3.
31. Sheila Kaye-Smith, *John Galsworthy* (London: James Nisbet, 1916) p. 103.
32. Marrot, p. 192. The comparison between the Squire and his wife is a regrettable simplification.
33. Kaye-Smith, *John Galsworthy*, pp. 19, 103.
34. Letter of 1910 (Garnett, *Letters from John Galsworthy*, pp. 199–200).
35. *The Forsyte Saga*, Manaton Edition, pp. xi–xii.
36. Marrot, p. 304.
37. This is an idea that is typical, if not of Romanticism, at least of many Romantics. Its origin in Galsworthy can be attributed mainly to Turgenev, whose life was marked by his submissive adoration of the great singer Madame Viardot-García. The theme of the strong woman and the weak man is to be found in his writings, particularly *Fathers and Sons*. Through Turgenev, Galsworthy underwent the Romantic influence of George Sand.
38. *The Patrician*, p. 250.
39. Ibid., pp. 117, 119.
40. *The Dark Flower*, p. 34.
41. *The Patrician*, p. 133.

42. Marrot, pp. 799–800.
43. 'The Creation of Character in Literature', p. 17; reprinted in *Candelabra*, p. 271.
44. 'What is Hilary? . . . He is a man of forty. A man of forty, unless he is a pathological case, must have a formed character, that sort of knowledge of his own weakness which (the knowledge I mean) is a sort of strength, and also some sense of moral independence and perhaps − surely it is not too much to ask − a certain power of resistance. But H. has no individuality as above defined, he is refined into a special monster. I don't think . . . you have realized the harrowing atrocity of his conduct. . . . He is a degenerate who is completely satisfied with the last scene with the girl, and therefore with incredible villainy and a total absence of moral sense will act as you make him act. The strain on the reader is tremendous and the whole thing borders on the intolerable. . . . Morbid psychology, be it always understood, which is a perfectly legitimate subject for an artist's genius. But not for a moralist' (Marrot, pp. 230–1).
45. Marrot, pp. 732–3.
46. *The Island Pharisees*, p. 45.
47. Ibid., pp. 45–6.
48. *Fraternity*, p. 234.
49. Ibid., pp. 13, 223.
50. Ibid., p. 223.
51. William Bellamy, *The Novels of Wells, Bennett and Galsworthy 1890–1910* (London: Routledge & Kegan Paul, 1971) p. 168.
52. *The Country House*, p. 29.
53. Marrot, p. 466.
54. Garnett, *Letters From John Galsworthy*, pp. 193–4.
55. In 1932 he wrote to Gilbert Murray: 'The war killed a terrible lot of − I don't know what to call it − self-importance, faith, idealism, in me' (Marrot, p. 803).
56. Frank Swinnerton, *The Georgian Literary Scene* (London: Heinemann, 1935) p. 201; St John Ervine, *Some Impressions of my Elders* (New York: Macmillan, 1922) p. 145.
57. 'Six Novelists in Profile' (lecture given at the Sorbonne in 1925), published in *Candelabra*, p. 133.
58. *The Patrician*, p. 13.
59. The point of using a small number of fictional place-names may be to display his independence with regard to reality, as well as reflecting his reserve and discretion. About fifteen place-names in the novels are fictional. Galsworthy does not invent them completely, but alters real names, showing far less imagination than when he makes up names for characters. For example, there is no Nettlefold in Sussex, but Nettlebush and Nettlestead are to be found in Kent.
60. It shows the vigour of their stock. The French critic Ernest Guyot, in *John Galsworthy* (Paris: Didier) p. xv, points out that Galsworthy uses this longevity as a way of keeping characters as long as possible as witnesses of different periods, the diversity of which contrasts with their own almost permanently identical nature. Frank Swinnerton also rightly praises Galsworthy's portraiture of the aged.

61. Marrot, pp. 699–700.
62. *Beyond*, p. 365.
63. *The Patrician*, p. 338.
64. Ibid., pp. 141–2, 144.
65. Ibid., p. 145.
66. Ibid., pp. 130–1.
67. Ibid., p. 201.
68. Galsworthy seems to have been aware of the great differences between his novels and plays. The forces behind the action in the novels and in the plays can be distinguished: there is more mystery in the novels, because of what is not expressed, and more suspense in the plays, because of the livelier action.
69. Wherever the method and criteria used by Percy Lubbock, in *The Craft of Fiction* (London: Jonathan Cape, 1921; paperback, 1965) are applicable to Galsworthy's novels, they have been used in this analysis of his art as a novelist, as well as certain terms employed by Lubbock, particularly 'panoramic' and 'dramatic'.
70. 'You often say that my chief merit is balance' (Garnett, *Letters from John Galsworthy*, p. 185). In *Four Contemporary Novelists* (New York: Macmillan, 1930) pp. 112–13, Wilbur L. Cross uses the word 'poise', attributing this quality to Turgenev's influence.
71. Galsworthy's own word.
72. Ould, *John Galsworthy*, p. 121.
73. Marrot, p. 317.
74. Conrad's anti-chronology corresponds to his wish to avoid omniscience and reduce introspection (see R. Las Vergnas, *Joseph Conrad* (Paris: Didier, 1938) pp. 129–31); Galsworthy uses it rather to contrast present and past, and introduce a note of nostalgia.
75. *The Country House*, p. 3.
76. *A Modern Comedy*, p. 819.
77. W. L. Myers, *The Later Realism* (Chicago University Press, 1927; Cambridge University Press, 1927) p. 114.
78. *Saint's Progress*, p. 10.
79. *The Country House*, p. 220.
80. Henry James, 'The New Novel' in *Selected Literary Criticism* (London: Heinemann, 1963) pp. 314, 337.
81. *The Forsyte Saga*, pp. 50–1.
82. *A Modern Comedy*, pp. 590–5; also pp. 942–7, where only a brief piece of dialogue interrupts a six-page monologue.
83. Ibid., p. 958.
84. *The Forsyte Saga*, p. 92.
85. *A Modern Comedy*, p. 864.
86. Ibid., p. 1034.
87. *Fraternity*, p. 192.
88. *The Country House*, pp. 245–6.
89. *End of the Chapter*, pp. 793–5.
90. I have calculated that the percentage of dialogue, which is 17.5 in *The Country House*, drops to 12% in *The Patrician*.
91. Robert Liddell, 'The Upholstery of Galsworthy, Contrasted with Henry James', in *A Treatise on the Novel* (London: Jonathan Cape, 1947) p. 125.

92. Arnold Kettle, *An Introduction to the English Novel*, vol. 2 (London: Hutchinson, 1953) p. 88.

93. *The Forsyte Saga*, p. 183.

94. There is a eulogy of trees in *The Dark Flower*, pp. 59–63, where Mark and Sylvia climb an oak. There is also the oak at Robin Hill in *The Forsyte Saga*, the beech wood in *The Patrician*, pt ii, ch. 14, and the delightful sketch 'The Lime-Tree' in *A Motley*, pp. 145–51; see also 'Silent Wooing', the interlude between *The White Monkey* and *The Silver Spoon*, in the second trilogy *A Modern Comedy*.

95. *The Country House*, pp. 24–5.

96. *The Forsyte Saga*, p. 207.

97. *The Country House*, p. 26.

98. *The Dark Flower*, p. 186.

99. Ralph Freedman, *The Lyrical Novels: Studies in Hermann Hesse, André Gide and Virginia Woolf* (Princeton University Press, 1963); Richard Church, *The Growth of the English Novel* (London: Methuen, 1951) p. 168.

100. They include 'The Runagates', 'Sheep-Shearing', 'Threshing', 'That Old-Time Place', 'Joy of Life', 'A Pilgrimage', 'The Kings', 'Riding in Mist', 'Gone', 'Wind in the Rocks', 'Buttercup Night', 'Bel Colore', 'The Japanese Quince', 'The Cime in Lavaredo', 'The Lime-Tree', 'Magpie over the Hill', 'Delight', 'Felicity', 'Romance — Three Gleams', 'Fairyland', 'A Green Hill Far Away'. Seven of these texts come from the collection *A Motley*, nine from *The Inn of Tranquillity*' and three from *Tatterdemalion*.

101. These include, in particular, 'Magpie over the Hill', 'The Lime-Tree', 'Romance — Three Gleams', 'Fairyland', 'That Old-Time Place'. There are others: 'The Muffled Ship', 'The Dead Men', 'Hey-Day', 'The Gibbet', 'The Road', 'Reveillé' and 'Reverie of a Sportsman', one of the most successful, together with 'The Lime-Tree'. The influence of Turgenev, and through him perhaps of George Sand, can be perceived. But Galsworthy's phantasmagoria has a personal character: he is usually himself the visionary recounting his vision.

102. Swinnerton, *The Georgian Literary Scene*, p. 204; Ould, *John Galsworthy*, pp. 139–45; Hugh Walpole finds irony but no humour in Galsworthy, in *The Post-Victorians*, pp. 183–4.

103. *The Country House*, p. 177.

104. Ibid., pp. 61–2.

105. From a letter of 1914 (Marrot, p. 720).

106. Diary entry for Christmas Day 1910, and Marrot, p. 308.

NOTES TO CHAPTER EIGHT: GALSWORTHY'S PHILOSOPHY AND OUTLOOK

1. Works by Samuel Butler that Galsworthy is known to have read are *Erewhon, God the Known and God the Unknown, The Authoress of the Odyssey* and *The Way of All Flesh* (see Marrot, pp. 687–8, 779); *The Authoress of the Odyssey* is included in the reading list Galsworthy gave his cousin Frank, who showed it to me; for *Erewhon*, see *Another Sheaf*, p. 111.

2. 'Evolution', in *The Inn of Tranquillity*, pp. 40–6. Darwin and natural selection are named or alluded to in *The Island Pharisees*, pp. 8, 10; *Fraternity*, pp. 73–4, 178, 204, 223; *The Patrician*, p. 140; *The Country House*, pp. 34, 183; *Saint's Progress*, pp. 106, 136; and in several Manaton Edition prefaces: *The Island Pharisees*, p. xii–xiii; *The Forsyte Saga*, p. xi; *The Burning Spear*, p. xi; *A Modern Comedy*, p. ix.
3. *The Plays*, p. 1068; also a doubt about the actual truth of natural selection, ibid., p. 557.
4. *Fraternity*, p. 118.
5. Houghton, *The Victorian Frame of Mind 1830–1870* (New Haven, Conn.: Yale University Press, 1957) p. 209.
6. *Addresses in America*, p. 100. Galsworthy is not even mentioned in *Darwinism in the English Novel, 1860–1910* (New York: Russell, 1963) by L. J. Henkin, although he should have been included in this thorough and abundantly-documented standard work. The omission is typical of the state of Galsworthy studies.
7. *A Sheaf*, p. 133.
8. There is an interesting allusion of an admiring nature to Bergson in *Loyalties* (*The Plays*, p. 661). The Galsworthy Collection contains a letter from Bergson to Ada Galsworthy about *The Man of Property* (ref. JG 962).
9. *The Burning Spear*, Manaton Edition, p. xi.
10. Bellamy, *The Novels of Wells, Bennett and Galsworthy*. This study, published in 1971, is extremely important: it is the most modern, by the methods he uses. Adopting a determinedly scientific standpoint, Bellamy applies psychoanalytical and certain sociological criteria and vocabulary to his investigation of the novels of the three 'Edwardians', studying them in relation to Freud and Darwin. Within the limits he has set himself, and which the title does not reveal, his merit is to have undertaken the scientific study of Galsworthy, hitherto awaited in vain.
11. Ibid., pp. 211–16.
12. *The Inn of Tranquillity*, Manaton Edition, p. x.
13. Bellamy, *The Novels of Wells, Bennett and Galsworthy*, pp. 19–20.
14. Marrot, p. 673.
15. Ibid., p. 43.
16. '. . . the social resurrection of 1906' (*Beyond*, p. 17).
17. Marrot, p. 675.
18. Barker, *The Man of Principle*, p. 130.
19. Marrot, p. 222; Garnett, *Letters of John Galsworthy*, p. 182.
20. *A Sheaf*, p. 262.
21. *The Island Pharisees*, p. 113. The term 'Imperialism' is used on the same page.
22. This information came from Dorothy Easton.
23. *A Sheaf*, pp. 179, 186.
24. Ibid., pp. 179. 180, 191.
25. Marrot, pp. 689–93, 696, 742.
26. *The Patrician*, p. 26.
27. *A Sheaf*, pp. 157–9.
28. 'Speculations (1917–1918)', in *Candelabra*, p. 89.

29. *A Modern Comedy*, p. 760. On Carlyle's anti-Parliamentarianism, see Houghton, *The Victorian Frame of Mind*, p. 328.
30. Marrot, *A Bibliography of the Works of John Galsworthy*, pp. 155–6, 168–70.
31. *The Freelands*, Manaton Edition, p. xi.
32. *Castles in Spain*, p. 13.
33. *Candelabra*, p. 84.
34. *Addresses in America*, p. 21; Marrot, pp. 42–3.
35. *The Island Pharisees*, ch. 18, pp. 155–63; *The Country House*, p. 131.
36. *Another Sheaf*, p. 15.
37. 'Diagnosis of the Englishmen', in *A Sheaf*, p. 201; reprinted in *Candelabra*, p. 52.
38. *The Island Pharisees*, Manaton Edition, p. xiii.
39. Marrot, p. 738.
40. Ibid., p. 749.
41. Ibid., p. 770.
42. Kettle, *An Introduction to the English Novel*, vol. 2, p. 87. There is very scant information about Galsworthy's philosophical and paraphilosophical reading. The list of authors he mentions comprises Carlyle, Arnold, Ruskin, Butler, William James, Mill, Spinoza, Hegel, Nietzsche, Bergson, Emerson, Renan, William Morris, Havelock Ellis, Reinach, Hollander, R. Hunter, John Morley, Froude, Pater and Lytton Strachey.
43. *A Sheaf* (1916), *Another Sheaf* (1919), *Addresses in America* (1919), *Castles in Spain* (1927) and *Candelabra* (1932).
44. John A. Lester, *Journey through Despair 1880–1914: Transformations in British Literary Culture* (Princeton University Press, 1968) pp. 62–5.
45. 'Rise of the Critical Spirit' in Houghton, *The Victorian Frame of Mind*, pp. 94–6.
46. For the letter to Hardy, see Marrot, p. 750. For 'product', see *The Plays*, p. 1070, and *Fraternity*, pp. 218, 234, 242.
47. *The Country House*, pp. 112, 114.
48. *Castles in Spain*, p. 15. The italics are Galsworthy's.
49. Ibid., pp. 170–1; *A Sheaf*, pp. 216, 295; *Glimpses and Reflections*, p. 313.
50. *Glimpses and Reflections*, p. 312.
51. Galsworthy gives, as his philosophical motto, the lines by Adam Lindsay Gordon quoted in *The Country House*:

> Two things stand like stone;
> Kindness in another's trouble,
> Courage in your own.

See *The Country House*, p. 78; *Glimpses and Reflections*, p. 27.
52. *The Plays*, pp. 453–4.
53. *The Inn of Tranquillity*, Manaton Edition, p. xi.
54. *Moods, Songs and Doggerels*, p. 7. 'A Dream' appeared in the *Atlantic Monthly* in March 1912.
55. Marrot, p. 706. See also *The Freelands*, p. 78; *The Dark Flower*, p. 50; Marrot, p. 754; *A Sheaf*, p. 177; *Castles in Spain*, p. 26.
56. *Another Sheaf*, p. 22. See also Marrot, p. 802. For another use of the word 'agnostic', see *The Plays*, p. 703.

57. The term 'agnosticism' was used for the first time in 1869 by Thomas Huxley. The two main works of Leslie Stephen on the subject are *The Science of Ethics* (1882) and *An Agnostic's Apology* (1893). On Victorian agnosticism, see Houghton, *The Victorian Frame of Mind*, pp. 82–4, 221–2, 238–9 *passim*.
58. *A Sheaf*, p. 157; *Glimpses and Reflections*, p. 315. See also *Candelabra*, p. 88.
59. Marrot, p. 754.
60. *A Sheaf*, p. 176.
61. Marrot, p. 369.
62. *The Patrician*, pp. 110–11. See also pp. 253, 348.
63. Marrot, pp. 651–2. The poem is not included in the published collections.
64. *A Sheaf*, pp. 95–119.

NOTES TO CONCLUSION

1. David Daiches, *The Present Age* (London: Cresset Press, 1958) p. 172.
2. E. M. Forster, 'English Prose between 1918 and 1939', in *Two Cheers for Democracy* (London: Edward Arnold, 1951) p. 290.
3. Schalit, *John Galsworthy: A Survey*, p. 13.
4. Louis Tillier, *Arnold Bennett et ses Romans Réalistes* (Paris: Didier, 1967) p. 325.

# Select Bibliography

## (a) BOOKS ON GALSWORTHY

Barker, Dudley, *The Man of Principle: A View of John Galsworthy* (London: Heinemann, 1963).

Bellamy, William, *The Novels of Wells, Bennett and Galsworthy: 1890–1910* (London: Routledge & Kegan Paul, 1971).

Coats, R. H., *John Galsworthy as a Dramatic Artist* (London: Duckworth, 1926).

Dupont, V., *John Galsworthy, the Dramatic Artist* (Toulouse and Paris: Didier, 1942).

Dupré, Catherine, *John Galsworthy: A Biography* (London: Collins, 1976).

Eaton, Harold T., *Reading Galsworthy's 'Forsyte Saga'* (New York: Charles Scribner's Sons, 1936).

Fisher, J., *The World of the Forsytes* (London: Secker & Warburg, 1976).

Garnett, Edward (ed.), *Letters from John Galsworthy, 1900–1932*, with an introduction by Edward Garnett (London: Jonathan Cape, 1934; New York: Charles Scribner's Sons, 1934).

Guyot, E., *John Galsworthy – I: Le Romancier* (Paris: Didier, 1933).

Holloway, D., *John Galsworthy*, 'International Profiles' series (London: Morgan-Grampian Books, 1968).

Kaye-Smith, Sheila, *John Galsworthy* (London: James Nisbet, 1916).

Marrot, H. V., *Bibliography of the Works of John Galsworthy* (London: Elkin Mathews & Marrot, 1928; New York: Charles Scribner's Sons, 1928).

———, *Life and Letters of John Galsworthy* (London: Heinemann, 1935; New York: Charles Scribner's Sons, 1935).

Morris, Margaret, *My Galsworthy Story* (London: Peter Owen, 1967).

Mottram, R. H., *John Galsworthy*, 'Writers and their Works' series, no. 38 (London: Longmans, 1953).

_____, *For Some We Loved: An Intimate Portrait of Ada and John Galsworthy* (London: Hutchinson, 1956).

Ould, Hermon, *John Galsworthy* (London: Chapman & Hall, 1934).

Reynolds, Mabel E., *Memories of John Galsworthy by his Sister* (London: R. Hale, 1936; New York: Frederick A. Stokes, 1936).

Sauter, Rudolf, *Galsworthy the Man: An Intimate Portrait by his Nephew* (London: Peter Owen, 1967).

Schalit, Leon, *John Galsworthy: A Survey*, translated from the German (London: Heinemann, 1929).

Smit, J. Henry, *The Short Stories of J. Galsworthy* (Rotterdam: D. Van Sijn & Zonen, 1948).

Stevens, Earl E. and Stevens, H. Ray, *John Galsworthy: An Annotated Bibliography of Writings about Him* (Northern Illinois University Press, 1979).

Wilson, Asher Boldon, *John Galsworthy's Letters to Leon Lion* (The Hague: Mouton, 1968).

## (b) GENERAL WORKS AND BOOKS OF SPECIAL INTEREST FOR THE STUDY OF GALSWORTHY

Budd, Susan, *Varieties of Unbelief, Atheists and Agnostics in English Society, 1850–1960* (London: Heinemann, 1977).

Cross, Wilbur E., *Four Contemporary Novelists* (New York: Macmillan, 1930).

*Fifty Years: Memories and Contrasts: A Composite Picture of the Period 1882–1932*, by 27 contributors to *The Times* (London, 1932).

Henkin, L. J., *Darwinism in the English Novel, 1860–1910* (New York: Russell, 1963).

Houghton, W. E., *The Victorian Frame of Mind, 1830–1870* (New Haven, Conn.: Yale University Press, 1957).

Hynes, S., *The Edwardian Turn of Mind* (Princeton University Press, 1968; Oxford University Press, 1968).

*Ideas and Beliefs of the Victorians: An Historic Revaluation of the Victorian Age*, a series of talks on the BBC Third Programme.

Jean-Aubry, G., *Joseph Conrad: Life and Letters*, 2 vols (Garden City, New York: Doubleday, Page, 1927).

Kettle, A., *An Introduction to the English Novel*, vol. 2 (London: Hutchinson, 1953).

Lawrence, D. H., *Phoenix: The Posthumous Papers of D. H. Lawrence* (London: Heinemann, 1936) pp. 539–66.

———, *Selected Essays* (Harmondsworth: Penguin, 1966) pp. 217–30.

Legouis, E. and Cazamian, L., *Histoire de la Littérature Anglaise* (Paris, 1939; London: J. M. Dent, 1964).

Lester, J. A. Jr, *Journey through Despair, 1880–1914: Transformations in British Literary Culture* (Princeton University Press, 1968).

Miller, J. Hillis, *The Disappearance of God: Five Nineteenth-Century Writers* (New York: Schocken Paperbacks, 1965).

Myers, W. L., *The Later Realism* (Chicago University Press, 1927; Cambridge University Press, 1927) pp. 114–18, 131–4, 146–7.

Phelps, G., *The Russian Novel in English Fiction* (London: Hutchinson, 1956).

Priestley, J. B., *The Edwardians* (London: Heinemann, 1970).

Smith, Warren S., *The London Heretics 1870–1914* (London: Constable, 1967).

Swinnerton, F., *The Georgian Literary Scene* (London: Heinemann, 1935) pp. 199–207.

Wells, H. G., *Experiment in Autobiography* (London: Jonathan Cape, 1934) pp. 410–24.

Willey, B., *More Nineteenth Century Studies: A Group of Honest Doubters* (London: Chatto & Windus, 1963).

Woolf, V., *Collected Essays*, vol. 1 (London: Hogarth Press, 1966).

*Fifty Years: Memories and Contrasts – a Composite Picture of the Period 1882–1932*, by 27 contributors to *The Times* (London, 1932).

*Ideas and Beliefs of the Victorians: An Historic Revaluation of the Victorian Age*, a series of talks on the BBC Third Program.

# Index